Colonial N~~~~~ Dialogues

Colonial Narratives/Cultural Dialogues demonstrates the continuing validity of the colonial paradigm as it maps the political, geographical, and imaginative space of "India/Indies" from the seventeenth century to the present. Breaking new ground in postcolonial studies, Jyotsna Singh highlights the interconnections among early modern colonial encounters, later manifestations in the Raj, and their lingering influence in the postcolonial Indian state.

Singh challenges the assumption of eye-witness accounts and unmediated experiences implicit in colonial representational practices, and often left unchallenged in the postcolonial era.

Essential introductory reading for students and academics, *Colonial Narratives/Cultural Dialogues* re-evaluates the following texts: seventeenth-century travel narratives about India; eighteenth-century "nabob" texts; letters of the Orientalist, Sir William Jones; East India Company petitions; and reviews of Shakespearean productions in colonial Calcutta and postcolonial, Indo-Anglian novels.

Jyotsna G. Singh is an Associate Professor of English at Southern Methodist University, Texas, and co-author of *The Weyward Sisters: Shakespeare and Feminist Politics* (1994).

THOMAS CORIATE
Traueller for the English
VVits : Greeting.

From the Court of the Great MOGVL, *Resi-*
dent at the Towne of ASMERE, *in*
Easterne INDIA.

Printed by VV. Iaggard, and Henry Fetherston.
1616.

Colonial narratives/cultural dialogues

"Discoveries" of India in the language of colonialism

Jyotsna G. Singh

London and New York

First published 1996
by Routledge
11 New Fetter Lane, London EC4P 4EE

Simultaneously published in the USA and Canada
by Routledge
29 West 35th Street, New York, NY 10001

Typeset in Times by BC Typesetting, Bristol
Printed and bound in Great Britain by
TJ Press (Padstow) Ltd, Padstow, Cornwall

British Library Cataloguing in Publication Data
A catalogue record for this book is available from the British Library

Library of Congress Cataloguing in Publication Data
Singh, Jyotsna G.
    Colonial narratives/cultural dialogues/"discoveries" of India in
the language of colonialism/Jyotsna G. Singh.
    p. cm.
Includes bibliographical references and index.
1. English literature—Early modern, 1500–1700—History and
criticism. 2. India—History—British occupation, 1765–1947—
Historiography. 3. Literature and anthropology—England—
History—17th century. 4. Literature and anthropology—England—
History—18th century. 5. English literature—Appreciation—India.
6. English literature—Indic influences. 7. Imperialism in
literature. 8. Colonies in literature. 9. Narration (Rhetoric).
10. India—In literature. 11. Renaissance—England. I. Title
PR129.I5S46 1996   96-7428
82-.9′358—dc20   CIP

ISBN 0–415–08518–7 (hbk)
ISBN 0–415–08519–5 (pbk)

Contents

Acknowledgements

Colonial Narratives/Cultural Dialogues has taken shape in three different locations—India, Britain, and the United States—and I am grateful to many people for their personal and intellectual support. I begin with Jean Howard, my mentor and role model since graduate school, and to whom I am indebted for introducing me to the challenges and pleasures of intellectual work.

This book has grown out of extended conversations about colonialism, race, gender, postcoloniality, the third world, and (in the mix) Shakespeare. In the past few years I have been particularly helped and challenged by Eric Cheyfitz, Dennis Cordell, Shanti Menon, Anindyo Roy, Ryan Bishop, Hala Asker, Dympna Callaghan, Andrew O'Shaughnessy, and Corey Capers.

To Dympna Callaghan, my "partner-in-crime[s]," I owe a special thanks for her friendship, intellectual support, and her astute critique of this manuscript at its early stages. As I also do to David Riggs, whose encouragement kept me going—and whose friendship I value.

I am grateful to Mark Burnett for his encouraging and useful comments on parts of the book—and for introducing me to the byzantine world of British libraries.

I would be remiss not to acknowledge with some warmth my parents, siblings, and extended family in India, who have always treated my intellectual work with good-humored skepticism. I also want to mention with great affection Aman and Amar Gujral, who are joyous reminders of early intellectual discoveries.

To Talia Rodgers, my editor at Routledge, I express my deep gratitude for her guidance and patience—which have made this a better book.

At SMU, I am grateful to the Dean of University Research, Dr Narayan Bhatt, for his support in the allocation of funds for travel and research. I also must thank my colleagues, Dennis Foster, for helping me with the manuscript and averting potential disasters with computer software, and Bruce Levy for his frequent prodding while I was writing. Greg O'Molesky, our graduate assistant, was magnificent in his prompt assistance—both in research and in proof reading. And Jill Bagwell's and Margaret Bookhout's daily, solicitous concern kept me going.

In India, I must thank Dr Suresh Awasthi, the former director of the National School of Drama, for generously sharing his research materials on Indian performances.

A special thanks to Ryan Bishop. Many of the ideas of this book were generated and refined by our conversations—and by Ryan's endless rhetorical questions. I am particularly grateful for his great support in the final stages of this project—in reading and editing meticulously. The book is vastly improved because of his help.

Finally, I would like to acknowledge all my students at SMU—from whom I have learnt a lot.

Permission to reproduce the title page from Thomas Coriate, *Traueller for the English Wits: Greeting from the Court of the Great Mogul*, 1616 [4°.L.62. Art (18)] was kindly given by the Bodleian Library, University of Oxford.

Introduction

> The cause of my coming hither [to India] is for foure respects. First, to see the blessed face of your Maiesty [the Great Mogul, Jehangir], whose wonderfull fame hath resounded ouer all Europe & the Mahometan Countries. . . . Secondly to see your Maiesties Elephants, which kind of beasts I have not seen in any other country. Thirdly, to see your famous river Ganges, which is the Captaine of all the Riuer of the World. The fourth is this, to intreat your Maiesty that you should vouchsafe to grant mee your gracious Passe that I may trauell into the Country of Tartaria to the Citty of Samarkand, to visit the blessed Sepulcher of the Lord of the Corners (this is a title that is giuen to Tamburlaine in this Country in that Persian language . . .) whose fame by reason of his warres and victories is published ouer the whole world: perhaps he is not altogether so famous in his own country of Tartaria as in England.
>
> (Thomas Coryate 1618: 1st verso after B2^v)

The "discovery" of India serves as a framing trope of this book. It begins with Thomas Coryate's wonderstruck evocations of the Mogul court in the seventeenth century and concludes with Jawaharlal Nehru's *The Discovery of India*, in which he defines the independent nation's identity by "discovering" both its mythic past and its claims to Western modernity. Since the early modern period, this discovery motif has frequently emerged in the language of colonization, enabling European travelers/writers to represent the newly "discovered" lands as an empty space, a *tabula rasa* on which they could inscribe their linguistic, cultural, and later, territorial claims. Geographically speaking, the English discovery of Indian territory was mostly accomplished in the seventeenth century. Rhetorically, however, the trope of discovery took on shifting, multiple meanings within British colonial discourse, being constantly refurbished and mobilized in the service of other colonizing enterprises, such as *civilizing, rescuing,* and *idealizing* or *demonizing* their Indian subjects as "others."

By frequently drawing on the idea of discovery, the British gained a privileged epistemological position, whereby as "discoverers" they could claim new knowledge which they could then process and circulate via the intractable colonial binarisms: civilization and barbarism, tradition and modernity, and Christianity and heathenism, among others. The legacy of these binaries has extended through history, passing through the enlightenment to the postcolonial era in India, where Jawaharlal Nehru co-opts the language in his own "discovery" of India.

From their earliest encounters with non-European natives, going as far back as antiquity, Europeans have described their travels in terms of discovering marvels and monstrosities. In doing so, they have often deployed the rhetorical strategy of mingling eye-witness descriptions with fables and myths derived from the poetic geography of medieval, classical, and biblical texts.[1] Samuel Purchas, for instance, in his "Preface" to *Purchas His Pilgrimes* (1625), aptly defines the generic expectations of travel narratives when he claims to be recapitulating the "rarities of nature" and the "extraordinary Wonders, which God's providence hath herein effected" (xliii). Thus, given such generic prerequisites, English travelers to India in the seventeenth century tended not to recognize the discrepancies between their roles as functionaries or beneficiaries of the East India Company and as compilers of knowledge of all that is curious and strange. Henry Lord, for instance (in his Dedication to the Governor of the Company, preceding his *A Discoverie of the Sect of Banians*, 1630), describes the members of the East India Company, as "worthy Adventurers," and praises their works that "have in them anything forraigne and exotick in the limit and confine of your Adventures" (1ᵛ). And Coryate, in his 1618 oration before the Mogul king, embellishes the account of his journey with the received narrative about the fabled Tamburlaine, "whose fame by reason of his warres and victories is published over the whole world."

As "adventurers," who were frequently also East India Company functionaries, early modern English travelers produced numerous narratives about India, claiming varying degrees of authenticity, but often revealing the role of fiction in the making of their "facts." Thus, despite their professions of veracity, these narratives point to the power of a *colonizing imagination* which "discovers" new lands via demarcations of identity and difference, often based upon ideological and mythical distinctions between civilization and barbarism and tradition and modernity. It is at this intersection between the "real" and an imagined India that I make my entry into the field of colonial/postcolonial cultural studies.

Not only do claims of "discovery" merge into fabrication and invention in this early colonial scene of writing, but this pattern reveals the resilience of the discovery trope as it takes varied and shifting forms through colonial and postcolonial history. For instance, the English endeavors to open trade routes for commercial profit were recorded as narratives of wonder and discovery in which "India/Indies" emerges through the prism of the exotic and barbaric. In the eighteenth century, as the mismanaged East India Company gave way to direct governance by the state, the first generation of British civil servants refurbished the trope of discovery. Learning Indian languages and forming the Asiatic Society of Bengal, for example, they attempted to recover India's classical past as a golden age, while setting it in contrast to images of disarray and decadence of a "fallen" eighteenth-century India—an India that had, in effect, corrupted the moral rectitude of the Company officials. In the nineteenth century, the evocations of India's ancient past went through several revisions. Among the Indian elite, the products of the British civilizing mission, the Orientalist movement gave an impetus to the Bengal Renaissance, an Indian cultural movement based in part on Western liberal humanism. But more importantly, the eighteenth-century Orientalist vision gradually gave way to a new "discovery" by James Mill in his *History of British India* (1815), in which he defines the ancient Hindu period as the ruin of a decadent civilization, rather than as a pristine Aryan society.

By the mid-nineteenth century, it seems, Britain had fixed and normalized its "discovery/discoveries" of India by defining the land as "an unchanging text" of a primitive and static Hinduism—one which continually reaffirmed the British Raj as a necessary moral and civilizing order.[2] And yet, the discovery motif continued beyond British colonial rule. When India gained independence in 1947, a centralized, class-based nation-state was buttressed by an idealist vision of India's glorious past wherein lay the universal "essence" of Indianness. In Jawaharlal Nehru's *The Discovery of India*, one of the founding texts of Indian nationalism, we once again find a dichotomy between the author's encounters with "real" Indians and his "discovery" of India's ideal past, the source of true Indianness that binds the citizens of the nation-state.

In following these interrelated strategies and themes of British colonialism—as a mode of *discovering, civilizing, rescuing,* and *cataloguing* the Indian empire—my study focusses on the intersection between historical narrative and rhetorical analysis, assuming a "metaphorical relation between colonizing and writing," as David Spurr explains:

> The problem of the colonizer is in some sense the problem of the writer: in the face of what may appear as a vast cultural and geographical blankness, colonization is a form of self-inscription onto the lives of a people who are conceived of as an extension of the landscape.[3]

Thus, if one recognizes that all colonial interactions are an effect of power relations inscribed within cultural and linguistic forms, then it becomes apparent how colonial representational practices draw on strategies of naming and classifying as implicit modes of political and territorial domination. These strategies are especially apparent in the many English travel narratives about India, which are my main sources.[4]

In thus examining this language of colonization in the making of "India," both during the growing English presence and in its aftermath, my purpose is to foreground how we (from the perspective of the Anglo-American academy) interrogate the West's colonial past, given that colonialism has now become a historical category, linked to the present by terms like *neo* and *post* rather than by any direct continuity (Dirks 1992: 5). In fact, colonialism may seem far removed from the postmodern displacements of late capitalism, so that, in effect, as Nicholas Dirks states, "Colonialism is now safe for scholarship . . . [and that] in calling for the study of the aesthetics of colonialism, we might end up aestheticizing colonialism"(5). Partha Chatterjee (1993: 14) addresses similar issues when he states:

> The idea that colonialism was only incidental to the history of the development of the modern institutions and technologies of power in the countries of Asia and Africa is now very much with us. In some ways, this is not surprising because we now

tend to think of the period of colonialism as something we have managed to put behind us, whereas the progress of modernity is a project in which we are all, albeit with varying degrees of enthusiasm, still deeply implicated.

Such reflections on colonial history in relation to the two poles of "tradition" and "modernity" typically show how any study of colonial/postcolonial institutions and practices must constantly choose its bearings between past and future. One cannot, of course, direct all necessary social criticism of contemporary realities to the irrecoverable world of imperialism as the originary moment—or even the prototype—of all current inequities. Yet why is it that the colonial paradigm persists, and even acquires an urgent, *contemporary* validity? In obvious terms, it shows how aspects of the language of colonization—the tropes of *discovery*, *civilization*, and *rescue*, for instance, have survived beyond the classic colonial era and continue to color our perceptions of the non-Western world.[5] More broadly, cultural, racial, and moral differences established by colonialism continue to have broad ramifications for the way in which marginal, subordinated races, cultures, economic groups, and sexualities are defined and figured as "others" in relation to dominant, privileged categories.

It is in this context of continuing political and cultural struggles that one has to consider the emergence of postcolonial studies, a discipline that has produced a new archive of revisionist colonial materials, forcing Western readers to *re-negotiate* their relationship to the history of colonialism—and to re-examine the continuities and discontinuities between the colonial and postcolonial eras. As a result, as has often been noted, this field has provoked a crisis in the contemporary North American and European sense of world hegemony. Challenging the liberal humanist notion of a "universal" history, postcolonial studies is a counter-disciplinary practice, analyzing literary texts, among other cultural forms, at the level of specific historical and discursive struggles by which they are shaped.[6]

Given these postcolonial influences on literary studies, Shakespeare's play, *The Tempest*, for instance, can never again be claimed as a purely Western text after the 1980s reappraisals of Prospero's role from that of a benevolent patriarch to an oppressive colonist. These critical revisions followed the decolonization movements in the former colonies of Africa, the Caribbean, and

Latin America, which imaginatively claimed Caliban as their ancestor while politically they re-claimed their lands.[7] More recently, some efforts have been made to remove or distance *The Tempest* from colonial history and ideology, as well as from its postcolonial appropriations, to bring the Western canonical work "home" so to speak—and to replant Shakespeare's play firmly "in European soil and in the European environment."[8] While these recent studies are useful in pointing to the play's multiple meanings and histories, they cannot retrieve the play from its non-Western contexts and return it to its singular canonical, "Western" status, considering that the story of *The Tempest* has proliferated into multiple versions in Africa, the Caribbean, and Latin America.

While postcolonial studies has been recognized as a field within the humanities, its orientation and influence have come under considerable critical scrutiny. Most typically, as Anne McClintock suggests, postcolonial theory runs the risk of being bogged down in a single binary opposition: colonial and postcolonial, "making colonialism the determining marker of history."[9] Other contemporary theorists have also addressed this dilemma of a Eurocentric teleology by describing colonialism and postcolonialism, not as monolithic, autonomous categories, but as part of an overdetermined discursive field. Critics such as Homi Bhabha and Lisa Lowe, among several others, have noted the dialogic strains within colonial narratives and called for anti-essentialist revisions of a previously monolithic history—ones in which colonial/postcolonial identity is always already overwritten by the differential play of colonialist ambivalence.[10] Conceptualizing colonial power as a discursive formation in the Foucauldian sense, they challenge the notion of colonial discourse as a closed system "that manages and colonizes otherness" (Lowe 1991: 10). Lowe, for instance (drawing on Foucault and Gramsci), offers a "de-essentialized understanding of power" to define it as "a hegemonic *process* rather than a static or monolithic condition" (16). In this sense, "hegemony does not refer exclusively to the process by which dominant groups exercise and maintain influence, but it denotes equally the process through which other groups organize, contest, or accommodate any specific kind of resistance."[11]

In exploring such instabilities and contradictions within colonial discourse—and thereby circumventing the colonial binaries—postcolonial critics have enabled readings of resistance and agency, often missing in the European accounts. Such concerns about agency and teleology have also come into play in studies of colonial and nationalist historiographies in which, for instance, there is little consensus about the role of colonial rule within Indian history: about the "transitions" between different periods in this history, and about the complex engagement of both colonial and nationalist narratives with the Western project of modernity (cast in opposition to shifting notions of tradition).[12]

It is within these complex strands of colonial history and historiography—grappling with issues of teleology and agency—that I map the discursive space of British colonialism in India and its aftermath. A postcolonial study such as this one faces an intellectual, political, and conceptual challenge in the way it positions itself toward the colonial past it is attempting to revise. As Raymond Williams puts it, "in every kind of radicalism the moment comes when any critique of the present must choose its bearings between past and future" (1973: 36). This search for historical bearings is, in fact, an on-going project in *Colonial Narratives/Cultural Dialogues*, and informs my analyses of diverse colonial materials.

My methodology involves interconnecting many different stories to explore the triangulated colonial themes of *discovery, civilization*, and *rescue*. Splicing together the terms "narrative" and "dialogue," I focus on the intersection between official, formal narratives deployed in the management of colonial and postcolonial institutions and unofficial, informal accounts, textual traces of individual, dissonant voices. I do not, however, undertake here a comprehensive history of empire or point to a direct correspondence between "reality" and its representations. Rather, I combine historical and rhetorical analyses to follow a web of signification weaving through a variety of colonial and postcolonial texts: seventeenth-century travel narratives about India, East India Company petitions, eighteenth-century "nabob" texts, letters of William Jones, nineteenth-century Mutiny novels, reviews of Shakespeare productions in colonial Calcutta, and postcolonial, Indo-Anglian novels, among numerous others. In eschewing a single, colonial source or perspective, I attempt to locate cultural interpretations in many sorts of reciprocal and oppositional contexts, spanning different historical moments.

In focussing on discrete historical moments in the seventeenth, eighteenth, nineteenth, and twentieth centuries, I do not wish to connect these periods in a teleology of empire. We cannot, for instance, consider Thomas Roe's and Thomas Coryate's early modern cultural encounters as originary moments in the trajectory toward the full-blown British Raj or read colonial history as a univocal and unbroken narrative. But still, it is apparent that as colonial and later, nationalist power re-inscribes itself, we can note a modality of colonialism from one historical moment to another, rhetorically structured by the trope of discovery often mediating the standard repertoire of colonial binaries: tradition and modernity, and civilization and barbarism. Such rhetorical demarcations between identity and difference are not incidental to colonization, but have consistently promoted the "modern regime of power" or institutional and cultural arrangements, which enabled the power of the colonial and, later, the nationalist state to expand and consolidate.[13]

The five chapters that comprise this book are varied and yet loosely interrelated. They all "speak" to shared concerns about the power of the colonial and nationalist state as it articulates itself via familiar and tenacious tropes of discovery, civilization, rescue, and progress, while revealing and containing challenges to its legitimacy. Overall, my aim is to join contemporary moves to de-naturalize history: to show that it is not objectively or providentially created and that it is yoked to specific, sometimes discrete agendas, whereby power re-inscribes itself in different linguistic, cultural, and political forms.

Chapter 1 charts the discursive space of the early modern European encounters in India. This period has drawn little interest among postcolonial critics, perhaps because it lacks the continuing political resonance of the year 1492, popularly labeled as the originary moment of Columbus's "discovery" of the Americas. As with the Western hemisphere, many Europeans left eye-witness accounts of their travels to the East. To reveal the geographical, political, and imaginative space of "India/Indies," as mapped by these early travelers, I juxtapose formal documents of the East India Company, the journals and personal letters of Sir Thomas Roe, King James's Ambassador to the Mogul court, with the histrionic representations of Thomas Coryate's letters. I use terms such as "encounter" and "discovery" with some ambivalence, sharing the skepticism of anthropologists who argue that the notion of an actual encounter or discovery is inevitably caught up in the process of imaginatively fabricating rather than representing the cultural "others."[14] That such fabrications constituted the imperatives of the European discovery narratives as they were shaped by the rhetorical and cultural conventions outlined by compilers of travelogues like Purchas's is obvious. Characterized by a blend of fact and fantasy, these narratives do not equally partake of an ideological consensus about the necessity or inevitablity of British commercial and political interests—a consensus that gathers force later, in the late eighteenth and early nineteenth centuries.

Yet these accounts, both empirical and fanciful, historians admit, establish a base of knowledge about local commercial networks, which later facilitated British inroads into existing structures of power. Furthermore, while colonial imperatives are not yet evident, the accounts of Roe, Terry, and others are nonetheless implicated in the religious, social, and ideological codes of the time, such as a belief in the natural superiority of "Christendome" over the "non-Christian heathens." Whether one considers Thomas Roe an early colonist or not, his struggles in interpreting proliferating cultural signifiers in the Indian society reinforce ideological divisions between "barbarism" and "civilization," so that English identity is often defined in relation to otherness.

In contrast to Roe's direct concerns with trade and political negotiations, Thomas Coryate represents his experiences in the Mogul court as spectacles of discovery with himself as a "character" in the scenario, implicitly evoking associations with the Elizabethan discourse of the "theatre of the world" and of Renaissance maps that theatricalized alien lands and peoples (Gillies 1994: 3–98). Yet even in his dramatic accounts, representations of otherness frequently define unfamiliar customs and sights by using Christianity as a mark of the normative, namely of civilization.

Roe's and Coryate's interpretive struggle with Indian languages and culture, in all its drama, was typical of the seventeenth-century discursive formation, where "India/Indies" was gradually caught in the web of European representations. With increasing success in the consolidation of trade and political power, the English began to approach their rule in India via the appropriation of Indian languages to create new systems of rule.

Chapter 2 discusses the formative period in this process—between the years 1770 and 1785—most notably in creating a discourse of Orientalism which converted Indian history and languages into objects of Western knowledge. The founding of the Asiatic Society of Bengal in 1784 marked the watershed of this movement, which was predicated on the "discovery" of India's classical past as an Aryan golden age. I examine recent critiques of Orientalists, which suggest that on the one hand, they idealized India's ancient past and drew resemblances between the East and the West, and on the other hand, they viewed contemporary Hinduism and Indian society as corrupt and fallen, and thus in need of reform. It was no accident that Orientalists were also colonial administrators whose indigenous acculturation made them more efficient, such as in translating and codifying Sanskrit law. With this knowledge the British transformed native laws into instruments of the new, colonial legal system.

If one strand in the ideological formation of "India" was an Orientalizing trend among colonial administrators, the general public in eighteenth-century Britain imagined another kind of Orientalism. This involved a complex picture of India that emerged via the figure of the *nabob*, the popular subject of eighteenth-century cultural and literary texts: of poems, pamphlets, orations, novels, and perhaps most notably, of Samuel Foote's play, *The Nabob* (1772). "Nabob" was the label given to East India Company employees who supposedly acted like stereotypes of Eastern potentates or *nawabs*, and through their corruption jeopardized the Company's future in India. However, while these denunciations of nabobs were supposedly administering a self-corrective on Britain's expanding colonial role in India, they also evoked images of a decadent East that bred dissipation among Englishmen. And these images were often transferred on to the natives as somehow being responsible for the corruption of the English nabobs, as in Foote's play, *The Nabob*. This chapter suggests an interplay of connections between the two seemingly distinct perspectives. For instance, popular denunciations of East India Company nabobs produced a vision of a weakened, decadent India in need of civilization. Yet this sympathy for the hapless Indians was not too far removed from the Orientalist civil servants' discoveries of India's glorious past from which the natives had fallen. In both instances, the appropriate goal for the British was to civilize and rule eighteenth-century India.

Chapter 3 focusses on the nineteenth century, mapping an ideological shift in British colonial attitudes, whereby the imperative of discovering the land and its culture gave way to the second phase of civilizing the natives. This change began in the early nine-teenth century and was marked by the arrival of British women in India to form colonial domesticity and to curb "decadence" or liaisons between East India Company officials and native women. By 1858, when Queen Victoria proclaimed the goals of empire, the custom of arranging the influx of marriageable British girls became an intrinsic feature of Anglo-Indian or British expatriate social life. This demographic change in the ruling population resulted in a significant *gendering* of the empire. By this term I mean that by the mid-nineteenth century the British mobilized the ideal of Victorian domesticity as an important corollary to their "civilizing mission" in India. In transporting the English family to the colonies, the rulers created a racially pure space that the colonial housewife guarded against contamination from native society. Thus, the main premise of the colonial gender system was a *rescue scenario*, whereby the sexual purity of British women, and by inference, of the colonial society, must be preserved by closed enclaves of domesticity or civilization. Ironically, however, the British women who were part of this narrative of imperialism were also constrained within a Victorian model of repressive domesticity.

I approach the concept of a gender system via the theories of feminist historians such as Joan Scott, who use the term "gender" not only as it refers to women's experience, but also as it buttresses other forms of cultural, political, and social organization and experience.[15] It is in this context that I examine the "women's question," a hotly debated topic within both official and unofficial discourses about the "civilizing mission" in nineteenth-century India. Debates on education and on social practices like *sati*, for instance, frequently provoked comparisons between the socially devalued position of Indian women with the assumed freedom and superiority of their British counterparts—and kept alive the convenient dichotomy between colonial definitions of tradition and modernity. Recent feminist criticism questions these official constructions of Indian women as perennial victims whose "rescue" from tradition, they argue, justified British interventions. And after the Mutiny of 1857, they add, the rescue of white women's bodies from the Indian male, a potential rapist, became included in the trope of chivalry.[16] To consider these claims, I explore the complexities of the rescue paradigm, especially how it reveals the relation between colonial motives for reform and their social effects. The native woman is most typically caught in a binary opposition: as the sacrificial victim, the *sati* who must immolate herself, or as the *nautch* girl, the prostitute/dancer, often conflated with the sexualized figure in the *zenana*, the women's quarters, which Europeans often inaccurately represented as a harem. In nineteenth-century texts ranging from Mutiny novels like *Seeta* and *On the Face of the Waters* to eye-witness accounts of the *nautch* performances of the courtesans, the native woman functions as a powerfully ambivalent figure. In the novels mentioned, she fleetingly becomes the alter ego of the *memsahib* in ways that undermine colonial sexual divisions. Usually, of course, these hierarchies are troubled but remain intact. They nonetheless reveal the fragile and disingenuous nature of the code of rescue. For the English woman, rescue entailed her entry into a de-eroticized realm of social segregation, while being reminded of the sexual threat of the native male. And the Indian woman's "rescue" never amounts to more than an English adventure romance told from the safety of a privileged social location.

Chapter 4 explores another cultural form that intervened in a variety of ways in the ideological formation of the British empire in the nineteenth century, namely the colonial theater in Bengal. More specifically, I examine how the material and discursive production of Shakespeare's plays in nineteenth-century Calcutta intersected with the "civilizing mission," particularly as it was manifested in English liberal education and more obliquely, in the Bengal Renaissance.[17]

Shakespeare's name figured prominently in colonial cultural discourses; in fact his works became a means of contextualizing and prescribing perceptions and expectations about the British "civilizing mission," and later of postcolonial reactions to it. One aspect of this process led to a cultural struggle that produced hybrid forms of theater. Among these, most notably, were the Company *nataks* in Bengal, a movement related to the Bengalis' rediscovery of their distinct cultural identity via English literary texts and liberal values. This strain of hybridity continued into the postcolonial era, emerging in a variety of indigenous postcolonial productions of Shakespeare. By hybridity, I mean a specific form of *transculturation*, or a process whereby "marginal or subordinate groups select and create new cultural forms from materials of the dominant culture" (Pratt 1992: 3–5).

Yet this hybrid theatrical idiom is only one aspect of the complex cultural phenomenon of Shakespeare in India, given his pervasive influence in the postcolonial era. Since the nineteenth century, Shakespeare, on the one hand, has become an accommodating ideal, echoing the claims of the civilizing mission into the era of independence. On the other hand, his works have also been appropriated within indigenous theatrical modes in ways that question Shakespeare's canonical Western status, with attendant ramifications for contemporary cultural politics. Thus from the time when Shakespeare's plays were first staged in Calcutta, they have been the site of an on-going cultural struggle in the formation of India's colonial and later, national identity.

Chapter 5 further examines the political implications of such postcolonial cultural struggles that have shaped the Indian nation-state. One feature that most independent nations seem to have in common is the central role of the state, though often caught in competing or new versions of tradition and modernity (Sunder Rajan 1993: 6). This idea of the postcolonial nation in its liberal form has been consistently buttressed by colonial notions of reform and progress, while it has materially "expanded and not transformed the basic institutional arrangements of colonial law and administration of the courts, the bureaucracy, the police, the army, and the various technical services of government."[18] While there have been efforts to reform institutions inherited from colonialism, they have been hampered either by Western "modernization" that is anachronistic or by indigenous forces of communalism and misogyny that spout an anti-colonial rhetoric.[19]

This chapter explores these competing views of Indian nationalism in a variety of literary and cultural texts by drawing on the theoretical assumption of a nation as a fictional construct. It begins with Jawaharlal Nehru's *The Discovery of India*. Signaling the independence of India, this quasi-autobiographical history produces a curiously contradictory nationalist discourse: on the one hand, it is anti-colonial in positioning itself vis-à-vis the British Raj against which most Indians had fought and won. On the other hand, in Nehru's standard nationalist account, while the figure of India or *Bharat Mata* symbolically erases the class and religious divisions among its "children," it does so within a colonial teleology of progress and modernity.[20]

If Nehru's "discovery" of a unified India is caught between the competing claims of tradition and modernity—and between its past and future—it also reveals India's coming into being as a system of cultural signification within a fractured discursive field of the "nation." In this context, the chapter also explores the relationship between literature and the formation of the Indian national identity from three perspectives: the Indo-Anglian realist novel; the magic-realist, postmodern fiction of Salman Rushdie; and the critical reception of *The Blind Age*, a postcolonial play by Dharamvir Bharati, expressing a postmodern skepticism regarding India's mythic past. In thus exploring these varied fictions that go into the making of the concept of the nation itself, this chapter concludes the book with some reflections on the competing, often ambivalent, definitions of India's national postcolonial identity.

Thus, reflecting on the complex discursive strands that go into the making of the real and imagined "India," one can see that postcolonial cultural studies is itself a highly mediated field. Like Coryate's speech before the Great Mogul, received by contemporary readers after it had passed through a complex process of translation, transcription, and second-hand accounts, colonial and postcolonial narratives also constitute a derivative discursive field—one from which we can learn how our knowledge is shaped by rhetorical tropes, generic expectations, and discourse styles as much as by the information conveyed. And caught in these multiple narratives, India becomes a palimpsest, continually being "discovered" and "re-discovered" (inscribed and re-inscribed) by colonialist and later nationalist forces for their specific agendas and goals.

NOTES

1 Many primary and secondary sources suggest that early modern travel narratives often drew on prior sources to embellish their accounts, so that, for instance, the Elizabethan taste for the exotic demanded accounts of monstrous races drawn from Pliny and Mandeville. See Gillies 1994: 1–39, for a full description of this process. Samuel Purchas, in the "Preface" to his monumental anthology of travel writings, also defines the expectations of wonder and marvel that such writings created in their European readers (1905: xliii).

2 Individual chapters in the book offer detailed accounts of the shifting uses of the discovery motif. For an account of the British rejection of an idealizing Orientalism in the mid-nineteenth century, see Sharpe, "The Violence of Light," 1993: 30–1. According to her, once "'India' was fixed and normalized as an unchanging text, Oriental learning

was no longer necessary" (30). In the eighteenth century, the British felt that Oriental learning was "of value for governing the natives" (30).

3 I am indebted to David Spurr's conceptualization of the rhetoric of colonization (1994: especially 6–7). By focussing on "twelve rhetorical modes, or ways of writing about non-Western peoples" (3), he establishes a convincing connection between colonizing and writing. My book is informed by his interest in the "cultural, ideological, or literary" assumptions underlying specific linguistic tropes found in colonial discourse. For a full account of his argument, see pp. 1–12.

4 Most relevant to my premise is Mary Louise Pratt's study of travel writing (1992) as a part of the history of European imperialism since the Renaissance. According to Pratt, among the representational conventions deployed by European travelers/writers was the strategy of naming geographical landmarks and cultural practices, while taking on the pose of objective witnesses. But Pratt views the main protagonist of the European travel narrative as a "seeing-man . . . whose imperial eyes passively look out and possess" (7). Pratt's paradigm is useful in understanding the pervasive assumptions about objectivity and veracity in British travel narratives about India.

5 While I focus on certain recurring colonial tropes similar to Spurr's, I do not divide them into the "twelve rhetorical modes" listed by him (1994: 2–4).

6 Patrick Brantlinger, in *Crusoe's Footprints* (1990), charts the history of cultural studies in the Anglo-American humanities. For his discussion of a "counterdisciplinary practice," see pp. 22–33.

7 Several essays in the 1980s persuasively show how *The Tempest* is imbricated in the discourse of colonialism and how critical responses to it have been complicit, whether consciously or not, with colonialist ideology. The seminal essay on this subject is Paul Brown's "'This thing of darkness I acknowledge mine': *The Tempest* and the discourse of colonialism" (1985). Cultural/literary critics and authors in the third world offered revisionary readings of the play even earlier, in which they identified Caliban as a revolutionary. For an important account of the play's relation with the decolonization movements, see Roberto Fernández Retamar 1989: 3–55.

8 For a fuller account of the long trend to locate Shakespeare's works firmly within European tradition, see Gillies 1994: 1–4, especially his discussion of J.D. Roger's essay, "Voyages and Exploration: Geography, Maps," in *Shakespeare's England* (1916). This essay claims that Shakespeare's "plots, themes, and scenes are almost exclusively European" (quoted in Gillies 1994: 1). For recent studies that make a case for "revising" the colonialist readings of *The Tempest* and drawing attention to the more "local" contexts, see Bruster (1995) and Skura (1989). While both of these are brilliant, insightful essays that suggest multiple contexts, they seem to overlook the fact that the play's place in colonial and postcolonial history has forever changed its status as a Western canonical text.

9 Anne McClintock (1995) pointedly questions the orientation of postcolonial studies as an emerging discipline because the two categories
   reproduce the binary opposition between colonial and postcolonial
   eras, thereby recuperating "linear European time," the cornerstone of
   the colonial teleology of "progress" and "civilization" (9–17). She
   also rightly critiques the monolithic and static use of the term "postcolonial," which blurs, among other issues, the political distinctions
   between cultures and the continuities in the "international imbalances
   in imperial power" (13) in the supposedly postcolonial era. Therefore,
   she suggests that "more complex terms and analyses of alternative
   times, histories, and causalities are required to deal with the complexities that cannot be served under the single rubric of postcolonialism"
   (13).
10 For an account of Bhabha's analysis of the discourse of colonialism
   as a signifying system marked by ambivalence, see Stephen Slemon's
   analysis (1994: 16–29).
11 Lisa Lowe (1991: 16–21) draws on Gramsci, among others, to make a
   persuasive case for the instability of colonial discourse, with its attendant possibilities for resistance. However, in making her elaborate
   case for the discursive instability of colonial discourse, she runs the
   risk of eliding resistance at the level of reading with material practices
   that block off all such possibilities.
12 See Partha Chatterjee (1993: 27–32), who discusses various competing
   readings of colonial history. One view of discontinuity between a
   precolonial and colonial period is challenged by various versions of a
   continuous history of "Indian capitalism," which supposedly simply
   merged into colonialism.
13 Partha Chatterjee (1993: 14–34) charts these shifts whereby the regime
   of power re-inscribes itself in new institutional arrangements.
14 For contemporary ethnographic theories of cultural encounters, see
   James Clifford, "Introduction" to *Writing Culture* (Clifford and
   Marcus 1986), 1–26. Here he discusses ethnography as a form of "cultural fiction" based upon "systematic and contestable exclusions" (6).
15 My use of the term "gender" as an analytic category in historical
   studies is drawn from Scott (1989).
16 Jenny Sharpe offers a good analysis of the colonial trope of rescue in
   Allegories of Empire (1993), as does Sunder Rajan (1993: 47–8). I am
   indebted to both these studies.
17 My reading of the collusion between empire and English literature
   draws on Vishwanathan 1989: 1–50.
18 Partha Chatterjee (1993: 14–18) offers a useful analysis of the continu-
   ance of colonial state institutions into the postcolonial era.
19 Sunder Rajan (1993: 23–7) discusses the *sati* debate in contemporary
   India, to illuminate the rise of indigenous reactionary movements.
20 Nehru's account does not challenge what Partha Chatterjee describes
   as a "standard nationalist history," in which the independence movement is seen in the context of the colonial enlightenment in the late
   nineteenth century, whose aim was to "modernize the customs and
   institutions of a traditional society" (1993: 5).

WORKS CITED IN THE INTRODUCTION

Brantlinger, Patrick. *Crusoe's Footprints: Cultural Studies in Britain and America*. London: Routledge, 1990.

Brown, Paul. "'This thing of darkness I acknowledge mine': *The Tempest* and the Discourse of Colonialism." In *Political Shakespeare: New Essays in Cultural Materialism*. Ed. Jonathan Dollimore and Alan Sinfield. Ithaca: Cornell University Press, 1985: 48–71.

Bruster, Douglas. "Local *Tempest*: Shakespeare and the Work of the Early Modern Playhouse." *Journal of Medieval and Renaissance Studies*, 25, 1, 1995: 33–53.

Chatterjee, Partha. *The Nation and its Fragments: Colonial and Post-colonial Histories*. Princeton: Princeton University Press, 1993.

Clifford, James and George F. Marcus. Eds. *Writing Culture: The Poetics and Politics of Ethnography*. Berkeley: University of California Press, 1986.

Coryate, Thomas. *Mr Thomas Coriate to his friends in England sendeth greeting*. London: 1618. STC 5811.

Dirks, Nicholas B. Ed. "Introduction." *Colonialism and Culture*. Ann Arbor: University of Michigan Press, 1992: 1–25.

Dyson, Ketaki Kushari. *A Various Universe: A Study of the Journals and Memoirs of British Men and Women in the Indian Subcontinent, 1765–1856*. Delhi: Oxford University Press, 1978.

Gillies, John. *Shakespeare and the Geography of Difference*. Cambridge: Cambridge University Press, 1994.

Greenblatt, Stephen. *Marvelous Possessions: The Wonder of the New World*. Chicago: University of Chicago Press, 1991.

Lord, Henry. *A Discoverie of the Sect of Banians Conteyning their Historie, Law, Liturgie, Casts, Customs, and Ceremonies*. London: 1630. STC 16825. New York: De Capo Press, 1972.

Lowe, Lisa. *Critical Terrains: British and French Orientalisms*. Ithaca: Cornell University Press, 1991.

McClintock, Anne. *Imperial Leather: Race, Gender, and Sexuality in the Colonial Contest*. London: Routledge, 1995.

Nehru, Jawaharlal. *The Discovery of India* (1945). New York: Doubleday, 1959.

Pratt, Mary Louise. *Imperial Eyes: Travel Writing and Transculturation*. London: Routledge, 1992.

Purchas, Samuel. "To the Reader," in *Hakluytus Posthumus or Purchas His Pilgrimes: Contayning a History of the World in Sea Voyages and Lande Travells by Englishmen and others* (1625), Vol. I. Glasgow: James MacLehose and Sons, 1905: xxxix–xlviii.

Retamar, Roberto Fernandez. *Caliban and Other Essays*. Trans. Edward Baker. Minneapolis: University of Minnesota Press, 1989.

Sangari, Kum Kum. "Introduction: Representations in History." In *Journal of Arts and Ideas*, 17–18, 1989: 2–16.

Scott, Joan W. "Gender: A Useful Category of Historical Analysis." In *Coming To Terms: Feminism, Theory, Politics*. Ed. Elizabeth Weed. London: Routledge, 1989: 81–100.

Sharpe, Jenny. "The Violence of Light in the Land of Desire; or, How William Jones Discovered India." In *boundary 2*, 20:1, 1993: 26–46.

——— *Allegories of Empire: The Figure of the Woman in the Colonial Text.* Minneapolis: University of Minnesota Press, 1993.

Skura, Meredith. "Discourse and the Individual: The Case of Colonialism in *The Tempest.*" *Shakespeare Quarterly*, 40, 1989: 42–69.

Slemon, Stephen. "The Scramble for Post-colonialism." In *De-scribing Empire: Post-colonialism and Textuality.* Ed. Chris Tiffin and Alan Lawson. London: Routledge, 1994: 15–32.

Spurr, David. *The Rhetoric of Empire: Colonial Discourse in Journalism, Travel Writing, and Imperial Administration.* Durham, N.C.: Duke University Press, 1994.

Sunder Rajan, Rajeswari. *Real and Imagined Women: Gender, Culture, and Postcolonialism.* London: Routledge, 1993.

Vishwanathan, Gauri. *Masks of Conquest: Literary Study and British Rule in India.* New York: Columbia University Press, 1989.

Williams, Raymond. *The Country and the City.* New York: Oxford University Paperbacks, 1973.

Chapter 1

Discoveries, encounters, spectacles: colonial beginnings

I

a people presented themselues to mine eyes, cloathed in linnen garments, somewhat low descending, of a gesture and garbe as I may say, maidenly and well nigh effeminate; . . . whose use in the [East India] Companies affaires occasioned their presence there.

Truth to say, mine eyes unacquainted with such objects, took vp their wonder and gazed; and this admiration the badge of a fresh Trauailar, bred in mee the importunity of a Questioner: I asked what manner of people those were, so strangely notable and notably strange? Reply was made, they were *Banians*, a people forraigne to the knowledge of the Christian world; their Religion, Rites, and Customes, sparingly treated of by any.

(Henry Lord, a Minister attached to the East India Company
Factory at Surat, 1630: B–B1)[1]

When the East India Company was granted its charter in 1600, the image of "India," often conflated with the "Indies," had already become a part of the collective European imagination. Images of India did not converge on a single geographic entity, but proliferated in a range of associations drawn from Columbus's misnaming of the Americas as the "Indies" to the "wonderfull fame" of the Mogul king, Jehangir, and his ancestors, who were the descendants of the fabled conquerer, Tamburlaine. In fact, most accounts of India and other non-European lands, described by Samuel Purchas as "uncouth countries of the World," were shaped by an informal repertoire of conventions and methods. In his Preface to his monumental anthology, *Purchas, His Pilgrimes*, Purchas (1625) articulates his interest in recapitulating the "Rarities of Nature" and the "extraordinary Wonders, which God's providence hath therein effected according to his good and just pleasure" (xliii). And in gathering information of "various Nations, Persons, Shapes, Colours, [and] Habits," he admits that his method "could not be therein exact . . . because I had such a confused Chaos of printed and written Bookes . . . [and] because this Method by way of Voyages often repeates the same Countries" (xliii–iv). As a result, he explains, the "vast Volumes" of information are "contracted, and Epitomised," so that the "nicer Reader might not be cloyed," and the travel narrative will serve as a form of edifying entertainment for a domestic audience (xliii). Thus, Purchas goes on to explain: "for [those] which cannot travell farre . . . I offer a World of Travellers to their domestike entertainment, easie to be spared from their Smoke, cup, and Butter-flie vanities . . . and to entertain them in a better Schoole to better purposes" (xliv).[2]

From Purchas and others we learn that what typically attracted both the writers and the readers of these travel accounts were expectations of the strange and the marvelous. Henry Lord aptly describes the way in which the trope of amazement and wonder casts its spell over all travel narratives when he identifies "admiration [as] the badge of a fresh Travailar" (Lord 1630: B2). In the quest for marvels, then, the geographic imagination of the Renaissance travelers/writers and ethnographers ranged freely, mingling their eye-witness descriptions with received accounts of the exotic from classical and medieval writers. Undoubtedly, their imagination was given an impetus as well as formed by descriptions of marvels and monstrosities in the texts of Pliny, Africanus, and Mandeville (who was still taken seriously at the time), by the atlases of Abraham Ortelius and Gerard Mercator, and by the voyage compilations of Richard Eden and Richard Hakluyt.[3] Thus, typically, these received conventions offered prescriptions for the travelers' expectations and provided a context for their behavior.

For instance, even the travelers employed by the East India Company saw an integral connection between their roles as Company functionaries and as compilers of strange and curious knowledge. Henry Lord makes this apparent in his two dedications, to the Archbishop of Canterbury and to the Goverer of the Company (1630): he informs the Archbishop that having arrived "in the forraigne parts of the East Indies (whither it pleased God to dispose me in a Ministeriall charge under the imployment of the East India Company)," he had noted Indian

sects such as the Banians "violating the divine law of the dread
Maiesty of Heaven, and with notable forgery Coyning Religion
according to the Minte of their owne Tradition, abusing that
Stampe which God would have to passe currant in the true
Church" (A2–A3). To the Governor he writes, "this sect of
Banians suggested unto me something novell and strange, and
gave mee hopes it would bee a present worthy and welcome to
your [Governer's] hands" (I^v). Lord wants this account to cross
the "Tropicks" to England, so that "together with the Transport
of Commodities from a forraigne Mart, you [the Governer
should] informe the home residers with the Manners and
Customes of the People in transmarine kingdomes of the world"
(I^v). Calling the members of the East India Company "worthy
Adventurers," he believes that their names lend weight to his
dedication to works that "have in them anything forraigne or
exotick in the limit and confine of [their] adventures" (A3). Lord's
account reveals an interesting connection between English commercial interests and the production of ethnographic knowledge—
a connection that was beginning to emerge at this time. Furthermore, he reinforces the generic expectations of the standard travel
record, namely the discovery of marvels and curiosities.

Similarly, in Theophilus Lavender's compilation, *The Travels of
Certaine Englishmen into Africa, Asia, Troy* . . . (1609), the writer
at the outset addresses his readers' eager expectations for adventures, while luring them to read about "sundrie Travellers of
great name, which have enterprised and taken in hand great
voyages, and dangerous journeys" (3). His travelers are William
Biddulph, a preacher, and his brother, Peter, a diamond-cutter,
who travel for "ten yeeres" to several "easterne" lands including
India. According to Lavender, William Biddulph "feares that
others will hardly beleeve anything but that which they themselves
have seene; and when they heare anything that seemeth strange
unto them, they reply that travellers may lie" (A). This emphasis
here on the Europeans' veracity as eye-witnesses, so pervasive in
travel narratives, privileges their act of *seeing* as a mode of unmediated access to experience, while implicitly ignoring the natives'
own ability to *see*. However, it becomes apparent that though
the compiler of the Biddulph letters testifies to the "trueth of
everything therein contained" (claiming the verification of other
"travellers of good judgment who have been in those parts"),
his reflections reveal the contradictions between the travelers'

(and compilers') desire to establish their veracity and their impulse to exoticize and often demonize the cultural "others" they encounter.[4]

This tension between the experiences of travelers/writers and their rhetorically embellished and often distorted accounts are evident in seventeenth-century English discovery narratives about the "East Indies." Yet the rifts between fact and fiction are ideologically held in check by the often unexamined European assumptions of "truth" underpinning the rhetoric of the marvelous and wondrous. Thus, not surprisingly, the English travelers/writers frequently fall back on naturalizing distinctions between themselves and the natives they encounter, representing the otherness of unfamiliar customs and sights as antithetical, and, thereby, inferior to Christian beliefs and practices. Implicated in these familiar strategies of representation is a sense of certitude, a faith in the all-encompassing power of Christianity. Thus, Christianity not only serves as the mark of the normative, but also crucially provides the moral imperative for the discovery, and later conquest, of the non-Christian, "heathen" lands. For instance, when Henry Lord brings to the attention of the Archbishop of Canterbury certain Indian sects who with "notable forgery" "coyne Religion according to the Minte of their owne Tradition," rather than of the "true [Christian] Church," he does so because he considers it his "bounden duty . . . to apprehend them and bring them before your Grace, to receive both censure and Iudgment" (A2–A3). Furthermore, while Lord is struck by the "strangely notable and notably strange" Banians, he defines their strangeness in terms of their exclusion from the "knowledge of the Christian world" (B1). And other accounts of the exotic, such as Thomas Coryate's vivid imaginings of the River Ganges, are also frequently predicated upon a binary opposition between Christianity and "superstition," which, in this instance, neutralizes the pleasures of the spectacle:

> I expect an excellent opportunity . . . to goe to the famous River Ganges, whereof about foure hundred thousand people go hither . . . to bathe in the River, and to sacrifice a world of gold in the same River . . . throwing into the River as a Sacrifice, and doing other notable strange Ceremonies most worth of obseruation, such a notable Spectacle it is, that no part of all Asia . . . [is] the like to be seen; this show doe they make

once euery yeere, comming hither from places almost thousand miles off, and honour their Riuer as their God, Creator, Sauiour; superstition and impiety most abominable . . . these brutish Ethnickes, that are aliens.

(Coryate 1618: C3)

Edward Terry, Chaplain to the English Ambassador (1615–19), in his well-meaning attempts at deciphering Indian customs and religions, also frequently reproduces this dichotomy between Christianity and its "others," sometimes through a desperate attempt to ensure the superiority of Christianity, despite the actions of those who practice it. For instance, while criticizing the "exorbitances of many [Christians] which come amongst them [the Indians]," the Chaplain feels that their lax behavior diminishes the moral superiority of their religion:

For truly it is a sad sight there to behold a drunken Christian, and a sober Indian, a temperate Indian and a Christian given up to his Appetite. An Indian that is just and square in his dealing, a Christian not so; a laborious Indian, and an idle Christian. . . . O what a sad thing is it for Christians to come short of Indians, even in Moralities, come shorte of those who themselves believe, to come shorte of heaven.

(Terry 1655: 419)

In setting such moral boundaries between the Christian Europeans and the "brutish" Indians, the English narratives were simply recapitulating the Renaissance poetic geography, itself drawn from texts of antiquity, whereby geographic distance from the European/Christian center implied a progressive degeneration and a "loss of cultural, moral, and linguistic integrity" (Gillies 1994: 32). Hence one can see why, in the Chaplain's eyes, a Christian typology of moral difference must be held in place in this land of moral confusion, reminding his readers that Indians come "shorte of heaven." Quite typically, then, the English travelers/ writers are often caught up in the ideological codes of the time, such as a naturalized belief in the superiority of "Christendome" over non-Christian "heathens," despite the fact that the latter might act in ways morally superior to certain Christians. Of course, these Englishmen do not emerge as static, allegorical figures, or simply as agents of the impending empire. Rather, we see them as historical subjects struggling to come to terms with a confusingly different culture that seems to threaten the stable categories and assumptions of English cultural identity. In response to their obvious disorientation, they often fall back on conventional divisions between "barbarism" and "civilization" which help to fix their identity in relation to otherness.

While seventeenth-century travel narratives about India constitute an archive frequently used by historians, they have drawn the attention of Renaissance and postcolonial literary critics much less. In fact, among literary critics, it is the nineteenth century that is cast as the defining moment of imperial power with little or no connection made with the periods preceding it. I suggest that while there is no direct trajectory toward empire from Sir Thomas Roe's arrival in India in 1615 to Queen Victoria's proclamation of direct rule in 1858, some traces of an incipient colonial ideology can be found in the language of colonization by which these English travelers/writers established their own dominance rhetorically and imaginatively, if not militarily and politically. In effect, these early modern representations of the non-European "others" served as a context for empire-building by prescribing actions and strategies, as well as laying out the advantages of trade. Drawing on this formulation, I examine how these travel narratives constitute a loosely connected system of cultural significance by which one culture (the English) came to interpret, represent, and gradually to dominate the other. While the repertoire of colonial discourse was broad and diffuse, even in the early modern period, one can nonetheless identify its strategy of domination via "a range of tropes, conceptual categories, and logical operations available for the purposes of representation" across a range of contexts and periods.[5]

Furthermore, as several studies have noted, these narratives of the early forms of economic and commercial penetration into Mogul territories were also appropriable by later imperial designs. Thus, in providing information about practical aspects of trade and commerce, among other things, narratives by Roe, Terry, and others related to Company affairs have enabled historians to chart the beginnings of the British colonization of India, as Bernard Cohn explains:

> The records of the seventeenth and eighteenth centuries reflect the Company's central concerns with trade and commerce; one finds long lists of products, prices, trade routes, descriptions of

coastal and inland marts, and "political" information about the
Mughal Empire and especially local officials and their actions
related to the [East India] Company. Scattered throughout
these records are mentions of names of Indians employed by
the Company or with whom they were associated, on whom
they were dependent for the information and knowledge to
carry out their commercial ventures.

(Cohn 1985: 276)

Cumulatively, then, descriptions of the development of English
trade in India are useful to historians in showing how the
merchants established a base of trading operations, one factory
after another. Again, according to Cohn, in these sources "we
can trace the changes in forms of knowledge which the conquerers
defined as useful to their own ends" (276). Overall, historians
agree that the early commercial ventures of the East India
Company combined with the gradually declining power of the
Moguls became the building blocks for the larger edifice of the
nineteenth-century British Raj.[6]

Some intimations of a developing colonial ideology, which is
only implicit in the seventeenth-century travel narratives, can be
traced more directly to official self-representations by the East
India Company at the time. For instance, "The Petition and
Remonstrance of the Governing Board of the East India Company," presented before the House of Commons in 1628, promoted trade as a moral imperative and a disinterested activity
bringing "commodities for Christendome" (3):

> This trade as it is thus great in itselfe; so doth it yet further
> enlarge our Traffique and strength, by furnishing this King-
> dome with all sorts of Indian wares not only for our owne use,
> but more especially for the necessary wants of Forraigne
> nations, which hath greatly increased the number of our warlike
> ships.

Profits for the merchants and the Company are justified by the
lowering of prices of new commodities—"Pepper," "Cloves,"
"Indico," "Maces," and "Nutmegs"—without giving any clue as
to why and how a need for such "staples" was created by their
availability.

What the merchants do disclose, however, is the link between the
"exportations of commodities for diverse parts of Christendome"

and the expansion of the number of warships and "marriners" added to Britain's growing naval forces. The Company's Petition reminds the authorities of the political stakes of trade when it refers to the "expulsion of our peoples" by the "Hollanders" who "do keep us by force from the trade in those Spices: in which wares . . . we enioyed the freedom in the Indies . . . " (3). Not surprisingly, then, these "price wars" are presented with an urgency that reveals the stakes of the conflict: "as the Dutch have raised the price of these commodities, so would they much more enhaunce them and all other rich Wares of those countries, if wee should abandon or be basely driven from the trade" (9–10).

The merchants conclude their petition by collapsing all the "Nations of the Eastern world" (36) into a single source of rich wares that will increase their own nation's "strength, wealth, and treasure" and prove "honourable" both to the "King and his Kingdomes":

> for when it shall be found that the trade to the East Indies is so good a measure to increase our strength, wealth, safety, and treasure, and that discoueries have spread his Maiesties fame into Persia, Japon, China, and the Dominions of the Great Mogull, and many other remote Nations of the Easterne world, there shall be no deniall, but that these great blessings are so precious and honourable both to the King and his Kingdomes that they out to be preserued with our best endeauours. . . . And for conclusion the East India Companie doe humbly declare unto this Honourable House that have not made their Petition and this Remonstrance for their owne *private* ends, but for the *publique* good.
>
> (ibid.; my emphasis)

Finally, the merchants elide the continued prosperity of the East India Company (for which they seek protection) with the prosperity of England as a nation, while subsuming their "owne private ends" within the benign discourse of the "publique good." Thus, in the Company's petition, "India/Indies" is both a site of "treasures" or "commodities," which have generated price wars among European merchants, and a crucial signifier in the formation of England's emerging identity as a "nation," significant to its later claims of imperial power. And in this formulation, the potential readers of the East India Company's document (and implicitly, the larger public) are produced as patriotic subjects who will accept the naturalized convergence of the interests of capital profit and the national prosperity. The tropological cast of this official petition is apparent in the way it represents its commercial intent via the *discovery* motif of finding "treasures/commodities" to which the English had both natural and moral claims. Thus, its disinterested stance is undermined by its ideological function in the emergence of nascent imperialism and capitalism.

However, it is important to note that though this document yokes the interests of the state to those of the merchants, it occludes an important aspect of this partnership, one that will become apparent in the eighteenth century, namely, that "the colonizing of government by speculative finance [was] far more at stake than the actual conquest of someone else's land."[7] While at this early stage of trading activities, mercantile and state interests rallied under the banner of the "great blessings" of trade, this relationship (as I discuss later) became progressively estranged with the growth of both colonial capital and political power in the eighteenth century.

The rhetoric of this document, unlike the travelers' narratives, is typically monologic, detailing political and commercial rivalries among Europeans, but ignoring the possibility of any dialogue with native perspectives. If the lands of the east are labeled "discoueries" and sources of "treasures," the sprawling Mogul empire (which did not hold uniform sway over the land) becomes an entity called "India" to which the East India Company seems to have a natural claim, as opposed to other Europeans such as the "Hollanders," and not to mention the peoples living there.

The official view of the East India Company, as found in the merchants' petition, is part of a complex, though unstable, discursive field of English representations of India in the seventeenth century. Overall, the English narratives, as mentioned earlier, do not coalesce into an ideological consensus around the necessity or inevitablity of direct political rule. The formulation of ideology used here stems from the Althusserian definition to mean that these accounts were not part of an ensemble of beliefs and practices by which *all* Elizabethans and later Jacobeans imagined themselves as empire-builders. Thus, the political/commercial agenda of the East India Company at this stage did not constitute an overarching ideology that "hailed" people, interpellated them into specific class positions as rulers, and provided them with appropriate subjectivities.[8]

Nonetheless, I believe, the stage for the British empire in India was set in the seventeenth century. This setting was provided by British travelers/writers who created "India" as a site of alterity and otherness vis-à-vis a European hierarchy of difference. Thus, despite the textual density of their record, we get no sense of an indigenous actuality except as mediated by English drives and desires, which in turn were conditioned by the expectations of the marvelous and strange. A vivid sense of this interpretive process can be found in the travel narratives of the men who came to India in a variety of roles: as emissaries of James I and the East India Company, like Sir Thomas Roe, as freewheeling adventurers, like Thomas Coryate, or as chaplains administering to English souls, like Edward Terry.

While the East India Company was the patron and protector of most English travelers—and was patronized in turn by James I— these travelers/writers often reveal the tensions between the imperatives of political and commercial interests and their efforts to interpret and master what they perceive as the intractable otherness of India. Some of these strains also emerge in the way in which the travelers' experiences are mediated by expectations of sights and customs that they consider unnatural and uncivilized. In different modes and degrees, these seventeenth-century eyewitness accounts show "India/Indies" emerging as a geographical and cultural entity within the British imagination via the rhetorical, figurative, and sometimes fictionalizing practices common to both history and ethnography. Thus, it becomes apparent that all these narratives depicting the East Indies and other non-European lands did so in a context and tradition familiar to their domestic audiences. Hence, naming and representing the geographical and imaginative terrain helped in the establishment of imperial claims in the late eighteenth century, when India was fully mapped as a crucial site in England's definition of its nationhood.[9]

Despite their varying roles—as Ambassador, adventurer, Chaplain, and others—the methodology of these writers reflects certain shared concerns: about cataloguing geographical features and social customs of the land, and about recording their day-to-day experiences. This impulse to catalogue easily enabled the establishment of detailed typologies of geographical, cultural, and moral categories, and in turn, became a crucial aspect of the project of colonial meaning-making from the earliest European encounters. Typologies mark identity and difference, thus usefully *determining* what will be perceived as different.[10] Therefore, not surprisingly, the English travelers/writers in seventeenth-century India drew on a repertoire of inherited typologies—geographical, cultural, and religious, among others—to which they had easy access. Overall, they function as both historians and ethnographers or "participant observers," revealing the way in which history, ethnography, and literature intersect in a blend of "fact" and "fiction." Within this context, the term "eye-witness" must be used with some care; far from being transparent, these narratives are inescapably figurative and polysemous, interwoven with familiar tropes of discovery, spectacle, and adventure, while stressing the opacity and "barbarism" of the cultural "others" the Europeans encountered. The highly mediated narratives of the two representative figures I study—Sir Thomas Roe and Thomas Coryate—vividly illustrate this intractable struggle, showing us how they are in part "caught up in the invention not representation of [Eastern] cultures."[11]

II

Sir Thomas Roe's journal and letters written from India[12]—from the site of the commercial and political exchanges—are constrained by official inscriptions of policy, as are his encounters with Indians with whom he negotiates trading privileges. When Thomas Best brought home glowing accounts of the possibilities of trade in India, the East India Company recognized the threats posed to such a venture by the Portuguese, who already had a base on the Western coast. Therefore Sir Thomas Smythe, the Governor of the Company in 1614, requested James I on behalf of the English merchants to send a man "of extraordinary partes to reside att Agra to preuent any plottes that may be wrought by the Iesuites [accompanying the Portuguese] to circumvent our trade" (quoted in Foster 1899: iii).

Thomas Roe was just this man of "extraordinary partes," having already sought adventure, as was then the fashion among aristocratic males, in a voyage to Guiana in 1610, under the patronage of Prince Henry. It is not incidental that Ralegh's founding narrative of the "discovery" of Guiana should have shaped Roe's self-image as an explorer and incipient colonist. He welcomed the offer of the East India Company, after the death of his patron, Prince Henry, and set sail in February 1615. At the time of his arrival he had found the English in a precarious position:

> threatened by the Portuguese, plundered by the native officials, and in imminent danger of expulsion owing to the ill-will of Prince Khurram (the King's heir) . . . their active competition injured the trade of the native merchants, while . . . the troubles caused by the hostilities between the Portuguese and the English estranged the great body of the inhabitants.
>
> (in Foster 1899: xliii)

But by the time Roe departed for England in 1619, the future of British influence in India was on a more secure footing. After a prolonged struggle to outwit the machinations of various unfriendly parties, the Ambassador succeeded in procuring a grant to establish a trading post at Surat, though with some constraints, as he states: "I was forced to relinquish many poynts often insisted vpon . . . to settle a trade . . . which might giue the least offence and might pass with ease" (xli).

Departing from India, the Ambassador did not foresee that he had established the foundation for later, colonial rule, though he made an uncanny prediction about the forces of unrest within the Mogul empire—and "of a tyme when all in these kingdomes will be in combustion."[13] Overall, while the English did not lay immediate claim to India, they gradually recognized a convergence of their commercial and political interests. Of course, Roe's role stands out in stark contrast to Columbus's, who had declared, "I found innumerable people and very many islands, of which I took possession in Your Highnesses' name" (Zamora 1993: 3). Such direct claims on India were beyond the imaginings of the Europeans in the seventeenth century. And the Mogul king Jehangir's memoirs reveal his indifference toward the English embassy and European rulers in general; in his mind, only the Persian and the Ottoman monarchs were his worthy rivals.[14]

Roe's impressions of India tell a complex story frequently cited in histories of the period. The fact that his account takes the form of a journal, interspersed with letters, is crucial in revealing the way in which he produces "facts" about the principal personages and their power struggles in the Mogul court. Roe's journal offers details of his day-to-day machinations to gain concessions for English traders, under the auspices of obtaining a pact of "constant love and peace" between the two monarchs. In it, we also get a vivid, dramatic picture of an autocratic, yet malleable and even amiable Jehangir, of the cold and haughty Prince, of a wily governer, "Asaph Chan," and even an imagined view of the powerful Queen "Normall" (and the women of the harem), whom he never meets. Roe frequently breaks away from the position of narrator to recapitulate his own interactions with his cast of characters. Despite his vivid descriptions, however, Roe's writings also reveal his considerable difficulty in reading the political and cultural world in terms of his own *system of meanings*. Like other European travelers/writers, the Ambassador represents the Mogul court in a series of *spectacles* that both exoticize and demonize the natives. Yet frequently, in detailing the complexities of unfamiliar customs, he defines his own culture as the norm and in opposition to "uncivilized" practices.

According to several historians, Europeans of the seventeenth century lived in a world where the written word had an established cultural hegemony and was also seen as a pragmatic vehicle of communication. Therefore, for them agreements inscribed in language, and thus constituting the law, implied a stability and certitude of meaning.[15] Bernard Cohn, for instance, explains this process in the context of seventeenth-century India as follows:

> Meaning for the English was something attributed to a word, a phrase or an object, which could be determined and translated, hopefully with a synonym which had a direct referent to something in what the English thought of as a "natural" world. Everything had a more or less specific referent for the English.
> (Cohn 1985: 279)

With the Indians, according to Cohn, "meaning was not necessarily construed in the same fashion" (279), as he explains:

> Hindus and Muslims operated with an unbounded substantive theory of objects and persons. The body of the ruler was literally his authority, the substance of which could be transmitted in what Europeans thought of as objects. Clothes, weapons, jewels, and paper were the means by which a ruler could transmit the substance of his authority to a chosen [person].
> (ibid.)

Thus the relations among persons, groups, and "nations" were constituted differently in Europe and in India. As a result, the English in seventeenth-century India had some difficulty in establishing a system of exchange value. They operated on the idea that

> everything and everyone had a "price" . . . They never seemed to realize that [among the Indians] certain kinds of cloth, jewels, arms, and animals had values that were not established in terms of a market-determined price, but were objects in a culturally constructed system by which authority and social relations were literally constituted and transmitted.

> (ibid.)

Given these differing perceptions about the social functions and relations of language, the English assumptions of unmediated representation inevitably came under some strain. As a representative of the Crown and the Company, Roe also views himself as master hermeneut—writing from the authority of an interpreter who must represent, categorize, and fix the culture and its practices for the benefit of his patrons. However, he faces obstacles in communication because his assumptions about cultural translation are based on a seamless relation between word and referent, language and reality.[16] And as he did not know Persian, the Court language, his own problems with linguistic and cultural translation, as described in his journal and letters, are transformed into a recurring complaint against Indian linguistic and legal practices. For instance, in trying to translate the letters he brought from James I to the Mogul king, Jehangir, Roe expresses his frustration to his employers: "For the Brokers here will not speak but what shall please; yea, they would alter the King's letter because his name was before the Mughals, which I would not allow" (quoted in Cohn 1985: 278). Repeatedly in his writings, Roe complains about a world of proliferating signs that does not correspond to fixed concepts inscribed in language, which can then be translated and verified in English. Thus, he laments in a letter to the Minister at Surat: "Religions infinite; lawes none. In this Confusion what can bee expected?" (in Foster 1899: 168).

In another letter to the Archbishop of Canterbury, Roe specifically protests against the Mogul king's lack of distinction between spoken edicts and written laws: "Lawes they have none written. The Kyngs judgment byndes, Who sitts and giues sentence with much patience, once [weekly], both in Capitall and Criminall

causes; wher sometymes he sees the execution done by his Eli-
phants, with too much delight in blood" (123). To Lord Carew,
he echoes the same criticism: "They have no written Law. The
King by his owne word ruleth, and his Gouerners of Prouinces
by that authoritie. Once a week he sitteth in judgment patiently,
and giueth sentences for Crimes Capitall and Ciuill" (110).

Roe's frustrations in the Mogul court were both linguistic and
cultural, as these two aspects were inextricably linked. The Indians
lived in a world where the body of the ruler, not any words he may
write, was literally his authority, an authority which could be
transmitted in what Europeans thought of as objects. The Mogul
king's "weighing ceremony," for instance, described by Roe and
others, would have such a symbolic and literal significance: on his
birthday every year, the King weighed himself on a pair of golden
scales, and when the ceremony was over, he distributed "among
the standers-by thin pieces of Silver and some of Gold made
like flowers of that country and some . . . [like] Cloves and . . .
Nutmegs, but very thin and hollow" (Terry 1655: 395). While par-
ticipating in a ritual with obvious symbolic significance, the King
could supposedly transmit the *substance* of his authority in some
of the silver and gold pieces with which he was weighed.

On other occasions, more complex transmittals of the king's
authority occurred as Edward Terry, Roe's Chaplain, reports:
"When the Mogul by Letters sends his Commands to any
Gouerners . . . Officers ride to meet the Messenger . . . and as
soon as he sees those Letters he alights from his horse, falls down
on earth, and takes them from the Messenger and lays them on
his head . . . [and] binds them [there]" (Terry 1655: 453). Here, it
seems, that the letters as objects, and not the written words on
them, are venerated and received as the person of the King himself. They were a means of sharing in the "authority and substance
of the sender" (Cohn 1985: 280). This conflation of the King's
person with his letters shows how the Indians had a radically different understanding of the social relations of language—one that
did not share the European preoccupation with words as signs,
especially by assuming a stable correspondence between words
and their referents. Therefore, not surprisingly, in the absence of
binding legal documents, coupled with a lack of knowledge of
local languages, the English merchants found it hard to establish
the *exchange value* of goods and presents.[17] These differing attitudes toward language and meaning underpinned the developing

ideological divide whereby English representatives saw Indian laws and customs as "barbaric," as opposed to their own "civilized" laws in written form. In fact, assumptions about the transparency of their own modes of representation were cast into a rhetorical strategy frequently deployed by English travelers/ writers, one in which the inscrutability of Indian languages and customs could be transformed to "barbarism" via the tropes of unrepresentability and mystery. Roe's recurring complaint of the "barbarism" of the unwritten laws and customs at the Mogul court typify this strategy.

Given these linguistic and ideological divisions, it is not surprising that a confusion about the personal, political, and commercial aspects of gift-giving greatly preoccupied the Ambassador in his dealings with the Mogul court. It "beeing the Custome," Roe reveals in his journal, that "when any body hath busines [with the King] to giue somewhat, and those that cannot come neere to speake, send in or hould up their guift, which he eccepts bee it but a rupie (single currency), and demands their bussines" (in Foster 1899: 115). Most gifts offered were certainly not as humble as a rupee, and Roe observes that such customary gifts seem to have some exchange value implicitly recognized by both parties. As on New Year celebrations when the Mogul king, Jehangir, comes abroad, there are "offered to him, by all sorts, great guiftes, though not equal to report, yet incredible enough; and at the end of the feast the King in recompence of the presents receiued, aduanceth some and addeth to theyre entertainment some horse at his pleasure" (144).

From the outset of his service, the English Ambassador expresses the urgency of giving suitable gifts to the Mogul king in order to bargain for trading privileges for his countrymen. And in a 1615 letter to the East India Company, Roe berates the merchants' choice of presents:

> The Presents you haue this yeere sent are extreamely despised by those who haue seene them; the lyning of the Coach and Couer of the Virginalls scorned . . . the Knives little and meane . . . the burning glasses and prospectiues such as no man hath face to offer to giue, much less to sell, such as I can buy for sixe Peence a peice, your Pictures not all woorth one Penny. . . . Here [in the Court] are nothing esteemed but the best sorts: good Cloth and fine, and rich Pictures, they comming

out of Italy ouerland and from Ormus; so that they laugh at vs
for such as wee bring. And doubtlesse they vnderstand them as
well as wee; and what they want in knowledge they are
enformed by the Jesuites and others [the Portuguese], that in
Emulation of vs provide them of the best at any rates.

(in Foster 1899: 97)

Getting gifts that pleased the King was not so much the issue as
exchanging them for a trade accord in which the *language* would
be binding. In his journal, Roe recounts a moment in 1616, when
he requested the King for an agreement "clear in all poynts and
more formall and Authentique confirmation than it had by
ordinarie *firmaens*, which were temporary Commandes" (146).
However, Roe writes, it took much negotiation overcoming the
machinations of the Prince and Asaph Chan to get a reasonably
satisfactory agreement in 1618.

A full sense of the English struggle with differing social relations
operative in language can be gained from Thomas Roe's letter to
James I, dated January 25, 1615:

To relate the Customes of this Cuntry, the state of the Court or
their gouerment, were fitter to beguile the weariness of the way
(like a tale) at your Majesties stirrop then for a discourse in
earnest. Fame hath done much for the Glory of this place. Yet
it cannot be denied that this King is one of the mightyest
Princes in Asia, as well in extent of territory as in revenew;
equall to the Turke, far exceeding the Persian. But the Gouerment so uncertayne, without written law, without Policye, the
Customes mingled with barbarisme, religions infinite. . . . The
trade here will doubtlesse in tyme bee very profitable for your
Majesties Kingdomes, and may vent much cloth; but as yet
our condition and vsadge is so bad (notwithstanding fayre
woords) that will require much patience, much Industry to sett
vpright.

(in Foster 1899: 120)

Once again, Thomas Roe takes the stance of a master hermeneut. And typically his definition of "barbarisme" hinges upon
his difficulty with the Indians' different understanding of the relation between written laws and the words of their King. Interesting
here is Roe's transformation of his *own* difficulties in communication and interpretation into a picture of the Mogul kingdom as a

site of political, legal, and moral confusion: the "Customes of this Cuntry" lack integrity and certitude and are best described as a beguiling tale for "your Majesties stirrop" rather than as a "discourse in earnest." And Roe devalues the power and revenue of one of the "mightyest" princes in Asia into a "Gouerment so uncertayne" whereby, in his eyes, the governing practices of the Mogul king lack any substance without "written law, without Policye." Ultimately, what seems most troubling about the culture of "India/Indies" is its defiance of convenient European typologies and practices via proliferating cultural signifiers: "Customes mingled with barbarisme, [and] religions infinite."

Ironically, Roe does not see any connection between his difficulty with the unwritten laws of the Mogul court and his *own* lack of knowledge of Persian or any other Indian language. Nor does he seem aware of the figurative cast of his own representations, while drawing on familiar tropes of wonder and mystery to catalogue the otherness of Indian customs and languages. Here and elsewhere, Roe often complains about the bad "vsadge" of the English by the Indian powers, despite "fayre woords," especially regarding the exchange value of gifts and presents. But the Ambassador rarely acknowledges the possibility of miscommunication arising out of antithetical *systems of meaning*, with their differing assumptions about language and meaning— miscommunications that are, in effect, exacerbated by the processes of linguistic translation. Thus, as he promotes "patience" in developing conditions of "profitable trade," Roe, nonetheless, accepts the ideological divide between "barbarism" and "civilization," based largely on the European practice of valorizing written inscriptions, preferably in their own languages.

The Europeans' struggle in establishing a one-to-one correspondence between words, both written and spoken, and their social meaning clearly emerges in the English Ambassador's record of the tortuous mediation of the exchange of presents between him and the Mogul king. However, Roe's journal also goes on to reveal that practices of gift-giving could playfully destabilize cultural otherness as much as they could obfuscate communication. In a 1615 letter to the East India Company, for instance, Roe recounts one such moment:

Then he [the King] sent to me, though 10 O'clock at night, for a seruant to tye on his scarfe and swoorde in the english fashion, in which he tooke so great pryde that he marched up and downe, draweing yt and flourishing, and since hath neuer been seen without yt. So that in conclusion, he accepted your presents well.

(in Foster 1899: 119)

On another occasion, the Ambassador's gift of a picture depicting Venus and a Satyr generated a lively discussion about the possibilities of disinterested, culturally neutral interpretation. Receiving this picture from the English, the Mogul "commanded [his] Interpreter not to tell [him] what it was, but asked his Lords what they conceiued should be the interpretation or morall" of the figures (386). When Roe suggested that it could be an allegory about the "invention of the painter," the King was not convinced, and at this point in his journal, the Ambassador warns his English readers (the merchants) to "be wary what they send may be subject to ill-interpretation; for in that point the King and his people are very pregnant and scrupulous" (387). By Roe's account it seems that the Mogul king, Jehangir, "understood the Morall to be a scorne of Asiatiques, whom the naked Satyre represented and was of the same complexion, and not vnlike; who being held by Venus, a white woman, by the Nose, it seemed that shee led him Captiue" (387). Yet significantly, according to the Englishman, the King "reuealed no discontent, but rould them vp and told me he would accept it also as a Presente" (387). Here, while Roe registers an awareness of the porous, manifold nature of interpretation, he nonetheless seems equally invested in controlling the interpretation for the consumption of his English readers.

Scenes such as these cast a different light on the uneven negotiations of meaning and intent which seem to preoccupy Roe in his journal, and which suggest the King's unceasing demands; instead, they show that the Mogul court was governed by a complex, though sometimes inscrutable system of reciprocity, which functioned even within a hierarchy of relationships. Thomas Roe was ambivalent about his participation in this arrangement of relationships, consistently refusing personal gifts from the King, as Edward Terry testifies: "the King [would] often ask [Roe] why he did not desire some good, and great giftes at his hands . . . the Embassador would reply, That he came not hither to beg anything of him; all he desired was that . . . the English might have free, safe, and peacable trade" (Terry 1655: 459). Despite the Ambassador's effort at distinguishing between personal gain and political favors, he nonetheless had a ceremonial relationship with his host, as he writes, "I went to visitt the King, who, as soone as I came in, called to his woemen and reached out a picture of him selfe sett in gould hanging at a wire gould Chaine . . . which [he presented to Roe, who recognized this as an] especiall favour, for that all the great men that weare the kings Image (which none may do but to whom it is giuen)" (244). However, the Englishman did not seem to be aware of the full significance of the event, namely, that receiving the imperial likeness was a symbol of a special bond or discipleship called *shast wa sabah*.[18] Overall, these curious exchanges point to the more interactive and playful aspects of cultural encounters—aspects that are often obscured in Roe's singular complaint about the inscrutable customs and lack of written laws. Ultimately, however, the English were able to establish their influence in the face of cultural differences and ambiguities, as Edward Terry so aptly sums up:

> The Mogul, sometimes by his Firmauns, or Letters Patents, will grant some particular things into single or persons and presently after will contradict those Graunts by other Letters. . . . Yet what he promised was usually enjoyed, although he would not be tied to a certain performance of his promise. Therefore, there can be no dealing with the King on very sure termes, who will say and unsay, promise and deny. Yet we Englishmen did not suffer . . . but there found a free Trade, a peaceable residence, and a very goode esteem with that King and People.
>
> (Terry 1655: 445)

In his letters to England, Sir Thomas Roe often describes his post as a backward place of hardship. Writing to Lord Carew in 1615, for instance, he states: "I shall be glad to do your Lordship seruice in England; for this is the dullest, basest place that euer I saw, and maketh me weary of speaking of it" (in Foster 1899: 113). The Ambassador's journal, however, frequently offers a counterpoint to this negative picture, especially when he depicts the events of the court as picturesque, theatrical scenes, in which he is an actor and spectator. Despite assumptions of authenticity running through his account, Roe falls back on conventional tropes of wonder and discovery—the familiar badge of European travelers so invested in the notion of origins and genealogies. While fabled, mythic expectations of the Mogul court were no doubt a part of the European imagination at the time, English travelers/writers like Roe (and Coryate) gave life to them by representing them as "discoveries." In Roe's account, for instance, we can see how he frequently attempts his cultural translation in the context of these received expectations of the marvelous and the inscrutable. Typically, then, scenes of grandeur and ritual at the court frequently filter through Roe's sense of amazement and he often uses the theatrical analogy, as, for instance, when he first witnesses the Mogul's *durbar* or formal court (109):

> The Place is a great Court, whither resort all sorts of people. The King sitts in a little Gallery ouer head; Ambassadors, the great men and strangers of qualety within the inmost rayle under him, raysed from the ground, Couered with Canopyes of veluet and silke. . . . This sitting out hath much affinitye with a *Theatre*—the manner of the king in his gallery; The great men lifted on a stage as actors; the vulgar below gazing on . . . the king preuented my dull interpreter, bidding me welcome as to the brother of my Master. . . . He asked me some questions . . . [and] dismissed me with more fauour and outward grace . . . than euer was showed to any Ambassador, eyther of the Turke or Persian.

Roe's account of the "weighing ceremony" reflects a similar amazement as a compelling spectacle (412):

> Here attended the Nobilitie . . . vntill the King came; who at last appeared clothed or loden with Diamonds, Rubies, Pearles, and other precious vanities, so great so glorious! . . . his fingers euery one with at least two or three Rings [with] Dyamonds, Rubies as great as Walnuts (some greater), and Pearles such as mine eyes were amazed at. Suddenly, hee entered into the scales . . . and there was put in against him many bagges to fit his weight.

This sense of wonder remains with the Ambassador during his contact with the court of the Mogul. It seems to offer a counterpoint to the ideological distinctions between "civilization" and "barbarism," only to temporarily elide "barbarism" into exoticism. While Roe's journal does not have the excessive rhetorical embellishments found in some other travel narratives, his representations of Mogul India reflect a continuing sense of wonder about, as well as desire for mastery over, its manifestations of otherness, both "exotic" and "barbaric." Thus, as he presents the scenario of Mogul sovereignty through a blend of wonder and disgust, he also sizes up, for the benefit of his successors, the extent, manifestations, and variety of the power with which they will have to contend: thus, he lays the grid of a European system of differences—a ground for later colonial rule—even though the collective dream of imperial power is yet to take shape.

III

If Sir Thomas Roe's narratives produce a discourse of difference centered on politics and commerce, Thomas Coryate constructs his narrative as an unending *spectacle*. Thus, unlike Roe, his more self-consciously theatricalized representations of the Mogul court reveal another, aestheticizing dimension of the colonizing imagination. While Roe's writings reveal his difficulties in interpreting a world of copious signifiers, and in enforcing a parity between words and actions in his encounters with Indians, Thomas Coryate's account seems to celebrate the same multiple "realities" experienced by him as a European traveler. Living in the Mogul court in part contemporaneously with Roe, Coryate did not represent any official interests—either of the East India Company or of the Crown—though he was implicitly under the protection of the Company. Richard Hakluyt does not include his letters in his compilations of voyages and discoveries and the Purchas collection has only a small excerpt about his travels. Yet the figure of Coryate emerges frequently in the accounts of other travelers, gaining a colorful notoriety for his ostensible idiosyncrasies and his self-posturings. If, as Purchas states, the aim of the Renaissance traveler was to "witness the Rarities of Nature" and the "extraordinary wonders which God's providence hath herein effected," then the flamboyant Coryate was himself transformed into a "character" wandering the landscape of the real and imagined "East" as described by him and others.

A recurring aspect of contemporary English accounts of Coryate is a bemused critique of his whimsical behavior and of his obvious love of fame and attention. In England, in the court of James I, he earned a precarious living as a kind of privileged buffoon. According to Thomas Fuller (1840), "he carried folly . . . in his very face . . . [and he exhibited] fancy and memory without any commonsense" (108). In fact, courtiers often amused themselves at his expense, once arranging his appearance at a masque in a trunk.[19] There is much evidence pointing to Coryate's posturings. Edward Terry, Roe's Chaplain, whom Coryate met in India, humorously compared Coryate to a "ship that hath too much sail, and too little Ballast" (1655: 72) and records that the Ambassador called him a "very honest poor wretch," and another "person of honour" also perceived him to be an "honest poor wretch" (73).[20]

While Coryate's contemporaries saw him as a source of universal mirth in the "Court and cities," they all testified to his "irrevocable addiction to travel" (Prasad 1965: 172–5). Thomas Roe also recorded in his journal his meeting with the "famous unwearied walker, Thomas Coryate (who on foot had passed on most Europe and Asya, and was now arriued in India)" (in Foster 1899: 103). One apocryphal story refers to a moment when Coryate went to his home church in Odcombe, Somerset, before leaving the country, and hung up a pair of shoes he wore on his Continental journey. An echo of this incident is supposedly found in Pompey's reference to "brave Master Shoe-tie the great Traveller" in Shakespeare's *Measure for Measure* (4.3).

Prior to his overland journey to India, Coryate set out for a walking tour of the Continent in 1608, the result of which was a curious, florid travel account called *Coryats Crudities Hastily gobled in five Moneths travells in France, Savoy, Italy. . .* In order to find a publisher, Coryate requested eminent men of the time— including Ben Jonson and John Donne—to write panegyric verses to be attached to the travel account. These mock-commendatory verses on the "single-soled, single-souled . . . Observer" testify to Coryate's love of attention accompanied by humorous self-deprecation. Overall, however, *Crudities* also reveals an avid curiosity about social and geographical minutiae which are brought to life in a vivid, though hyperbolic style—one which enabled Coryate to cast himself as a traveler with keen and grandiose aspirations.

In this persona of flamboyant traveler Thomas Coryate describes his overland journey and stay in the court of the Great Mogul in India, from 1613 till 1617. His narrative consists of a compilation of his letters into two short volumes: *Traveller for the English Wits* (1616) and *Mr. Thomas Coriate to his Friends in England sendeth greeting* (1618). A distinguishing feature of these narratives is the way that Coryate's eye-witness experiences are so wholly imbricated within the conventional embellishments of the travel genre. For instance, he repeatedly recapitulates a sense of wonder associated with "exotic" places such as "Troy," "Constantinople," "Aleppo," "Jerusalem," and "Agra." And when responding to the geographical locations associated with mythic names, Coryate displays the influence of standard travel narratives, drawn from classical history, biblical stories, and epic fictions, often imaginatively re-creating the journeys and personae of legendary figures such as Aeneas, Ulysses, and Tamburlaine.

One such occasion, when Coryate takes on a mythical persona, occurs in his description of receiving a "knighthood" in Troy:

> Master Robert Rugge observing that I had taken paines for some few hours in searching out the most notable antiquities of this worthiest part of Troy . . . in merrie humour . . . knighted me . . . the first English knight of Troy . . . [with] those witty verses:
>   Coryate no more, but now a Knight of Troy,
>   Odcombe no more, but henceforth England's joy.
>   Brave Brute of our best English wits descended
>   Rise top of wit, the honor of our Nation,
>   And to old Illium, make a new oration.
>   (Coryate 1616: quoted in Purchas 1625: 1816)

While such moments of theatrical self-posturing typically color most of Coryate's cultural encounters, they also crucially reveal how mythical allusions and tropes of the discovery genre prescribed the experiences and interactions of the self-aggrandizing traveler. Thus, we can see the creative uses of fiction in the representation of "facts." Here, with some unwitting irony, Coryate flaunts the role of the new Aeneas, the "first English Knight of Troy." From his historical perspective, he cannot recognize that while he is not going to found a new empire as Aeneas did, he will nonetheless be an important, if naive, witness to the beginnings of Britain's empire in India.

Throughout his narrative, Coryate's self-aggrandizing impulses remain caught up in the received narratives of heroic travelers, even though he rarely perceives himself as a potential colonizer or as a political/mercantile representative of England. In his "Address to the Reader," for instance, Coryate identifies with another mythic figure, Ulysses, in his role as an insatiable seeker of experience and wisdom: "I have enrich't my feete. . . . With measuring millicents of Townes and Towres/. . . [yet] Meane [I] to trauaile still,/Till I haue equald in some seauen years more,/For who can purchase wisedome? Ten years? No./Before I get it, I will go and go" (A3). Coryate's posturings remain constant, even when he is not identifying himself with mythic heroes, as when he states: "Erasmus did in praise of folly write; and Coryate doth, in his self-praise endite" (A3). Or, when he rides an elephant in Ajmere, he determines: "one day [by God's leave] to have my picture expressed in my next Booke, sitting upon an Elephant" (26).

Given Coryate's flamboyant fictionalizing of his eye-witness experiences, one is not surprised to learn that what drew Coryate to India was the hope of journeying further into Central Asia to behold Tamburlaine's tomb in Samarkand. He requests the Mogul king in his address to "grant mee your gracious passe that I may trauell into the country of Tartaria to the citty of Samarkand, to visit the blessed sepulchre of . . . Tamburlaine" (Coryate 1618: 1st verso after B2^v). It is ironic and telling that his journey to India was framed by the quest for the fabled Tamburlaine, a powerful embodiment of otherness in the Renaissance imagination. Edward Terry (1655) testifies to the mythic diffusion of this story in Europe: "that most famous Conquerer called in our stories Tamberlain, concerning whose birth and original Histories much differ . . . but, in this, all that write of him agree, that he . . . made very great Conquests in the South-East parts of the World" (446). By the seventeenth century, the Tartar's name was widely known in the English popular culture as the Oriental conquerer; yet, as the "other," who stirred terror, he also inspired awe and fascination, especially when cast as Marlowe's romantic "Overreacher."[21]

A feeling of wonder drew Coryate to the cultural memory of Tamburlaine and in this sense typifies his mode of narration. An historian notes that Coryate's hyperbolic descriptions

> seem to be written by one who was either much too dazzled by the superb brilliance of the scene or was deliberately exaggerating to create a grand impression [on others] . . . he has chosen to describe only those objects which were likely to create a grand sensation.
>
> (Prasad 1965: 190)

Thus, Coryate's mode of dramatic description is permeated by references to *seeing*—and to his role as a spectator. In this emphasis on unmediated access to experience, Coryate deploys a rhetorical strategy of "discovery" narratives so that his mode of *seeing* is strangely imbricated in the prior poetics of travelogues. Their pervasive faith in "the hegemony of the visual" clearly mirrors the faith in representation that operates in European travel accounts.[22]

Coryate offers considerable evidence to reveal his obsessive preoccupation with seeing. Describing the Mogul king's birthday celebrations, he remarks, "I *saw* the same day (a custom that he obserueth most inuiolable every year) laying so much golde in the other scale as counteruaileth the weight of his body, and the same he afterward distributed to the poore" (1616: 20). Or, on another occasion, he declares himself a witness to unusual animals (24–5):

> Hee [the King] keepeth abundance of wilde Beasts and that of diuers sorts, as Lyons, Elephants, Leopards, Bears, Antelops, Vnicornes; whereas two I have *seene* at his Court the strangest beasts of the world: they were brought hither out of the Countrie of *Bengala*, which is a kingdom of most singular fertilitie.

Edward Terry, who was Coryate's close contemporary, testifies to the latter's keen and insatiable appetite for new sights and spectacles: "he was a man of a very coveting eye, that *could never be satisfied with seeing* . . . though he had seen very much; and I am perswaded that he took as much content on *Seeing* as many others in the enjoying of Great and Rare Things" (1655: 17).

Coryate not only reveals himself as an avid spectator, but also as a daring actor who frequently takes on a native persona while also learning the classical and vernacular languages (Terry 1655: 412). Thus, writing to England, Coryate states, "I haue beene at the Mogul's court three moneths already and am to tarry heere (by God's holy permission) five moneths till I haue gotten the foresaide three tongues [Persian, Turkish and Arabian]" (1616: 30). And Terry testifies to Coryate's claims:

> At Agra our Traueller made a halt . . . where he staid till he had gotten to his *Turkish*, and *Morisco* or *Arabian* Languages, some good knowledge in the *Persian* and *Indostan* tongues, in which study he was alwaies very apt and in little time shewed much proficiency. The first of those two, the Persian, is the more *quaint*; the other, the *Indostan*, the vulgar Language spoken in

East India: In both these he suddenly got such a knowledge and mastery that it did exceedingly afterwards advantage him in his Travels up and down the *Mogul*'s Territory, he alwaies wearing the Habit of that Nation and speaking their *Language*.

(Terry 1655: 69)

Coryate's participation in Indian culture, especially in taking on a native persona, enabled him to display his love of histrionics and shape his account as a dramatic fable. He embraced a variety of roles with a flourish, whether giving an oration of artful flattery in Persian before the Mogul king, for which he was rewarded with 100 rupees by the King, or responding in "Indostan" to a "laundress [in Roe's house, who] would sometimes scold, brawl, and rail from sunrise to sunset . . . [until] one day he [Coryate] undertook her in her own language [and] . . . so silenced her, that she had not one word more to speak" (Terry 1655: 70). Here, of course, his linguistic versatility also enabled Coryate to gain mastery over the native, constructing the laundress as domestic, English shrew and subversive servant, whom he could then silence.

What remains constant in Coryate's varied accounts is his keen sense of drama as he casts the world into a theatrical mode—a world divided into actors and audiences. Furthermore, given that this theatricalized account is implicated in the fabled discovery narratives featuring mythic figures such as Ulysses, Aeneas, and Tamburlaine, how do we judge the veracity of his view of Jehangir's court? Overall, as an eye-witness, Coryate sticks pretty closely to actual events without being aligned to any official Company policy. However, he is also a historicist whose theatrical sense of history is largely based on his desire to be remembered in posterity.[23] It is the mythical Mandeville, noted for his fabulous tales of discovery in the fourteenth century, with whom Coryate seeks an identity rather than with Thomas Roe. The nature of his ambition is apparent in a poem written by a John Brown, and based on Coryate's epistles. The opening stanza is a blatant praise of his subject's travels to the East as distinguished from his "Cruder" travels to Europe. The poet asks: "Have not thy glorious acts thereby ascended/Great Brittaines stage, even to the Princes Palaces . . . ?" After recommending places Coryate should visit on his return, the poem arrives at the following conclusion:

This done at Alexandria seeke your passage
For England's happy shores, wher How and Mundy

Will strive to make your trauels out-last age
So long as stand their Annals of our Country
For *Mandeville* wil come of thee farre short,
Either of trauell, or a large report.

(Coryate 1616: 34)

Sending these verses to Lawrence Whittaker, Coryate wanted them to be read to the members of the Mermaid Club in London. If Coryate's ambition was to outshine Mandeville, it was because in the seventeenth century *Mandeville's Travels* was still the proto-type for capturing the celebrated marvels of the East, leading Purchas to declare that Mandeville was the "greatest Asian traveller."[24] This blend of fantasy, spectacle, and geographic/ ethnographic detail found in Mandeville's accounts (though little is known about him) had an obvious appeal for the vain traveller, given to fictional self-aggrandizement. Thus, not surprisingly, he imaginatively drew on the Renaissance trope of man as actor— both in his life and writings—freely moving in the marvelous land-scapes described by him. Coryate died in India in 1617, without fulfilling his dream of paying homage to Tamburlaine's tomb at Samarkand. While he was a memorable figure to his immediate contemporaries, he was largely lost to posterity. Thus he became a footnote in the imperial script in which Thomas Roe later figured as an early foot soldier.

To conclude, if colonial discourse serves the forces of commer-cial and political power in Roe's writings, it assumes divergent, *seemingly* more benign forms in Coryate's letters. Yet, I believe, his travel writing is also a form of knowledge, precisely because of its particular mode: as Thomas Coryate views the court through the prism of the "exotic," he displaces the historical dimension by isolating the story as *story* (or drama as drama), apart from rela-tions of political and economic power. Thus, in effect, his writings also foreground the status of all English narratives, official and unofficial, as *inventions*. The role of the innocent, wonder-struck protagonist taken by Coryate is reminiscent of a character who emerges later in the colonial landscape: he is the "seeing-man," who, according to Mary Louise Pratt, represents the act of dis-covery as a form of "anti-conquest," whereby the European bour-geois subject can secure his innocence in the same moment that he asserts, or, in this case, assumes European superiority.[25]

Coryate, Roe, and other Englishmen represent their cultural encounters in India as both eye-witness accounts and as spectacles of discovery and amazement, and as such their views are hardly benign. They function as both actors and spectators in the early colonial scene of writing. And with the hindsight of history, we can read their picturesque scripts as part of the production of the "real" and imagined "India/Indies" which later became the property of the British Raj.

NOTES

1 In his evocative description of the sect of Banians he encounters in India, Lord (1630) shows how the mercantile interests of the English converged with his quasi-ethnographic impulse to catalogue a community whose "use in Company affairs," by all accounts, proved invaluable. Traditionally, a trading community among Hindus, the Banians aided the English merchants in the seventeenth century as functionaries and cultural interpreters in their factories.

2 For a typical account of medieval and Renaissance definitions of the discovery genre, see Purchas's Preface "To the Reader" (1905: xxxix–xlviii).

3 Purchas's emphasis on expectations of the strange and marvelous is reinforced by several recent studies of European discovery narratives, most notably by John Gillies (1994: 1–39), who argues that these narratives were shaped by classical and medieval poetic geography and ethnographic discourses. Thus the new lands were not only geographically mapped but imaginatively possessed via received notions of the "exotic" and "monstrous," terms generally used to describe non-European "others." Greenblatt (1991: 22) also offers a useful definition of the trope of the marvelous within European systems of representation:

> The marvellous is a central feature . . . in the whole complex system of [European] representation, verbal and visual, philosophical and aesthetic, intellectual and emotional through which people in the late Middle Ages and the Renaissance apprehended and thence possessed or discarded the unfamiliar, the alien, the terrible, the desirable.

Greenblatt's formulation is useful in its emphasis on the tropological cast of European discovery narratives, though I think he applies the term "marvelous" somewhat sweepingly to describe the experiences of *all* Europeans uniformly.

4 Most studies of European discovery narratives point to the recurring use of a binary opposition between Europeans and their "others" as a rhetorical device in the structure of colonial or proto-colonial

discourse. Gillies, for instance, traces the persistent trope of otherness spanning classical, medieval, and biblical narratives (1994: 1–39). David Spurr (1993: 3–7) suggests that the "colonizer's traditional insistence on difference from the colonized establishes a notion of the savage as *other*, the antithesis of civilized value" (7). This ideological distinction, according to Spurr, underpins the different rhetorical modes used to write about non-Western peoples, both in the colonial and postcolonial eras (1–12).

5 For a full account of "twelve rhetorical modes" used to define non-Western peoples as well as their relationship to the establishment and maintenance of colonial authority, see Spurr 1993: 1–12.

6 Spear (1978: 61–92) charts the decline of the Mogul empire and the expansion of the East India Company's power. While he notes, with some irony, that to seventeenth-century Indians, the Europeans "seemed heavy, shrewd and dull, and in no context dangerous" (69), he then goes on to detail how by the mid-eighteenth century India had become the site of a power vacuum which facilitated the expansion of English power.

7 For an astute analysis of the complex, and sometimes contradictory relationship between state and mercantile interests in England, see Suleri 1992: 24–7.

8 My understanding and application of the term, "ideology," here and throughout this chapter (and the book), derives from Louis Althusser's essay, "Ideology and Ideological State Apparatuses" (1971).

9 I am indebted to Mary Louise Pratt's discussion of the "rhetoric of travel writing" (1992) in which she persuasively argues that among the conventions of representation that constituted European travel writing the use of typologies was significant, whereby the "naming, the representing, and the claiming are all one" (33). Some elements of the rhetorical paradigms she finds in eighteenth- and nineteenth-century travel writings can also be found in the earlier narratives.

10 Pratt (1992) succinctly describes one aspect of typologizing as a strategy of colonial "meaning-making" as follows: "Navigational mapping exerted the power of naming as well, of course. Indeed, it was in naming that the religious and geographical projects came together, as emissaries claimed the world by baptizing landmarks and geographical formations with Euro-Christian names" (33).

11 I am indebted to contemporary, poststructuralist perspectives on ethnography developed by James Clifford, George Marcus, and others for my reading of the early modern European narratives about India. Also see above, Introduction, pp. 1–26.

12 These are anthologized in Foster 1899.

13 See Foster's Introduction (1899: i–lxviii), for a fuller background on Roe's life and place in British colonial history.

14 Foster draws on native sources like the *Tuzk-i-Jehangiri* (Rogers and Beveridge 1909) as a context for the Mogul king's responses to the British Ambassador (1899: x–xxiv).

15 For a detailed account of the differing systems of signification of the Indians and Europeans, see Cohn (1985), especially 276–9. Washbrook

(1991) also discusses the differing social relations of language between the two races in their early encounters with each other, especially 183–4.

16 I am indebted to Ryan Bishop for this formulation.

17 These incidents of the literal power of objects belonging to the Mogul king can be understood in the light of Washbrook's (1991) and Cohn's (1985) analyses.

18 Richards (1993: 104–5) offers an illuminating account of this custom of discipleship, revealing how Roe was unaware of the significance of the event. The bonds of a disciple spread far. For instance, Jehangir was a disciple of the dead Khwaja Chisti, a saintly man, and thus the links of discipleship reached from the Chisti saint to the emperor to his own disciple.

19 As an aspiring courtier, Coryate (also spelt Coriate and Coryat) was known for his idiosyncrasies. For a detailed account based on a variety of sources, see Prasad 1965: 170–5.

20 Terry seems more aware than Coryate himself of the general reputation of his countryman's idiosyncrasies, the object of humorous mockery.

21 Several studies discuss the mixture of fact and fiction in the popular Renaissance representations of Tamburlaine, especially as they relate to Marlowe's play. See Bakeless 1964: 25–7 and Levin 1984: 51–66.

22 Stephen Tyler (1987: 149–70) offers a persuasive account of the "hegemony of the visual" in European modes of representation.

23 In describing Coryate as a historian, I draw on Hayden White's formulation of the "rhetoric of history" (1978: 101–19).

24 See Greenblatt 1991: 54–115, for his subtle analysis of the fictions that went into the making of Mandeville's "identity," vividly illustrating how travel writers like Coryate were heavily invested in creating fictional personas. For *Mandeville's Travels*, see Letts 1953.

25 In suggesting "connections between travel writing and forms of knowledge," particularly during the Enlightenment, Mary Louise Pratt (1992) defines one European strategy of representation as "anti-conquest" (6–7). She also identifies this as a strategy of "innocence" whose central protagonist is a figure she names the "seeing-man." While seventeenth-century travelers did not reflect direct connections between seeing and possession, their roles are reminiscent of the figure of the "seeing-man," even though he emerges later on the colonial landscape.

I am grateful to Richmond Barbour for introducing me to Thomas Coryate's writings.

WORKS CITED IN CHAPTER 1

Althusser, Louis. "Ideology and Ideological State Apparatuses." In *Lenin and Philosophy and Other Essays*. Trans. Ben Brewster. New York: Monthly Review, 1971: 127–86.

Bakeless, John. *The Tragicall History of Christopher Marlowe*, Vols I and II. Hamden, Connecticut: Archon Books, 1964.

Clifford, James. "Introduction: Partial Truths." In *Writing Culture: The Poetics and Politics of Ethnography*. Ed. James Clifford and George E. Marcus. Berkeley and Los Angeles: University of California Press, 1986: 1–86.

Cohn, Bernard S. "The Command of Language and the Language of Command." In *Subaltern Studies: Writings on South Asian History and Society*, Vol. IV. Ed. Ranajit Guha. Oxford: Oxford University Press, 1985: 276–329.

Coriate, Thomas. *Traveller for the English Wits: Greeting from the Court of the Great Mogul*. London: 1616. STC 5809, 5811. (Also spelt "Coryat," "Coriat," and "Coryate.")

—— *Mr. Thomas Coriate to his Friends in England sendeth greeting*. London: 1618. STC 5811.

Foster, William. Ed. *The Embassy of Sir Thomas Roe to the Court of the Great Mogul. 1615–1619*, Vols I and II. London: The Hakluyt Society, 1899.

—— *Early Travels in India*. London: Humphrey Milford, 1921.

—— *England's Quest of Easterne Trade*. London: A. & C. Black, 1933.

Foster, William and F.C. Danvers. Eds. *Letters Received by the East India Company from its Servants in the East* (1602–17). 6 vols. London: 1896–1902.

Fuller, Thomas. *The History of the Worthies of England*, Vol. III. London: Thomas Tegg, 1840.

Gillies, John. *Shakespeare and the Geography of Difference*. Cambridge: Cambridge University Press, 1994.

Greenblatt, Stephen. *Marvelous Possessions: The Wonder of the New World*. Chicago: University of Chicago Press, 1991.

Hulme, Peter. *Colonial Encounters: Europe and the Native Caribbean 1492–1797*. London: Routledge, 1986.

Lavender, Theophilus. "Preface." *The Travels of Certaine Englishmen into Africa, Asia, Troy, Bythinia, Thracia, and to the Black Sea*. London: 1609. STC 3051.

Letts, Malcolm. Ed. *Mandeville's Travels: Texts and Translations*. London: The Hakluyt Society, 1953.

Levin, Richard. "The Contemporary Perception of Marlowe's Tamburlaine." In *Medieval and Renaissance Drama in England*, 1984: 51–70.

Lord, Henry. *A Discouerie of the Sect of Banians Conteyning their Historie, Law, Liturgie, Casts, Customs, and Ceremonies*. London: 1630. STC 16825. New York: De Capo Press, 1972.

Middleton, Henry. *The Last East-Indian Voyage*. London: 1630. STC 16825.

The Petition and Remonstrance of the Governor and the Company and Merchants of London trading to the East Indies: Exhibited to the Honourable House of Commons assembled in Parliament. London: 1628. STC 7449.

Prasad, Ram Chandra. *Early English Travelers in India: A Study of the Travel Literature of the Elizabethan and Jacobean Periods with particular reference to India*. Delhi and Patna: Motilal Banarsi Das, 1965.

Pratt, Mary Louise. *Imperial Eyes: Travel Writing and Transculturation*. London: Routledge, 1992.

Purchas, Samuel. *Hakluytus Posthumous or Purchas His Pilgrimes: Contayning a History of the World in Sea Voyages and Lande Travells by Englishmen and others* (1625), Vol. X, STC 20509.Vol. I, Glasgow: James MacLehose and Sons, 1905.

Qaisar, Ahsan Jan. *The Indian Responses to European Technology and Culture, 1498–1707*. Delhi: Oxford University Press, 1982.

Richards, John. *The Mughal Empire*. Cambridge: Cambridge University Press, 1993.

Riggs, David. *Shakespeare's Heroical Histories: Henry IV and its Literary Tradition*. Cambridge, Mass.: Harvard University Press, 1971.

Rogers, Alexander and Henry Beveridge. Eds. and trans. *The Tuzk-i-Jehangiri*. London: The Asiatic Society, 1909.

Spear, Percival. *A History of India*, Vol. II. London: Penguin (rev. edn), 1978.

Spurr, David. *The Rhetoric of Empire: Colonial Discourse in Journalism, Travel Writing, and Imperial Administration*. Durham, N.C.: Duke University Press, 1993.

Suleri, Sara. *The Rhetoric of English India*. Chicago: University of Chicago Press, 1992.

Terry, Edward. *A Voyage to East India*. London: J. Martin, 1655.

Tyler, Stephen A. *The Unspeakable: Discourse, Dialogue, and Rhetoric in the Postmodern World*. Madison: University of Wisconsin Press, 1987.

Washbrook, David. "'To Each a Language of His Own': Language, Culture and Society in Colonial India." In *Language, History, and Class*. Ed. Penelope J. Corfield. Oxford: Blackwell, 1991.

White, Hayden. *Tropics of Discourse: Essays in Cultural Criticism*. Baltimore: Johns Hopkins University Press, 1978.

Zamora, Margarita. "Christopher Columbus's 'Letter to the Sovereigns': Announcing the Discovery." *New World Encounters*. Ed. Stephen Greenblatt. Berkeley: University of California Press, 1993.

Chapter 2

The English nabobs: eighteenth-century Orientalism

I

LADY OLDHAM: With the wealth of the East, we have too imported the worst of its vices.
(Samuel Foote, *The Nabob*, 1772: 14)[1]

When Thomas Coryate postured on the seventeenth-century stage of Mogul India, his aim was to acquire fame on the basis of his exotic "discoveries" of the fabled "India/Indies." While Coryate was largely forgotten by the mid-eighteenth century, India itself began to loom large in the popular imagination in Britain. The power of the East India Company had grown considerably by this time. And in 1757, when Robert Clive defeated Siraj-ud-Daula, the ruler of Bengal, in the famous battle of Plassey (replacing him with a pliant substitute), his victory opened the way for an untrammeled, monopolistic, and often ruthless, profiteering among Company officials. Such activities caused a widespread concern about the proper governance of India, leading to reforms in the trading practices of the Company officials undertaken by Lord Cornwallis in the 1790s. And an important consequence of these developments was the gradual replacement of Company officials by civil servants, which in turn led to direct British rule in the nineteenth century. It is clear, then, that while in the seventeenth century the interests of the state and the Company were closely related—coalescing, for instance, in the embassy of Sir Thomas Roe—by the mid-eighteenth century they were fraught with tensions "between the merchant's desire to act as a state and the state's desire to own the power of the merchant" (Suleri 1992: 25).

It is not surprising that this transition from the Company's commercial activities to direct political rule in the late eighteenth century also marked a period of colonial self-questioning within British society. However, while examining what its proper relationship to India should be, Britain did not relinquish its power; instead, the nation made necessary political and ideological adjustments to justify its "rescue" of India. To get a sense of these ideological shifts, one has only to examine the complex and often contradictory images of India that emerged in the colonial discourses of eighteenth-century Britain. On the one hand, popular literary and cultural texts often represented India as a site of Eastern decadence and despotism, breeding corruption and dissipation among Company functionaries who assumed roles of Eastern despots or "nabobs" and exploited the hapless natives. On the other hand, another perspective on India came out of the Orientalist studies of the first generation of British civil servants in India, such as Sir William Jones and H.T. Colebrooke. This view entailed a "discovery" of India's classical past as a Hindu golden age, or a pristine Aryan society which had fallen into decline and decadence. In this chapter, I examine what seems to be a tangential relation between these two visions of India, and show how they coalesce, leading the way to the nineteenth-century "civilizing mission"—the cornerstone of the British empire.

The interplay of connections between the two perspectives is almost tautological. For instance, the popular denunciations of "nabobs," or corrupt East India Company officials, produced a vision of a weakened, decadent East in need of civilization. One step further and this sympathy for the hapless Indians was not far removed from the Orientalist evocations of India's ancient, glorious past, from which the natives had fallen. In both instances, the appropriate goal for the British was to civilize and rule eighteenth-century India. This imperative blocked off any possibility of returning India to its glorious past, and instead, was aimed at saving the Eastern colony from itself, that is from its fallen state.

The concern for the good governance of the Indian colony also exposed the growing anxieties about the attendant social and economic dislocations that were taking place within British society. To examine both the colonial self-questioning and the social disruptions, let us now turn to the figure of the nabob who emerges frequently in eighteenth-century literary and cultural texts: in poems, pamphlets, orations, novels, and perhaps most notably, in Samuel Foote's play, *The Nabob* (1772), which I will discuss at length. The nabob is both a liminal, yet polarizing, figure who emerges from the murky horizon of the Eastern colony as a stereotypical Eastern despot. And despite the humorous, often satiric, depictions of him, the nabob seems to pose a threat to the social and moral certainties of the British aristocracy adapting to Britain's colonial rule.

The title "nabob" was given to East India Company employees—merchants, factors, soldiers—roughly between the years 1757 and 1785, and before the reforms undertaken by Cornwallis in the 1790s by which he banned private trading among Company officials. These nabobs, so called because they acted like stereotypes of Eastern potentates or *nawabs*, differed from both the early traders of the seventeenth century and the civil servants of later years; by most accounts they were seen as merchant/adventurers and opportunists who were in India solely to acquire wealth.[2]

The figure of the nabob first appeared during what Percival Spear (1963) defines as the "transition period," between the years 1757 and 1785, during which the English in Bengal had changed "from pettifogging traders quarrelling over their seats in church . . . into imperialist swashbucklers and large scale extortionists" (23). Tracing this historical transition and the emergence of the new Anglo-Indian gentry, the nabobs, Spear explains its effects as follows (32):

> Before 1750 the few Company's servants who acquired fortunes did so as merchants living in European settlements. On their return they invested their money in land as any successful London merchant might have done, and we hear no tales of extraordinary extravagance or pomp. It was the migration of the factor to the country districts after [the battle of] Plassey [1757] that changed their outlook from that of merchants desiring to get rich quickly to that of gentlemen desiring titles and deference, prestige and social distinction. Nabobs first appeared in England after Plassey. They entered Parliament in force at the election of 1768, and they were first publicly exposed by Foote in his play, "The Nabob", in [1772–3].

Returning nabobs caused a stir in England by proclaiming themselves "gentlemen," implying, somewhat subversively, that "commerce and trade should be compatible with gentility," while acting like "oriental prince[s]" (Spear 1963: 37). Given the social dislocations caused by the return of these Anglo-Indian "gentle-men" with their ostentatious living, it is not surprising that the figure of the nabob is the focus of the first English literary dis-courses about India in the mid-eighteenth century. The denuncia-tion of nabobs featured in the following untitled and anonymous poem of 1773 is characteristic of the tenor of this theme:

[NABOB]: Concerns it you who plunders in the East,
In blood a tyrant, and in lust a beast?
When ills are distant, are they then your own?
Saw'st thou their tears, or heard'st their oppressed groan?
What others feel, if we must feel it too;
If for distress, we give the tribute due,
Not *Heraclitus* could with tears supply
The constant spring of sorrow's flowing eyes
[POET]: I hate this apathy—This stoic plan
Seems sullen pride; as man, I feel for man,
My country's honour hath received a blot
A mark of odium ne'er to be forgot:
A larger country still I boast; embrace
With a warm heart all Adam's wretched race.[3]

The nabob here blatantly justifies his "plunder in the East" through a cavalier indifference toward "ills" that are "distant" and therefore not his "own." While he does not repudiate the conventional titles of "tyrant" and "beast," the poet criticizes him as one who has stained his "country's honour" with a "mark of odium." Also in keeping with the conventions of this literature, the poet represents the Indians as nameless, absent victims of nabobery, while granting them an abstract humanity as part of a "larger country," and belonging to "Adam's wretched race."

Such denunciations directed against nabobs were fairly standard and appeared in a variety of literary forms: in satirical poems, such as the anonymous "The Nabob or the Asiatic Plunderer" (1776) and "Tea and Sugar: or the Nabob and the Creole" by Timothy Touchstone (1772), in Robert Bage's novel, *Man As He Is* (1792), and in Samuel Foote's play, *The Nabob* (1772), among numerous other works.[4] Literary denunciations of mercantile adventurism as opportunistic, immoral, and un-English were further reflected in the widespread negative perceptions of the East India Company in the mid-eighteenth century. A typical sense of the British public's moral outrage can be found in "The Asiatic Plunderer":

> Could [the nabobs], if conscience were not quite asleep,
> Each day, a *Saturnalian* revel keep?
> Each day, a *nuptial* feast before their sight,
> If angry conscience did, or lash, or bite?
> 'Tis a strong symptom they forget to feel;
> Their breasts are stone, their minds are hard as steel.
>
> (quoted in Holzman 1926: 19)

The returning nabob with his ostentatious living, was indeed, a significant figure on the eighteenth-century scene of colonial self-examination in the light of Britain's growing role in India. Edmund Burke's famous speech on December 1, 1783 in the House of Commons aptly captures the controversy swirling around the role of the East India Company as well as the behavior of its representatives in India.[5] Burke, perhaps, knew more about India than did any public figure at the time. And as a noted parliamentarian, he spent much time formulating theories about the "proper relationship between Britain and India, and by implication between any imperial power and any subject people" (Marshall 1981: 1). His criticism of the nabobs centers on what he perceives as a deformation of their Englishness while in India. Furthermore, Burke implicitly reminds his readers, when these young nabobs acquired attitudes and habits that were inappropriate among British aristocrats, they also imperiled the comfortable class hierarchies at home:

> There is nothing in the boys we send to India worse than the boys whom we are whipping at school, or that we see trailing a pike, or bending over a desk at home. But as English youth in India drink the intoxicating draught of authority and dominion before their heads are able to bear it, and as they are full grown in fortune long before they are ripe in principle, neither nature nor reason have any opportunity to exert themselves for remedy of the excesses of their premature power.
>
> (in Marshall 1981: 402–3)

Not unlike the literary conventions shaping the literary images of nabobs, Burke also bases his disapproval of the Company representatives in terms of his professed sympathy for the natives, who are, once again, the silent victims of the foreign predators:

> The natives scarcely know what it is to see the grey head of the Englishman. Young men (boys almost) govern there, without

society, and without sympathy with the natives. They have no more social habits with the people, than if they still resided in England. . . . Animated with all the avarice of age, and all the impetuosity of youth, they roll in one after another; wave after wave; and there is nothing before the eyes of the natives but an endless, hopeless prospect of new flights of birds of prey and passage, with appetites continually renewing for food that is continually wasting.

(ibid.: 402)

Burke's powerful organic metaphors of birds of prey with insatiable "appetites," like his earlier references to the "intoxicating draught of authority" available in India, create a suggestive picture of a land *breeding* immorality in Englishmen who then became its exploiters and plunderers. Burke seems to have some anxiety about the nature of the nabobs' authority and the way they assert it, both in India and in Britain; thus, I believe, his Orientalist tropes illustrate the reification of the British class structure as much as they do the decadence of India.

Overall, however, Burke's suggestion that the East has corrupted these men and is somehow implicated in their dissipation and decadence is pervasive in a variety of literary and cultural texts of the time. For instance, in the anonymous poem, "The Asiatic Plunderer," we hear the suggestion that despotism belongs to India, where it must remain: "in Asia's realms let slavery be bound,/Let not her foot defile this sacred ground, Where Freedom, Science, Valour fixed their seat" (quoted in Juneja 1992: 191). The dichotomy between the backward, decadent East and a morally upright West is held in place here by a nostalgic desire to contain the contagion of slavery within Asia—where it rightly belongs. Thus, nabobery is often represented as a morally fallen, diseased condition, as in Colin Maclaurin's "Ode Inscribed to the Conquerers of the East":

Behold this predatory Lord [the nabob]
By sycophantic fools adored,
Magnificence displays:
But yet his melancholy air,
Shows discontent, if not despair,
Upon his vitals preys.

(quoted in Holzman 1926: 96)

Given their general dismay at what they perceived as the aber-
rant lives of the nabobs, the British public, especially the gentry,
viewed them as nothing more than upstarts like Sir Matthew
Mite in *The Nabob*. He "from the Indies, came thundering . . .
and profusely scattering the spoils of ruined provinces, corrupted
the virtue and alienated the affections of all the old friends of the
family." Clearly the source of Sir Matthew's vices, as of his
wealth, lies in the Indies, as Lady Oldham remarks: "With the
wealth of the East, we have too imported the worst of its
vices" (14).

In considering these recurring implications that the East has
corrupted Englishmen, can one infer, as Juneja (1992) does, that
the eighteenth-century discourse about nabobery "deftly reverses
common conceptions about British civility and Eastern barbarism" (195)? She views these attitudes toward Indians as "free of
any overt and even implicit racism" (195), which only emerges
later in the nineteenth century. While offering nuanced readings
of the individual texts, the critic somewhat blithely views this discourse as "remarkable for its overt criticism of English behavior
in India" (195). And in "showing a developing conscience about
the treatment of colonial subjects," she argues, "it reveals some
of the best features of the emerging, enlightened, humanitarianism
of the British" (195). I believe Juneja reads these works too
literally, taking the discourse at its face value, while downplaying
the Orientalist impulse apparent in the essentialist images of the
"decadent East." Images of nabobery often simply re-enacted
stereotypical scenes of Eastern luxury and despotism, which rhetorically, if not literally, played out Britain's colonial relation to
India. For instance, a curious prologue to a play entitled "A new
tragedy call'd Alonzo" (1773) is particularly responsive to the
role of the nabobs in discussions about reform in India:

Whilst ardent Zeal for India's Reformation,
Hath fir'd the Spirit of a generous Nation;
Whilst Patriots of presented Lacks complain,
And Courtiers Bribery to Excess arraign;
The Maxims of Bengal still rule the stage,
The Players are your Slaves from Age to Age.
Like Eastern Princes in this House you sit,
The Souhabs and Nabobs of suppliant wit;
Each Bard his Present brings when he draws near

With Prologue first he soothes your gracious Ear.

(quoted in Holzman 1926: 95)

Here we can see how during the widespread debates about the future of India and the decadence of the nabobs—accompanied by frequent literary, or rather satirical, denunciations—images of Eastern luxury and despotism may have shaped the popular imagination. And the predominance of such images, I believe, cannot be dismissed at a time when the political and mercantile forces in the nation were reappraising their relation to India. There was a widespread perception of the Company's abuses of power in India, heightened no doubt, by Warren Hastings's impeachment before the House of Lords, which opened in 1786 and lasted eight years. In 1783, Edmund Burke summed up the growing mood for re-form when he stated in his oration on Fox's India Bill: "Our Indian Government is in its best state a grievance. It is necessary that the correctives should be uncommonly vigorous . . . it is an arduous thing to plead against abuses of power which originate from your own country, and affect those whom we are used to consider as strangers" (in Marshall 1981: 403).

Literary texts such as "The Asiatic Plunderer" and *The Nabob* called for precisely the same remedy as Burke: administering a social and moral corrective on the extravagances and corruption of the East India Company representatives in India. Yet while these works questioned the nature of Britain's authority in India, they also evoked in the popular imagination a picture of India as site of decadence, decline, and in need of reform. As a result, their criticisms of nabobery re-affirmed the *categories of representation* by which the dichotomy between civilization and barbarism—or specifically between Western enlightenment and Eastern "decadence"—remained intact. These were the characteristic Orientalizing tropes of difference producing an ontological distinction between West and East, defining the Orient in terms of everything the Occident is not: decadent, weak, barbaric, feminine. I use this term in the context of Edward Said's definition of Orientalism as the European "impulse always to codify, to subdue the infinite variety of the Orient to a 'complete digest of laws, figures, customs, and works.'"[6] Sympathy for the natives expressed in the denunciations of the plundering nabobs did not rhetorically alter the terms of definition established by the Europeans.

This becomes apparent when we consider how this binary opposition between West and East also bears the marks of classical, medieval, and Renaissance imaginative geography—a geography in which the physical distance of the non-European lands from the European and Christian center of civilization also signaled a moral disparity between the two. Similarly, eighteenth-century literary discourses about nabobs designated India as a place of corruption, while defining England as the site of normative, civic virtue, which must be protected and rescued from "foreign," immoral influences. In fact, by their logic, the moral failing of the nabobs lay precisely in the way they collapsed these categories by taking on native personae, so to speak, which led to lapses in character considered "un-English."

Such binary oppositions between nabobery and civilized behavior, although deployed here in the condemnation of the East India Company's abuses of power, also reinforce the superiority of British civilization and society, the ideological mainstay of later colonial rule. While literary works express moral outrage at the actions of Englishmen staining "Hindustan's plains with human gore," what is really at stake in their criticism is the loss of the nabobs' Englishness. Prevailing criticism of nabobs assumed that Eastern excesses had weakened their natural moral rectitude and cautioned against transporting these excesses to civilized British society. The crass Sir Matthew Mite in *The Nabob* clearly embodies such a threat. Quite typically, for instance, he boasts to Mrs Matcham, the procuress: "I have had some thoughts of founding in this town a *seraglio*: they are of singular use in the Indies: Do you think I could bring it to bear?" (33). To which Matcham replies: "Why a customer of mine did formerly make an attempt; but he pursued too violent measures at first; wanted to confine the ladies against their consent; and that too in a country of freedom" (33). Here, once again, forms of slavery and decadence are represented as intrinsically Eastern and have no place in Britain, the "country of freedom," even in a setting like a brothel.

Typically, then, the shared concern of many of these literary and social texts is simply how to distinguish between the "real" British gentry and the nabobs—the latter being the intruders and usurpers who taint the society at home. Burke warns his countrymen with a vivid picture of such an intrusion and its related social dislocations:

In India all the vices operate by which sudden fortune is acquired; in England are often displayed by the same persons, the virtues which dispense hereditary wealth. Arrived in England, the destroyers of the nobility and gentry of a whole kingdom will find the best company in this nation, at a board of elegance and hospitality. Here, manufacturer and husbandman will bless the just and punctual hand, that in India has torn the cloth from the loom, or wrested the scanty portion of rice and salt from the peasant of Bengal, or wrung from him the very opium in which he forgot his oppressions and oppressor. They marry into your families; they enter into your estates by loans; they raise their value by demand; they cherish and protect your relations which lie heavy in your patronage.

(in Marshall 1981: 403)

Burke's sympathy for the Indian subjects is ideologically held in place by fundamental differences between the two societies, Indian and British, each having a different set of expectations for human behavior. Furthermore, if Indians figure as nameless victims—wretched peasants in the thrall of opium—English domesticity, with its "board of elegance and hospitality," embodies the civic virtues of a civilized, developed society. From Burke's account here, with its uneasy mingling of vice and virtue in terms of location, we can sense a complex range of anxieties that beset the nation trying to grapple with its colonial role. The widespread disgust at the ostentation, decadence, and corruption of the nabobs signifies an implicit, two-fold threat to the nation: to the profitable and efficient governance of India and to the established social and class hierarchies within Britain. Whereas in India this period marked the transition from factory to settlement life, in Britain the returning nabobs with their commercial wealth stirred the prejudice and hostility of the landowning gentry (Spear 1963: 37).

Despite a recognition of such social disruptions, the literary attacks on the immorality of the nabobs generally focus on individuals. There seems little recognition and no more than a simplistic understanding of the economics of colonialism.[7] For instance, in Foote's play, Thomas Oldham suggests that some nabobs did acquire their wealth honestly in India: "there are men from the Indies, and many too . . . who dispensed nobly and with hospitality here, what they have acquired with honour and credit elsewhere; and at the same time they have increased dominions and wealth, have added virtues too to their country" (14–15). This is a precursor to the nineteenth-century ideal of colonialism as a site of wealth governed by a natural system of beneficence and virtue. Burke, Fox, North, and others tried to do precisely the same via their legislative correctives; they attempted to establish a viable economics of colonialism so that India would become a prosperous, untroubled dominion, a source of wealth for both the merchants and the state. Fox's India Bill, with the strong influence of Burke, was an attempt to administer such a corrective, as Suleri explains:

> Fox's India Bill . . . attempted to warn both state and merchant of the dangers inherent in their desire to perceive India as a land of perpetual surplus; in order to preserve better the potential imperialist interest in India, the bill argued, the British government and the East India Company should coalesce into a governing body that could serve as a prudent conduit between the merchant's desire to act as a state and the state's desire to own the power of the merchant.
>
> (Suleri 1992: 25)

This desired balance of interests, according to Edmund Burke, had to be achieved by the elimination of British greed and corruption in India, and by assuming that the "interests of the Natives of India" and those of Great Britain "are in Effect, one and the same."[8] Throughout Burke's long engagement with Indian affairs, the good governance of India was his main prescription, as explained by Marshall:

> In political terms, [according to Burke] "every means, effectual to preserve India from oppression, is a guard to preserve the British constitution from its worst corruption". In economic terms "all Attempts, which in their original System, or in their necessary Consequences, tend to the distress of India, must, and in a very short Time will, make themselves felt, even by those in whose Favour such attempts have been made". . . . "The Prosperity of the Natives must be previously secured, before any Profit from them whatsoever is secured".
>
> (Marshall 1981: 23)

Burke's narrative of the colonization of India was marked by an unconvincing simplicity: because the East India Company, run by the profligate nabobs, combined a mismanagement of affairs with greedy and extortionist policies, it jeopardized the well-being and dignity of the natives as well as the viability of Britain's political and commercial interests. And Burke seems to consider that only greed and corruption were preventing a natural convergence of interests between Britain and India from functioning. Thus, the *individual* morality of the East India Company nabobs became a convenient issue, both in official policy and literary discourses, ideologically erasing the inherent conflicts between the mercantile drive of the Company and the interests of the natives. And, as P.J. Marshall puts it, the

> later history of British India would show that abuses stemming from the pursuit of personal advantage by men in power could be virtually eliminated, but that the control of corruption would by no means resolve the moral dilemmas of British rule. To its later critics, the abuses of the Raj were inherent in its very being.
>
> (ibid.: 24)

By all accounts, in his lifetime, Burke never confronted this dilemma in the belief that compromise and balance were possible (ibid.: 23–5).

Fox's Bill was defeated on December 13, but Burke's ideas articulated in the oration created in the collective imagination the shape of the British empire to come. Comparing the British entrance into India with previous, more bloody, conquerers, the "Arabs, Tartars, and Persians," Burke praises the latter for their investments in India:

> the Asiatic conquerers very soon abated of their ferocity, because they made the conquered country their own. They rose or fell with the rise or fall of the territory they lived in. Fathers there deposited the hopes of their posterity; the children there beheld the monument of their fathers.
>
> (in Marshall 1981: 401)

Britain's empire, according to Burke, lacks a foundation and cause:

> Every rupee of profit made by an Englishman is lost for ever to India. With us are no retributory superstitions by which a foundation of charity compensates, through ages, to the poor,

for the rapine and injustice of a day. With us no pride erects
stately monuments which repair the mischiefs which pride has
produced, and which adorn a country, out of its own spoils.
England has erected no churches, no hospitals, no palaces, no
schools. . . . Every other conquerer of every other description
has left some monument, either of state or beneficence, behind
him. Were we to be driven out of India this day, nothing
would remain, to tell that it had been possessed during the
inglorious period of our dominion, by any thing better than an
orang-outang or the tiger.

(ibid.: 402)

Burke's call for a "foundation" in India meant an assertion of
British colonialism as a new moral order, bringing with it the
edifices of civilization. The contradiction in Burke's broad, expan-
sionist vision (here and elsewhere) is apparent: while promoting a
humane, universal vision of civilization, which he earlier bases on
a "natural equality of all mankind" (385), Burke's main endeavor
is the consolidation of Britain's rule in India. Thus, he sees no
conflict of purpose between the monuments of "beneficence" and
those of "conquest." Rather, his purpose is to show them as necessarily enabling one another.

II

Burke's (and others') lament over the East India Company's
extraction of capital from India, with its attendant mismanagement and dissipation, together with the literary denunciations
of the nabobs' decadence and greed, come together to form an
Orientalist discourse in the late eighteenth century. As a corollary
to this call for reform in the governance of India, with its
sympathy for the natives, there emerged another related, though
seemingly separate, move to idealize India's ancient past.
Edmund Burke intimates such an attitude when he describes
Indians as follows:

a people for ages civilized and cultivated; cultivated by all the
arts of polished life, whilst we were yet in the woods. There,
have been (and still the skeletons remain) princes once of great
dignity, authority, and opulence. There, are to be found the
chiefs of tribes and nations. There is to be found an [ancient]

and venerable priesthood, the depository of their laws, learning
and history, the guides of the people whilst living and their con-
solation in death: a nobility of great antiquity and renown . . .
merchants and bankers . . . whose credit had often supported a
tottering state, and preserved their governments in the midst of
war and desolation.

(in Marshall 1981: 389–90)

Hearkening to India's ancient, pre-European past, Burke also
hints at both a timeless, almost atrophied, culture of the "ancient
and venerable priesthood" and a later decline, referring to "skeletons" of powerful rulers and the "desolation" of war and unrest.
Using their veneration for India's ancient past as a context for
framing their concerns about the eighteenth-century transformation of colonial power was a typical ploy of British public figures.
Such a rhetorical move, as is well documented, was the basis
of the famed "Orientalist" movement, an important feature of
eighteenth-century colonial discourse about India. As the East
India Company servants were undergoing a transformation from
commercial adventurers to civil servants, from the year 1773 to
the early nineteenth century, they were also beginning to re-define
their role in India via, curiously, a "discovery" of the ancient
Hindu classical age. When literary denunciations of nabobs "plundering" the "wretched" victims of the "decadent East" were at
their height in Britain, the elite Company servants in India began
to create a new discourse about an "Indo-Aryan period as an age
of gold."[9] The originator of this movement was Warren Hastings,
who himself represented a complex transition from merchant to
ill-starred empire-builder; like Robert Clive before him, he was a
nabob who attained a huge fortune and unlimited, despotic
power in India, but later, he was appointed the first Governor
General, ending the dual system of power sharing between the
state and the Company in 1773. Yet Hastings could not easily
shed his role of nabob or end the rapacity of the extortionist
system he inherited; thus he was tried in long-drawn-out impeachment proceedings before the House of Lords, which began in
1788 and dragged on for eight years, though it was obvious after
the first year that he was likely to be acquitted. It is not incidental
that Edmund Burke was the instigator of these proceedings, viewing Hastings as a despot who was a blight on the continued
health of Britain's colonial power.[10]

Despite the mixed responses to his rule in India, Warren Hastings left a distinct mark on eighteenth-century colonial rule through his cultural policy. Himself proficient in several South Asian languages, he aimed at creating "an Orientalized service elite competent in Indian languages and responsive to Indian traditions" (Kopf 1969: 17). By 1784, when Hastings founded the Asiatic Society, the knowledge of Indian languages opened the way to professional advancement as well as to the literary treasures of Oriental civilization. A name widely celebrated and most closely associated with the Orientalist movement was that of William Jones, civil servant and first President of the Asiatic Society until his death in 1794. He is best remembered for discovering links between Sanskrit, the language of ancient Hindus, and the European language family, thus re-animating a resplendent Hindu past by identifying it as the source of Western civilization. Jones's comparative linguistic work not only "discovered" Europe's ancient heritage, but also gave birth to the modern science of philology. Thus as an Orientalist, he was a typical product of the eighteenth-century Enlightenment, a rationalist and universalist who sought "to explain cultural unity through common origins" (Kopf 1969: 38).

As Orientalists such as Jones and Colebrooke constructed India's ancient past as an object of Western knowledge, they seemed to depend on the earlier and well-worn tropes of *discovery* and *wonder*. This was not surprising considering that the trope of discovery is, in part, based on the belief in origins as the foundation of all knowledge. Furthermore, the Orientalists' "discovery" was not only of an ancient and different India, but also of the lost heritage of the Europeans. Not surprisingly, then, Hastings, Jones, Colebrooke, and other Orientalists were also classicists who saw their study as a simulated re-discovery of classical works via analogies with Sanskrit literature. Thus, like the earlier British travelers/writers who came to India, the Orientalists also drew on literary tradition to contextualize and prescribe their own interactions in India, this time as civil servants.

William Jones describes this appropriation of India's classical past, with its attendant universalizing impulses, in a letter to Earl Spencer, dated August 23, 1787:

To what shall I compare my literary pursuits in India? Suppose Greek literature to be known in modern Greece only, and there to be in the hands of priests and philosophers; and suppose them to be still worshippers of Jupiter and Apollo: suppose Greece to have been conquered successively by Goths, Huns, Vandals, Tartars, and lastly by the English; then suppose a court of judicature to be established by the British parliament, at Athens, and an inquisitive Englishman to be one of the judges; suppose him to learn Greek there, which none of his countrymen knew, and to read Homer, Pindar, Plato, which no other Europeans had even heard of. Such am I in this country; substituting Sanscrit for Greek, the *Brahmans*, for the priests of *Jupiter*, and *Valmic, Vyasa, Calidasa*, for Homer, Plato, Pindar.

(in Cannon 1970: 755–6)

Or, in another letter in the same year to Earl Spencer, Jones points to even clearer connections between Sanskrit and Latin:

Sanscrit literature is, indeed, a new world . . . the *Latin* of *India*, and a sister of Latin & Greek. In Sanscrit are written half a million of Stanzas on sacred history and literature, Epick and Lyrick poems innumerable, and (and what is wonderful) Trage-dies & Comedies not to be counted, above 2000 years old, besides Works on Law (my great object), on Medicine . . . and so on to infinity.

(ibid.: 747)

A second feature of the Orientalist quest for historical knowl-edge was the premise, as Jones explains, that Indians had buried their glorious history "in a cloud of fables"—a history that Orien-talists were now supposedly discovering, somewhat to their amaze-ment, as Jones remarks: "how degenerate and abased so ever the Hindus may now appear, [it was a certainty] that in some early age they were splendid in arts and arms, happy in government, wise in legislation, and eminent in . . . knowledge."[11] Here, and elsewhere, the Orientalists' sense of wonder at India's glorious classical past is accompanied by a lament for the Eastern country's debased and fallen present.

H.T. Colebrooke, another noted Orientalist, also reiterated this relationship with India's past. Acknowledging that "civilization had its origins in Asia," he also believed that while the West was taking great strides forward, India was in a state of decline (Kopf 1969: 39). Colebrooke was particularly interested in Vedic India, in part because he believed that "modern Hindus seem to misunderstand their numerous texts" (quoted ibid.: 41). In Colebrooke's mode of analysis, "each discovery or recovery of Vedic India was dramatically and metaphorically contrasted with the peculiarities of contemporary Hindu society" (ibid.: 40). Thus, for the Orientalists acquiring knowledge of the ancient world, which lay buried in old texts, meant setting up a parallel authority to the Brahmins, who controlled, and according to Colebrooke and others, obfuscated the meaning of the traditional texts.

Overall, we cannot, with the hindsight of history, pre-judge the motives and intentions of men like Colebrooke and Jones. By all accounts, it would be fair to consider William Jones a liberal, and a humanist, albeit with an intensely romanticizing imagination. The Sanskrit language and literature obviously captured his imagination and sympathies; and his translation of works such as Kalidasa's classical play, *Shakuntala*, not only influenced and improved European conceptions of the Eastern world, but also had a lasting impact on generations of Indian scholars. An Indian editor, Moni Bagchee, explains this influence in a preface to the 1984 collection of Jones's work: "[Indians should] try to preserve accurately and interpret the national heritage by treading the path chalked out by Sir William Jones" (quoted in Niranjana 1992: 13). Jones's interest in Indian culture was accompanied by an abiding concern for the Indian natives. For instance, Jones, like his patron, Warren Hastings, strongly advocated that Indians should be ruled by their own laws, and acknowledges (in many of his letters) that "particular circumstances of our [Indian] judicature have produced new and crying evils" (in Cannon 1970: 662). He laments the conditions produced by the British prison system in India: "a place of close confinement in this climate must be worse than the worst dungeon of our western world" (661), and recognizes that the "notions of impurity peculiar to . . . [their] religion . . . must render the Hindu prisoners completely miserable" (661). Jones also refers to his Brahmin teachers with respect and affection. He describes his "favourite Pandit" ("the venerable sage") whom the British government on Jones's "recommendation have given . . . a pension of 300 rupees a month; and, I believe," he goes on to state, "no pension was ever better bestowed" (923). Such moments of empathy are frequent in Jones's writings, both in his "discoveries" of India's ancient past and in his concerns about justice for the natives over whom he governed. Yet these moments are countered by (and contained within) the pervasive ideological assumption about the British rulers' role as inter- preters, translators, and mediators of Indian culture, language, and laws in the face of the Hindus' inability to carry out these tasks, as Tejaswini Niranjana (1992: 13) explains:

> The most significant nodes of Jones' work are (a) the need for translation by the Europeans, since the natives are unreliable interpreters of their own laws and culture; (b) the desire to be a lawgiver, to give Indians their "own" laws; and (c) the desire to "purify" Indian culture and speak on its behalf.

Jones's letters and other writings offer much evidence of such attitudes. For instance, he repeatedly questions the natives' ability to rule themselves or to accurately interpret their own laws. According to him, manifestations of native insincerity were best found in the "frequency of perjury" and the "oath of a low native" had little value because they all committed perjury "with as little remorse as if it were a proof of ingenuity or even a merit."[12] My point here is that the main aspects of Jones's well- intentioned efforts—aimed at the "discovery" of Indian tradition and the reform of its society—fed into a larger liberal, yet colonial, discourse of civilization and rescue that interpellated the Indian subject. Predicated on a Western, historicist, and teleological model of civilization and progress, the eighteenth-century Oriental- ist discourses were caught in a paradox of historical transition: on the one hand, Orientalists such as Jones judged the present as "fallen" in terms of a historical past while simultaneously natural- izing Hinduism as unchanging and timeless.

The effects of the Orientalist movement have been a subject of debate among historians and scholars. The generous view is that the first generation of Oriental scholars worked in India with a new tradition of cultural empathy and public service, one that was missing in their predecessors in the East India Company. More importantly, as some would argue, "they brought into being a new concept of the Hindu golden age as a legacy for the rising Indian intelligentsia" (Kopf 1969: 31). A link is also established between the work of the Asiatic Society of Bengal and the evolution of a new historical consciousness among Indians recovering their "forgotten past" (Kejariwal 1988: 232). Most importantly, historians have traced connections between the dis- covery of a rich past and a sense of nationalism and patriotism among Indians. According to A.L. Rowse, "It was one of the long-term ironies of history that it was British rule that led to the renaissance of India, consciousness of her identity and her past, [and] the ultimate emergence of Indian nationalism."[13]

An opposing, more pervasive argument notes a complicity between Orientalism and colonialism. Recent historians frequently view Orientalism in negative terms, defined by Edward Said as a form of colonial discourse, or a "Western style for dominating, restructuring, and having authority over the Orient" (Said 1979: 3). From this colonial perspective, Orientalism had an administrative function, most notably in the instance of Sanskrit law, which Jones, also a Supreme Court judge, translated and transformed into an instrument of the new, colonial legal system. Jones often testifies to the administrative uses of his translation work, for instance, when he states:

> it has . . . been my earnest endeavour to draw a knowledge of Hindu and Musilmen jurisprudence from its fountain head . . . and hope to do my part towards compiling a complete Digest of Indian laws. The fruit of my labour I have already reaped in some degree by giving judgment in a Hindu case of importance, in which, after a difference of opinion between the Pandits, I translated the original tracts and decided on that which had the best reason as well as the highest authority.
>
> (in Cannon 1970: 718)

The issue for the British administrators was not so much a cultural sensitivity to Hindu laws as that the *principle of law* represented the new colonial order. In a letter to Pitt the Younger in 1785, Jones explains his interest in getting translations of Hindu laws, so that he may be "a check on the Pundits of the Court" (ibid.: 664). He then goes on to affirm to Pitt that a "good system of laws, a just administration of them, and a long peace" will "render this country a source of infinite advantage to Great Britain" (ibid.).

Acquiring historical and linguistic knowledge of India's classical past was not simply a disciplinary activity, but also an administrative imperative of colonial rulers mapping and securing a new political and cultural terrain (Sharpe 1993: 34–41; Cohn 1985: 288–95). This imperative is most evident in Jones's focus on the translation of Sanskrit texts of Hindu law so he could verify interpretations of his Indian interpreters, as he states in a letter: "Pandits and

Maulvis [Muslim holy men] few of whom give opinions without a culpable bias" (quoted in Niranjana 1992: 16). Jones's preoccupations with Indian laws reflect less empathy with Indian culture than do his translations of Sanskrit literary works, because in the legal treatises the Hindu is constructed as "a subject of law rather than as an object of knowledge."[14]

Overall, the scholarly work of colonial administrators who were also Orientalists was founded on a paradox: on the one hand, the Orientalists as civil servants shared the standard colonial belief in the superiority of Western knowledge and institutions. On the other hand, these Indologists "re-discovered" a glorious India by identifying a certain resemblance between East and West in a shared ancient past. This interplay between similarities and differences characterized the dissonant relationship between administrative and academic, or disciplinary, aspects of Orientalism, producing in turn, the pervasive instability in British colonial discourse in the eighteenth century.

What these schisms revealed was not so much the confusions or insufficiencies in attitudes of individual civil servants serving in India, but rather, the confusions about Britain's changing role in India, with all its attendant moral and social dilemmas. As the flamboyant and profligate East India Company nabobs gave way to the more enlightened civil servants like William Jones in the late eighteenth century, colonialism, it seems, was administering a self-corrective. One aspect of this corrective was, of course, the British commitment to indigenous acculturation, and by inference, to the efficiency of the civil servants in India. Among other manifestations of colonial self-examination in Britain itself were the literary and social denunciations of the nabobs, intense parliamentary debates, and the long public trial of Warren Hastings for alleged corruption. All such self-correctives were simply efforts at making the necessary ideological adjustments, whereby the British public could justify colonial rule, without directly confronting the social and economic displacements caused by the influx of colonial/mercantile capital into Britain. What these different efforts at colonial reform had in common was a vision of eighteenth-century India as the decadent and fallen East in need of Western civilization. However, what these colonial discourses could *not* fix was an appropriate relationship or distance between British society and the multifarious encroachments of colonialism. To get a sense of how the popular imagination in Britain made the necessary historical and ideological adjustments to the Indian empire, let us now turn to Samuel Foote's play *The Nabob*, first staged in London in the Haymarket Theatre on June 29, 1772.

III

It is not coincidental that Samuel Foote's play, *The Nabob*, was staged in 1772, after public interest in the East India Company had reached its peak in April, 1771, when Robert Clive's practices in India were investigated for their legality. In fact, Clive himself may have inspired Foote by defending the East Indians as follows: "There has not been one character found amongst them sufficiently flagitious for Mr. Foote to exhibit on the Haymarket Theatre" (quoted in Holzman 1926: 96). Foote seems to have taken up this challenge and created the caricature of a nabob in Sir Matthew Mite, modeled on General Richard Smith, the son of a cheese-monger, though probably incorporating traits of Robert Clive and Nabob Gray, Boswell's schoolmate (Trefman 1971: 204).

The plot of the play is both simple and sentimental: Sir Matthew Mite, a recently returned, wealthy nabob from India, places the Oldham family in debt to him through devious tactics in order to foreclose on their estate and force their daughter, Sophy, to marry him in repayment. Sophy is in love with young Oldham, a cousin, but Mite threatens to bring her family into financial ruin if she refuses him. At the last minute she and her family are saved by Sir Thomas Oldham, who appears with the necessary cash, checkmating Sir Matthew Mite's schemes. And Lady Oldham, who had sneered at her brother-in-law for being a merchant, allows her daughter to marry his son.

The thrust of this plot is the exclusion of an outsider, an intruder who attempts to contaminate British gentility with his "tainted" money from the "Indies." The happy ending seems somewhat contrived to foil Sir Matthew's attempts to control the Oldham family. And the play concludes with a reminder of the staying power of rich nabobs. When Thomas Oldham warns Sir Matthew of "his hour of retribution" (58), the latter retorts with a cautionary truism:

> You must, Master Oldham, give me leave to laugh at your prophetic effusion. . . . Now-a-days, riches possess at least one

magical power, that, being rightly dispensed, they closely conceal the source from whence they proceeded: That wisdom I hope never to want.

(ibid.)

Thus, despite Mite's temporary rout, Foote's play does not entirely quell the unease created by the influx of colonial capital into Britain. Yet the dramatist seems to suggest that if the nabobs and their "Eastern" practices literally cannot be excluded from the English society and economy, at least rhetorically and ideologically they can be cast as "others" by being conflated with natives and heathens. And so the social anxieties about the effects of Britain's developing colonial role in India could be diffused. It is this process of "othering" via demarcations of identity and difference that makes Samuel Foote's *The Nabob* a social satire that is also a form of colonial discourse. What is at stake in this very "English" social satire is, once again, a vision of a decadent Anglo-India—evoked by an appropriate jargon of "lacks," "roupees," and "jagghires"—a source of wealth, yet implicitly in need of correction and reform.

From the outset, the plot of *The Nabob* unfolds via an interplay of identity and difference in which the "Indies" are marked as a place of corruption and decadence, even though the Indians are the nameless victims of the nabobs' plunder. In the opening scene, Lady Oldham reminds her husband of the cause of their impending financial crisis: "At this crisis, preceded by all the pomp of Asia, Sir Matthew Mite, from the Indies, came thundering amongst us; and, profusely scattering the spoils of ruined provinces, corrupted the virtue and alienated the affections of all the old friends to the family" (7). Later, reflecting on Sir Matthew's "infernal" motives in initially advancing them a large sum of money, Lady Oldham ascribes his behaviour to an Eastern lapse of morality: "With the wealth of the East, we have too imported its vices. What a horrid crew" (14). Foote's play also gives expression to popular British perceptions about East Indian nabobs through Sir Matthew's own admissions of decadent practices alien to British society, as he mentions "founding in this town a seraglio . . . of singular use in the Indies" (33); and for the "direction" of this proposed seraglio, Sir Matthew rejects the services of Mistress Matcham with the following retort:

In the East we never confide that office to your sex or complexion. I had some thoughts of importing three blacks from
Bengal, who have been properly prepared for the service; but
I sha'n't venture till the point is determined whether those
creatures are to be considered as mere chattels or men.

(ibid.)

Once again, in keeping with the conventions of the nabob literature of the period, supposedly Eastern practices such as slavery
and despotism were unacceptable in Britain, which Matcham
reminds Mite is the "country of freedom" (33).

The characters' desire to distinguish between East India and
Britain is further accentuated by their repeated denunciations of
Sir Matthew's commercial and business practices tainted by the
Indian atmosphere of corruption, but supposedly alien to the
aristocracy at home. The Oldhams repeatedly take the morally
superior position over the nabob. Thomas Oldham refuses Mite's
offer of marriage to his niece with a lofty dismissal: "They [the
Oldhams] are, Sir Matthew, no strangers to your power and
wealth, but . . . there are superior spirits living, who would disdain
an alliance with grandeur obtained at the expensce of honour and
virtue" (41). Lady Oldham also questions the respectability of
East Indian nabobs. Despite her snobbery, for instance, she
accepts "merchants [in England] to be a useful body of men" (9)
and considers commerce "in this country, as a pretty recource for
the younger shoots of a family" (9). But when Sir Matthew offers
to settle a *jagghir*, or an annual income, on the Oldhams, Lady
Oldham declares, "What strange jargon he deals in" (11).

Other members of the Oldham family share her opinion about
Mite's questionable business dealings, typical of East Indian
nabobs, as Thomas Oldham reflects on Mite's "artful project" of
taking control of his brother's fortune: "so much contrivance and
cunning has been an overmatch for a plain English gentleman, or
an innocent Indian" (13). And later, he describes to his niece
what he considers Sir Matthew's suspicious rise to power: "these
new gentlemen, who from caprice of fortune, and a strange chain
of events, have acquired immoderate wealth, and rose to uncon-
troled power abroad, find it difficult . . . to admit of any equal at
home" (18).

Repeatedly, the Oldhams try to distance themselves from Sir
Matthew and his impending takeover of their family. In their

efforts, the play enacts a pervasive social anxiety about the money flowing from the East Indian colony, which they believe is ill-gotten, tainted at the source, and leading to socio-economic disruptions at home. This is in contrast, of course, to the inherited wealth of the British aristocracy, of which Lady Oldham reminds her husband: "You succeeded, Sir, to a patrimony, which though the liberal and hospitable spirit of your predecessors would not suffer to encrease, yet their prudence took care should never be diminished" (6). In comparison with this seemingly providential and natural transference of money, with its established social stratification, Lady Oldham portends that Mite's rapaciously gained treasures cannot last. She would rather see her daughter in "an indigent state, than voluptuously rioting in pleasures that derive their source from the ruin of others" (54). As in Burke's rhetoric, the Oldhams' evocations of Oriental decadence elide into an anxiety about how the nabobs gained their wealth and its ill-effects back home.

Furthermore, her strong rejection of Mite's offer of marriage to their daughter is buttressed by intimations of moral justice, which she believes will bring about his downfall. Thus, toward the end of the play, while stating that she "only echoes public opinion," Lady Oldham prophesies a dire future for the colonial nabobs: "The possessions arising from plunder very rarely are permanent; we everyday see what has been treacherously and rapaciously gained, as profusely and full as rapidly squandered" (55).

By foiling Sir Matthew's attempted financial takeover, Thomas Oldham can take a high moral stance at the end of the play. Blessing the impending marriage of Sophy with his son, he imagines the ideal boundaries of domesticity and nationhood, implicitly excluding the colonies: "For, however praiseworthy the spirit of adventure may be, whoever keeps his post, and does his duty at home, will be found to render his country best service at last" (59). Despite the Oldhams' tactical victory, Sir Matthew Mite's fortunes and spirits are left intact at the end of the play. The highly comic sub-plot of the work also testifies to the growing corruption spawned by East Indian money in London. For instance, the members of the Christian Club of the parish of "Bribe'em" enter into negotiations with Mite to sell their votes, declaring a bond between "Bribe'em" and "Bengal."

If anything, Samuel Foote's *The Nabob* forces on its British audiences a recognition of the widespread tentacles of colonial affluence and influence. As a defeated Sir Matthew Mite ceremoniously takes his leave of the Oldham family whom he "wished to make happy in spite of themselves" (58), he resists the family's denunciations of nabobs—the "common cry of the times"—by reminding them, as well as Foote's domestic audiences, of the benefits of colonialism: "such is the gratitude of this country to those who have given it dominion and wealth" (55). Clearly if this play reveals the faultlines in the emerging eighteenth-century colonial discourse in Britain, it does so by dramatizing the familiar binaries: the civic metropolis versus the corrupt colonies, and upright British rectitude assailed by the "voluptuously rioting pleasures" of the East. And in calling for a corrective to the reform of colonial practices, a work like *The Nabob* also shares the larger cultural consensus about the wretched and backward conditions of India in the eighteenth century—conditions which the East India Company exploited, but which the civil servants/ Orientalists attempted to correct. However, what was crucial about this consensus about India's current backwardness was a belief in a civilizing mission as its salvation. Thus, a call to "civilization" became an accommodating ideal in the nineteenth century, repressing the tensions and conflicts between the merchants and the state that dominated the eighteenth century.

NOTES

1 In *The Dramatic Works of Samuel Foote*, Vol. II, 14. All subsequent quotes from the play will be taken from this edition of the text and cited in parenthesis.
2 For a historical definition of the term *nawab*, see Juneja 1992: 196, who states: "Nawab was the title of those Muslim officials of the Mogul Empire who functioned as deputy governors of the provinces and districts." While it is true that in the eighteenth century, during the rapid decline of the Moguls, the local feudal lords or *nawabs* were often corrupt and rapacious, the English were sometimes responsible for dethroning legitimate and well-governing rulers and setting up corrupt puppets in their place. See Edmund Burke's complaint about the machinations of the English vis-à-vis Indian rulers in his "Oration on Fox's India Bill" (in Marshall 1981: 391–401), as when he states, "the Company has never made a treaty which they have not broken. This position is so connected with that of the sales of provinces and kingdoms" (394). My point here is that in the English imagination the figure of the *nawab* or nabob was a static representation of all Eastern rulers as decadent despots, but the reality was more complex, as I will discuss.

3 This anonymous poem is quoted by O.P. Kejariwal 1988: 22. It consists of a dialogue between the poet and his friend, who is a typical English adventurer of Clive's generation given to carefree plunder, to whom the poet responds with moral disgust.

4 For a full discussion of the treatment of nabobs as a literary subject in a variety of texts, see Juneja 1992: especially 184–9.

5 For a background to this speech, published on January 22, 1784, see the note in P.J. Marshall 1981: 378–80. Burke's speech was a defense of the pending legislation proposing limits to be placed on the power and independence of the Court of Directors of the East India Company.

6 Throughout this chapter, I use the terms, "Orientalizing" and "Orientalist" in the context of Edward Said's definition of Orientalism (1979: 78).

7 I paraphrase Juneja (1992) and I am indebted to her for bringing this fact to my attention, 188.

8 For a full account of Edmund Burke's vision of reform in India, see P.J. Marshall's Introduction (1981: 1–31).

9 See David Kopf 1969: 1–42, for a detailed account of the genesis of this movement, especially as he shows the connection between Orientalism as a discipline and its administrative function in creating acculturated, and hence more efficient civil servants.

10 Hastings's trial and alleged misdemeanors are not the subject of this chapter as my focus is on his role as the originator of the Orientalist movement in India and as a nabob involved in the misdeeds and mismanagement of the Company. For an account of his trial, see Suleri 1992: 49–74. Also see Kopf 1969: 13–21 on Hastings's cultural policy, which gave rise to the Orientalist movement among the empire-builders in India.

11 William Jones, "Third Annual Discourse," Asiatic Researches, I 1788, quoted in Kopf 1969: 39.

12 William Jones, "Charge to the Grand Jury, June 10, 1787," quoted in Niranjana 1992: 17.

13 I cite O.P. Kejariwal's use of A.L. Rowse's statement to endorse his own praise of the Orientalist movement (1988: 233).

14 See Sharpe 1993: 33–4, for a discussion of the paradoxical role of the Orientalists.

WORKS CITED IN CHAPTER 2

Belden, Mary Megie. The Dramatic Work of Samuel Foote. New Haven: Yale University Press, 1929.

Cannon, Garland. Ed. The Letters of Sir William Jones. Vol. II. Oxford: Clarendon Press, 1970.

—— The Life and Mind of Oriental Jones. Sir William Jones, the Father of Modern Linguistics. Cambridge: Cambridge University Press, 1990.

Cohn, Bernard S. "The Command of Language, the Language of Command." In Subaltern Studies: Writings on South Asian History and

Society, Vol. IV. Ed. Ranajit Guha. Oxford: Oxford University Press, 1985: 276–329.

Foote, Samuel. *The Dramatic Works of Samuel Foote*, Vol. II. London: Benjamin Blom, 1809.

Holzman, James. *The Nabobs in England: A Study of the Returned Anglo-Indian, 1760–1765*. New York: Columbia University Dissertation, 1926.

Juneja, Renu. "The Native and the Nabob: Representations of the Indian Experience in Eighteenth-Century English Literature." In *Journal of Commonwealth Literature*, 27, 1, 1992: 183–98.

Kejariwal, O.P. *The Asiatic Society of Bengal and the Discovery of India's Past 1784–1838*. Delhi: Oxford University Press, 1988.

Kopf, David. *British Orientalism and the Bengal Renaissance: The Dynamics of Indian Modernization, 1773–1835*. Berkeley: University of California Press, 1969.

Marshall, P.J. Ed. *The Writings and Speeches of Edmund Burke*, Vol. V. Oxford: Clarendon Press, 1981.

Niranjana, Tejaswini. *Siting Translation: History, Post-Structuralism, and the Colonial Context*. Berkeley: University of California Press, 1992.

Said, Edward. *Orientalism*. New York: Vintage Books, 1979.

Schwab, Raymond. *The Oriental Imagination: Europe's Rediscovery of India and the East*. New York: Columbia University Press, 1984.

Sharpe, Jenny. "The Violence of Light in the Land of Desire; or, How William Jones Discovered India." In *boundary 2*, 20, 1, 1993: 26–45.

Spear, Percival. *The Nabobs: A Study of the Social Life of the English in Eighteenth Century India*. London: Oxford University Press, 1963.

Suleri, Sara. *The Rhetoric of English India*. Chicago: University of Chicago Press, 1992.

Trefman, Simon. *Sam Foote, Comedian 1720–1777*. New York: New York University Press, 1971.

Chapter 3

The gendering of empire

I

"I think if any Englishman married a Hindoo or a Mohamedan girl, after the customs and beliefs of her sect, and in the good faith that such a marriage would be binding on him—why! have not many of our old dignitaries done this and lived happily all their lives?—and many others—. What a grand effect had the marriage of Akbar to a Rajpoot princess over the people at large! . . . but . . . I am putting the case hypothetically. I don't suppose it will ever be; but for all that there is many a Hindoo girl like Seeta, who would be an ornament and blessing to any man . . . though perhaps it is best, after all, that it is not attainable . . . because of our social prejudices, which you and I can't overcome . . . because our perceptions are narrowed with our isolated positions . . . and because if a man, one of us, married a native lady—married I say—he must exclude himself from society, which would require a strong mind."

"Then the thing is impossible, Philip?"

"I did not say that," he replied.

(Colonel Meadows Taylor, *Seeta*, 1872: 87)

This suggestive exchange between two Englishmen, Philip Mostyn and Cyril Brandon, from the novel *Seeta*, vividly brings to life the symbolic relationship between British and native women within the colonial gender system in the nineteenth century. The "Hindoo girl" whom they refer to is Seeta, a native widow and a witness at the trial of her husband's murderer. Both Mostyn and Brandon, the judge and magistrate, are immediately struck by Seeta's presence: "It was impossible for the judge not to be struck by her exceeding beauty and grace. . . . He had never seen such an Indian woman before . . . and could fully understand Cyril's warm description of her after [his early] enquiries" (Taylor 1872: 84). Thus, early in the novel, the scene is set for a rescue fantasy.

Here, the British officials are represented as Seeta's hope for impartial justice, after which the two men engage in their curious discussion of interracial marriages in colonial India. Such unions, "hypothetically" speaking, seem appealing in an imagined scenario, of living "happily all their lives," yet conveniently, are "impossible" and "not attainable." While Mostyn expresses the unspeakable in legitimating interracial sexual unions, his logic defers the possibility indefinitely, as he offers the "arguments for and against," yet without real concern because he concludes, "if the question arises, it will only be after many, many years" (88).

What is left unsaid in this exchange reveals more about the imperatives of the colonial social formation than about Mostyn's deflected idealism. If one reads these gaps and silences symptomatically, it becomes clear that they are not incidental, but necessary to the gendering process of colonial hierarchies.[1] Cyril Brandon, for instance, cannot articulate the socially forbidden, namely his developing desire for the Indian widow, and instead declares, "they [native women] could not be married," though he also adds in Seeta's defense, "such a girl as that could not be a mistress" (87). While Brandon also interjects with the claims of British women to their countrymen ("the spinsters would be up in arms"), both men tellingly repress the fear of miscegenation implicit in this scenario. When Mostyn extols the positive political effects of the "marriage of the Mughal [emperor Akbar] who married a Rajpoot [Hindu] princess [in the sixteenth century]," or when he refers to "our old dignitaries" who had native partners, he takes liberties with history by eliding the practice of taking native mistresses, which was widespread until the nineteenth century, with legitimate unions, and more significantly, skirts around the issue of racial "contamination" through the progeny of such illicit relationships.

By the nineteenth century, British colonialism, as most Victorian readers of *Seeta* would have known, was based on strict divisions of race, and unlike the Mogul emperor, the rulers did not assimilate with the local population in legal alliances, as Kenneth Ballhatchet (1980: 5) points out:

[as] improved conditions [by the early nineteenth century] encouraged more Englishwomen to live in India. . . . As wives they hastened the disappearance of Indian mistresses. As hostesses they fostered the development of exclusive social

groups. . . . As women they were thought by Englishmen to be in need of protection from lascivious Indians.

Thus, not surprisingly, the figure of the native male is absent in this discussion of interracial marriages.

Mostyn's vivid imaginings transgress the limits of colonial history by representing the unrepresentable, an Englishman's marriage to an Indian woman, legitimated "by the customs of our [British] society and by the legislature" (Taylor 1872: 87). More importantly, it signals an actual enactment of this scenario in the interracial marriage of Cyril Brandon and Seeta. While critics (and the author himself) generally view *Seeta* as a quasi-historical Mutiny novel, they note that this is perhaps the only sympathetic British account of such a union within the empire. Of course, other colonial writers like Rudyard Kipling often suggest possibilities for such unions with "hill women," for instance, but they rarely end happily. In one instance, a short story illustrating a British planter's marrying a hill woman after rejecting his fiancée back home, the ironic title of the story—"Yoked with an Unbeliever"—reveals the moral ambiguities Kipling grappled with.[2] Taylor's novel also ends with some ambivalence about interracial unions. Even though Brandon marries Seeta, the author eventually finds a melodramatic ploy for her death so her husband can remarry a woman of his own race in England.[3]

Overall, *Seeta* plays out a complex version of the colonial rescue fantasy, revealing the different, yet overlapping, functions of British and Indian women within the structure of colonial discourse.[4] Varied articulations of this rescue scenario emerged in a broad range of nineteenth-century colonial texts, among which I draw on the following: policy documents, Mutiny novels, *sati* narratives, and "picturesque" accounts of courtesans or *nautch* girls, among others. However, this rescue scenario not only figured as a frequent theme in literary and cultural works, but more crucially, it also revealed the gender inflections of Britain's civilizing mission—the overarching basis of its colonial rule in nineteenth-century India. There is some evidence to suggest that colonialism's benevolent face in the nineteenth century was premised on the assumption that both the British and native women needed to be "rescued" from the native male. Especially since the Mutiny in 1857, the rulers had cast him as a beast and a potential rapist, while representing white women as convenient icons to be valued, yet protected and segregated.[5] Furthermore, Indian women were also to be saved, not from the literal figure of the Indian male, but from their oppressive social conditions through utilitarian reform. And animating this triangulated dynamic which frequently appears in colonial texts are the familiar imperial binaries: barbarism versus civilization, tradition versus modernity and progress.

Reform—social, educational, and moral—was the ostensible imperative of the British rulers through the nineteenth century. If the early modern colonial narratives focussed on the "discovery"/ "discoveries" of East India, by the mid-nineteenth century, as stated earlier, British accounts had normalized and fixed India as decadent, backward, and in need of civilization. Thus, having laid their initial claims to India via the discovery trope—implying European entry as a point of origin—the British could now justify subsequent colonizing enterprises such as *civilizing* and *rescuing*. And the rescue of women—both British and native—became a synecdoche for the larger premise that the entire Indian culture needed saving from itself, which was an urgent concern of the nineteenth-century civilizing mission to India.

My premise here is that though the women of the rulers and the ruled faced different kinds of social constrictions, living in separate worlds, both were assigned specific, and generally restrictive and subordinate, gender functions within colonial discourse. By most accounts, British women in the colonies experienced the "privileges and contradictions of imperialism very differently from men."[6] According to one sympathetic Englishman: "In her drawing room for the chief part of her day, the Anglo-Indian lady [ironically] is as much a prisoner by reason of the heat as the zenana [or secluded] woman is by custom. . . . She is by herself all day long and thrown to her own resources" (quoted in Barr 1976: 13). The implications of such issues of identity and difference among Indian and British women, I believe, are crucial in understanding the dynamics of the rescue scenario, and more broadly, the gendering of the civilizing mission of the British Raj.

Throughout this chapter the term "gender" is used as an analytic category for historical analysis, not simply to refer to the arrival of British women and the establishment of domesticity, or to label the earlier, mostly male social formations among the colonists as somehow gender-neutral. Traditionally, historians approach the subject in terms of women's history, often substituting "gender" for women, and separating topics such as children and family from other social systems of economy, politics, or power. A more productive approach, as historian Joan Scott (1989) argues, is one that attends to signifying systems, that is "to the ways societies represent gender, use it to articulate rules of social relationships, or to construct the meaning of experience" (90). Thus, in expanding the conceptual and rhetorical scope of this term, while connecting it to "other social systems of economy, politics, or power," Scott establishes gender as a "primary way of signifying relationships of power" (93–4). Scott's concept of gender is clearly useful in both a historical description and a rhetorical analysis of the rescue scenario. And within this context we can better understand the colonial power dynamic by exploring how the gendered subjectivities of the colonizers and the colonized were produced, re-produced, or altered within the differing needs of colonialism.

Ostensibly this chapter focusses on the experience of women: English housewives, Indian *satis* and *nautch* girls, among others. However, in doing so, it maps the production of the gendered subjectivities of *both* men and women in the context of the colonial rescue paradigm. Male heroes and villains are intrinsic to this chivalric scenario. So even though the presence of British and especially Indian men seems peripheral in the varied texts, their *function* in the colonial script—as potential saviors and rapists respectively—is quite evident.

Let us see how this rescue scenario is played out in some depth in *Seeta*. It is obvious that the novelist had to bridge the cultural gap between Indian and European women before he could represent an interracial marriage. Meadows Taylor arranges for Cyril Brandon to rescue Seeta in a number of different ways: initially, he wears native disguise while joining a police party to protect her from the attack of her husband's murderer, the prototype of the Mutiny rebel-cum-terrorist/rapist, Azrael Pande, whose intentions are to capture "Seeta and [make] her [his] slave" (Taylor 1872: 96). More significantly, Cyril Brandon marries Seeta, in an act that is constructed not as a lapse into decadent, eighteenth-century nativism, but as a triumph of benevolent liberalism. Cyril's choice is presented as a chivalrous one as he tells himself: "I can give scores of instances of native connections in far higher places than mine . . . [but] few have dared as I have, to avow marriage" (240). He faces the additional temptation in the form of a suitable English girl, Philip Mostyn's sister Grace, so he tries to shut out "poor little Seeta and her claims on his love and protection" while basking in the thought of a different marriage "which his mother and sister [in England] would hail with delight" (240). His honor, more than his earlier passion, finally prevails in making Brandon stand by his Indian marriage, as he writes to his superior: "The lady you allude to is my wife: married to me by the Hindoo rites of her faith, which cannot be broken and which I respect" (241).

While the couple face both British racism and Hindu bigotry in their marriage, Brandon hopes to remarry her in a Christian ceremony, expecting his wife to be gradually convinced of conversion. On her death bed, after sacrificing herself to save her husband from the spear of the mutinous Azrael Pande, Seeta melodramatically enacts a synthesis of the two religions, mixing "snatches . . . of Sanscrit prayers . . . with lines of simple Christian hymns" (382–3). It is not incidental that Taylor's critique of religious intolerance and dogma on both sides came at a time when the empire's historical memory of the Mutiny was still alive. As Patrick Brantlinger (1988) remarks, in perhaps the only contemporary study of the novel: "the love affair between Brandon and Seeta is Victorian fiction's only approach to an adequate symbolic antithesis to the Mutiny" (216). By overcoming prejudice and superstition, they demonstrate liberalism's fantasy about how the Mutiny could have been avoided, without questioning Britain's claims to empire.

Seeta reflects the beliefs of utilitarian reformers, and in Cyril Brandon, the author has created the ideal servant of the empire. As Taylor explains in an interjection within the story: "If you, gentle reader, wish to know [Brandon's] views of Indian policy, I must request you to read Her Majesty's Proclamation of 1858 in which he is a true believer. He sees what has been done for the advancement of the people in education, and indeed in every other respect" (439). That Taylor's "daydream of justice, service, and loyalty . . . looks backward to the ideals of utilitarian reformers [of the 1820s and 1830s] with whom he began his career" is evident in Brandon's philosophy (Brantlinger 1988: 215). The British magistrate believed that after the uprising of 1857 was quelled, "the people rejoiced in the return to old laws and customs [of the British rulers]. They might be hard . . . but they were just" (Taylor 1872: 399). Given the novel's vision of a benevolent liberalism that naturalizes the empire, what role does Seeta, an Indian woman, play in this ideal, other than in briefly demonstrating a resistance to religious prejudice? After all, it is Brandon who speaks for and to Taylor's Victorian readers.

It is remarkable that Meadows Taylor does not mention the interracial marriage in his Introduction to the novel; instead, he presents *Seeta* as a quasi-historical novel relating to the period around the Mutiny of 1857. According to him, the uprising occurred because Indians resented "new and powerful elements of Western civilization" and wanted to "regain what had been lost" (viii). Thus, he describes the role of Azrael Pande in the context of the Mutiny rebels: "in [him] I have endeavoured to depict the character of the rebel and treasonable emissaries of the time" (ix). The relationship between the Mutiny and liberal justifications of the empire implicitly revealed by the author in the Introduction is perceptively brought to light by Brantlinger (1988), whose analysis includes the cross-cultural marriage: according to him, *Seeta* is about how "religion even of the highest sort . . . can create obstacles to love and sympathy" as well as about the struggling idealism of the British "civilizing mission" (215). Overall, however, Brantlinger's analysis of the novel's treatment of liberalism does not adequately address the gender inflections of the reform movement, which Taylor occludes in the Introduction, but ironically illuminates through his construction of Seeta's unconventional role within the novel.

If India served as the focus of humanitarian concern for the utilitarians such as Macaulay, Bentham, and James Mill, from the 1820s and 1830s onwards, the people who embodied the "civilizing mission" most literally were the young, male civil servants as portrayed by Cyril Brandon. These agents of empire were faced with a dual task of justifying colonialism on the ground that backward societies need to be civilized and insisting that only Europeans could do this, ironically implying both that the liberal principles were universally valid and that they were uniquely European in their origin.[7] Thus, as large numbers of British young men in the varied services of colonial rule—administrative, judicial, military—found themselves authorized in the untrammeled exercise of power, they were driven to live up to their assumed superiority over the natives through exceptional acts. According to one observer, "the colonizer's racial superiority, however flagrant skin colour or the appurtenances of power may have rendered it, had also to be demonstrated by acts of valour and authority," hence the savior paradigm mentioned earlier.[8]

Thus, seen through the prism of this rescue scenario, the colonial power dynamic assumes a clearly gendered form. Male colonizers could implicitly draw on the old chivalric code, so intrinsic to Western culture, as a way of contextualizing and prescribing their actions concerning the "protection" of women.

In this light it is understandable that Brandon must save an Indian widow, or even marry her to demonstrate his male chivalry through this noble gesture. What is ironic, however, is that the author constructs Seeta's identity, not in terms of colonial stereotypes of Indian women such as the *sati* or the courtesan, but rather as a refined "English" woman, embodying the ideals of liberalism. On his first encounter, Brandon sets her apart from her race and describes her beauty in terms of Western aesthetic traditions (61):

> For a native woman, Cyril Brandon had never seen any one so fair or of so tender a tone of colour. Such, he remembered, were many of the lovely women of Titian's pictures—a rich golden olive, with a bright carnation tint rising under the skin. . . . One particular [image] came to his memory as a flash—the wife of the Duc d'Avalos in the Louvre picture; or Titian's Daughter, carrying fruits and flowers, at Berlin.

The author also distinguishes her from other native women, and potential *satis*, in her situation: "Seeta might have settled down into a dull, usual widowhood of Hindoo life; pious, absorbed in household cares . . . with no hope for the future" (50). Instead, she refuses to perform the ascetic ceremonies of Hindoo widow-hood and declares: "It is not a shaven head or a coarse garment that makes a virtuous widow . . . what I am I will remain" (49). Further conforming to liberal expectations, she also displays literary and scholarly interests as well as a sensuous imagination derived from the tradition of English romanticism. Here we can see how Taylor places Seeta within literary and artistic practices, which the audience would know. In this gesture, the author clearly recapitulates a pervasive European rhetorical strategy of contex-tualizing and prescribing responses to their native subjects via Western literary and cultural conventions (50):

> Though she read only the sacred texts and some poems and dramas, yet there were thoughts recorded in them which seemed to leap up to her own mind, to set her brain aching

and her heart throbbing. . . . There were passages in which she
revelled; the rich descriptions of natural scenery by Kalidas
and Bawa Bhut. . . . She could hear the rushing winds and
waters of the poems, watch the glowing skies and smell the
perfume of the beauteous flowers.

If an understanding of metaphysical issues eluded her, and she
asked her Brahmin teacher for elucidation, she would hear, "they
were not fit for the tender minds of women" (50). By making her
challenge such cultural assumptions, the author separates Seeta
from her race, setting the stage for her rescue from the primitive
treatment of women at the hands of "traditional" Indian institutions. Interestingly, however, his description is also inflected in
terms of class, as he implicitly distinguishes her from the common
Anglo-Indian women, not belonging to the aristocratic classes.
As Brandon's sister writes to him of his noble family's fears:
"with nobody but natives about you . . . we fear lest some bright
young damsel . . . should captivate you . . . [and] what should we
know of her people. . . . I would rather you married an Indian
princess" (77).

Seeta, a goldsmith's widow, is not a princess or even a high-
caste Indian, but in the novel she represents both a liberal and
enlightened European woman and a desirable colonial subject. In
eschewing the superstition of the Indians, as well as the prejudices
of the Anglo-Indians, while venerating Brandon as "my English
Lord," Seeta embodies the hope of the post-Mutiny empire,
articulated in Queen Victoria's manifesto in 1858. Promising a
glorious and prosperous future for the Raj, this document erases
differences by assuring all "ranks and classes of Her Majesty's
Indian subjects" of their ruler's "protection and good will," and
yet at the same time, it reinscribes and naturalizes imperial power
by pronouncing the Indians as Queen Victoria's subjects rather
than as employees of the East India Company (Barr 1976: 142).
Thus, as a woman, Seeta can conveniently represent both the
civilized and the feminized Indian subjects whom the liberal
empire will rescue.

But ultimately who is Seeta? An embodiment of enlightened
behavior who offers a corrective to the excesses of Indian tradi-
tion/superstition as well as to Anglo-Indian provincialism? In
part, yes, but there is another curious dimension to her function
in the novel: she seems to play the role of an alibi or even a

"double" of the British woman, Grace Mostyn, Brandon's future wife, but in a complex interplay of identity and difference.

Seeta, the Titianesque, Europeanized beauty, is unlike "other native women," but the social divisions between her and British women remain unshakeable, as she finds out when "the English ladies [including Grace] did not consider [her] married [to Cyril]" (200). But after Seeta's heroic death, the novel ends with a curious scene in Hylton Hall in England, where, ten years later, Grace stands before a picture and a strand of hair of "a fair Indian lady," a kind of mirror image for her own beauty. Yet the author quickly establishes a contrast: "looking at these objects [is] Grace, Lady Hylton, whose beauty is great, though not greater than that of the picture, yet of a very different character" (441). To stabilize the difference between the two women, Taylor concludes by re-locating Seeta within an indigenous world, to the "native altar" of her memorial: "Ah far away—Brahmins offer flowers and sing hymns today. And many a girl lays a garland there . . . [for] the sweet spirit, whose death she commemorates" (442). Seeta's earlier, "English" identity is now subsumed within images of Indian religious orthodoxies, which venerate the self-sacrificing woman; and Grace takes her rightful place beside her aristocratic husband and child.

Interracial, colonial romances were not entirely unknown, though few ended in a legitimate marriage as depicted in *Seeta*. Critics often identify such narratives as an adventure genre in which the promise of cultural reconciliation fails: the European [male] is reabsorbed by Europe, and the non-European dies an early death (Pratt 1992: 87). Chris Bongie (1991) further describes the structure of an "imperialist exoticism" intrinsic to the notion of interracial unions. He defines the rejection of the native as a retreat from the exotic, whereby it is a given that the object one desires can never be fully experienced. In this context, the dead Seeta is ultimately designated "as a dream given over to the past" (22).[9] While Taylor certainly seems to conform to such expecta-tions at the end, it is significant that he does not allow a lack of historical precedents to limit and restrict what he can imagine and represent as a possibility if not as a "fact." Like Victoria's proclamation, the novel certainly gestures toward a liberal vision that erases cultural difference. But it nonetheless leaves intact the dichotomy between a superior British civilization and a backward

and primitive Indian culture—a dichotomy totally dependen\
the colonial gender system with its rescue scenario.

Yet, it is interesting that while Taylor cannot sustain the r\
paradigm through an interracial marriage, he nonetheless reveals,
if not resolves, the social contradictions embodied in it. Central
among these is that while Indian women were to be saved from
their backward institutions and their lives and characters improved
according to the expectations of British liberalism, their refurbished image could not overcome the anxiety of miscegenation.
Thus, at the end of the novel Cyril Brandon has a child by
Grace, a woman of his own race and class. An English novel written in the mid-nineteenth century could not break free from the
colonial gender ideologies. However, it is to Taylor's credit that
the novel opens the way for considering the broader justification
of empire on the pretext that women were in need of saving.

II

By the mid-Victorian period, the British Raj began to stabilize its
power through a frenzy of liberal reform known as the "civilizing
mission." This sense of the "white man's burden" intensified after
1857, and reformers and writers ranging from Macaulay and
Trevelyan to Bentham and Taylor called for the colonial rulers to
create and sustain in the Indians "a strong, deep-lying attachment
to English rule, to English faith and honour" (Taylor 1872: 315).
In his now famous statement, Macaulay expresses the need to
create a whole new class of persons who were "Indian in blood
and colour but English in tastes, in opinions, in morals, and in
intellect" (quoted in Loomba 1989: 31). Such sentiments were, of
course, a reflection of the concept of mass education gaining
ground in mid-Victorian Britain, as a result of which, dreams of
universal literacy began to spread to the empire. Lord Mayo, the
Viceroy of India from 1869 to 1872, for instance, was a keen
educator who expressed the goal of "teaching the 3 R's to rural
Bengal" (Barr 1976: 161).

An important aspect of this "civilizing mission" was the
"women's question," a fiercely discussed topic in official and
social debates about Indian women's education and social
reform.[10] In fact, the category of "woman" became an important marker in colonial discourse, the foundation for colonial

demarcations between so-called Western modernity and Eastern backwardness. And this dialectic between tradition and modernity became the nexus at which the debates about the "women's question" were played out, as Partha Chatterjee explains:

> the so-called women's question in the agenda of Indian social reform in the early nineteenth century was not so much about the specific condition of women within a specific set of social relations as it was about the political encounter between a colonial state and the supposed "tradition" of a conquered people . . . a tradition that . . . [in the case of *sati*] was itself produced by colonialist discourse. It was colonialist discourse that, by assuming . . . the complete submission of all Hindus to the dictates of [Brahmanical religious] texts, defined the tradition that was to be criticized and reformed.
>
> (Chatterjee 1993: 119)

In following the trajectory of the British concern for the upliftment of their female subjects, one can see that it was directly related to the importation of Victorian domesticity to the colonies. Travel narratives of the seventeenth century are primarily tales of male pioneers marking new frontiers of discovery and trade. Women are mentioned peripherally in some quasi-ethnographic accounts of their presence in the Indian court and society. Through the eighteenth and early nineteenth centuries, the East India Company nabobs and soldiers saw India as a more permanent location, but lived by self-indulgent social rules, freely taking on "dusky mistresses," as English women were a rarity in India (Dyson 1978: 88). A Captain Williamson, writing in 1810, notes: "The attachment of many European gentlemen to their native mistresses is not to be described. An infatuation beyond comparison often prevails" (quoted ibid.: 344–5). Furthermore, he goes on to justify the practice of keeping mistresses as more convenient than maintaining European wives, given the exigencies of expatriate bachelorhood:

> I trust this detail will convince, even the sceptic, that matrimony is not so practicable in India as in Europe; [and that] it is impossible for the generality of European inhabitants to act in exact conformity with those excellent doctrines, which teach us . . . "to avoid fornication and all other deadly sins." There are

certain situations and times, in which the law must be suffered
to sleep since its enforcement would neither be easy nor wise.
(ibid.)

A description of a later scene in Calcutta forms a contrast of
perspective and circumstance: "[as] more English ladies had
arrived on the scene, and at rows of mansions at Chowringhee,
Calcutta's richest quarter, no expense was spared to re-create for
them the ambience of . . . western-style comfort" (Barr 1976: 12).
With the arrival of British women and the ensuing changes in the
organization of social and sexual arrangements, colonial discourse
became more explicitly gendered. While discovery and adventure
narratives were predominant in the seventeenth- and eighteenth-
century colonial accounts, they were later subsumed within a
broader vision of transforming the empire into a Victorian domestic idyl. This cultural shift was, of course, enabled by the changing
demographics of the British population, which now consisted of
large numbers of woman.

Thus, the practice of keeping Indian mistresses, which continued
among some men, was now judged more strictly in terms of
colonial edicts which marked European women as repositories of
morality, in contrast to the Indian women whom they had
replaced. As Mrs Sherwood, a prolific writer who lived in India
for several years, remarked in 1854:

All these Englishmen who were beguiled by the sweet music
[of the Indian dancing girls/courtesans] had had mothers at
home . . . who, in the far distant land of their children's birth,
still cared, and prayed, and wept for the once blooming
boys . . . slowly sacrificing themselves to . . . the witcheries of
the unhappy daughters of heathens and infidels.
(Sherwood 1910: 449–50)

In comparing Captain Williamson's flippancy toward the moral
imperatives of European marriages with Mrs Sherwood's denigra-
tion of the Indian "daughters of heathens and infidels," one can
trace a trajectory toward an intensified gendering of the discourse
of empire, albeit with some contradictions in its logic. In the eighteenth century, as Captain Williamson suggests, functionaries of
the East India Company were not bound by the imperatives of a
European marriage. Therefore, he seems oblivious to any connection between appropriate sexual conduct and British interests in

India. In fact, by openly keeping Indian mistresses, nabobs and soldiers like Williamson flaunted a certain amount of sexual exploitation of the natives, without having to assume a position of moral superiority.

The ethical stance, with all its contradictions, took hold at a later phase in British rule in the guise of a "civilizing mission." Mrs Sherwood's response to the English male patronage of Indian courtesans is premised on precisely such a high moral ground; she distinguishes the "daughters of infidels" from the "mothers" of the "blooming boys" representing the domestic ideal on which the Raj was based. By the mid-Victorian period, this ideal had been decisively mobilized in the service of the empire, as the rulers (at least in public) began to uphold English family structures, which restricted women to the home as a sign of national virtue and superior morals. However, what her diatribe does not mention is the attendant concern for the moral and social rescue of Indian women, the daughters of "heathens."

According to several studies, when the Victorian family was transported to the colonies, a restricted domestic sphere also served as a space of racial purity that the colonial housewife guarded against contamination from the native society.[11] Once British femininity was declared to be vulnerable and pure, then a direct connection could be established between authoritarian power and the protection and rescue of women. And, as the next step, this impulse could be extended to include the native woman, who would nonetheless function as a crucial category of difference in designating relations between the "civilized" colonizers and their subjects.

Within this context, the debates about the upliftment of the Indian woman take on an added political resonance; she does not function at all times as the "subaltern shadow" of the white woman. But often, as we saw in *Seeta*, the native female has a complex symbolic relevance within colonial discourse. Let us begin with a brief account of how the "women's question" took hold in the colonial imagination. Even in recent histories, the mission of empire is often seen entirely in benevolent terms, as one study suggests:

> During [Lord Mayo's] term of office more government funds were diverted into primary education, though still little was done to instruct girls, for fear of offending the conservative

prejudices of Hindu and Moslem. A few Indian men themselves
however began to profess anxiety about the state of their young
womenfolk, and even visited England in the hope of gaining
support for the changes they wanted to make in Indian
society—such as the abolition of child marriages and of keeping
of women in conditions of ignorant seclusion.

(Barr 1976: 161)

The fact that a certain class of Indian men—Macaulay's ideal
colonial subjects and mostly products of the Bengal Renaissance—shared in the reformist impulses of British liberals, without
questioning the empire, would not be surprising at the time. Such
a naturalization of the dichotomy between "civilization" and
"backwardness" was a function of colonial ideology in which
Indians were constituted as consenting subjects. The term ideology
is used in the Althusserian sense to define a set of representations
by which we imagine our relationship to the real conditions of
our existence.[12] In this context, the work of colonial ideology was
to beckon the Indians, interpellate them into their positions
within the existing hierarchy, and provide them, in this case, with
suitably gendered subjectivities which held them in these places.
Thus, British political and military power perpetuated itself, not
entirely through brute force, but rather, through cultural representations and practices that cast this power into a benevolent light.
And even the self-critique of liberals like Taylor, or later Kipling,
did not question the validity of the "civilizing mission," but only
the limitations of some of its agents, for whom, they believed, the
Mutiny had been a timely lesson.

Hence, not surprisingly, British "civilization" had many fol-
lowers among Indian subjects. But it must be noted that the
"women's question" generated a complex and often contradictory
cultural struggle between the rulers and the ruled, especially
among members of the growing nationalist movement. As Chatterjee (1993) explains: "Indian nationalism, in demarcating a political
position opposed to colonial rule took up the women's question as
a problem already constituted for it: namely, as a problem of
Indian tradition" (119). The Indian male's ambivalence toward
colonial rule with its intimations of "modernity" mirrored his attitudes about modernizing the condition of women—the imperative
of British liberalism.

We can get a fuller sense of the complexities of this debate about women—oscillating between competing notions of tradition and modernity—as we observe the varied articulations of the "rescue paradigm" with specific concerns about women's education and social conditions, which enabled practices such as *sati*. The dominant colonial/official position on gender roles was one that implicitly compared the socially devalued lives of the native women with the supposedly superior existence of their British counterparts, as Keshub Chunder Sen of the Indian Reform Association declared on August 1, 1870. At a meeting of the Victoria Discussion Society in London, he asked for the services of "well-trained, accomplished English ladies" who would go to India to impart to Indian women an education "that will not be subservient or subordinated to the views of any religious community, an education free, liberal, and comprehensive in character, calculated to make Indian women good wives, mothers, daughters."[13] Sen's views were defined by colonial liberalism, hence his confidence in the abilities of "accomplished English ladies" as models and teachers for Indian women.

Sen's ideals were also crucial to the colonial promotion of a Western-style education for the more "enlightened" Indian subjects, who would then serve as a conduit between the rulers and the Indian masses, while upholding the superior, "universal" values of British culture and institutions.[14] While the Indian men quickly saw the connection between an English education and material prosperity and employment under the Raj, many among them were not always convinced, unlike Sen, of the need to educate their women. On official occasions, as recorded in the *Evidence taken before the Bengal Provincial Committee* (1884), this issue was debated in all its complexities. The witnesses before the committee included Indian and English educators, some of them missionaries and elite Indian men. All the Indian witnesses unequivocally seemed to accept Macaulay's edict of an English-language education as opposed to an Oriental curriculum, seeing the former as a mark of progress. As Moulvi Syed Amir Hosain Khan Bahadur (a Muslim leader) summed up before the committee:

> India is quite different . . . [now] there [is] . . . a network of roads, railways, and telegraph lines. Commerce and trade have considerably expanded. . . . The administration of justice has

much improved. Natives of the country are declared eligible for
the highest legislative assembly. . . . But the growth of this
happy state of things has augmented the necessity of a thorough
knowledge of the language of the rulers by the ruled and a suffi-
cient proficiency with Western sciences and arts through the
medium of that language.

(*Evidence* 1884: 228)

In this scenario of progress, the Moulvi seems little concerned
about the education of women in his community: "At the present
moment, the number of [Muslims] who are in favour of female
education in public schools [is very few]. The time, I hope, is not
in the distant future when we may count on the increase in such a
number, but till then I wish to speak as little on the subject"
(ibid.: 229). The official view on such issues often presented some
divisions between Muslims and Hindus in their acceptance of this
colonial policy. Evidence from missionaries seems to suggest that
it was more difficult for educators to follow the progress of
Muslim women "after they [left] school to carry on their education
in the [secluded] zenanas [women's quarters]" (291). But it would
be fair to assume that the orthodox elements in both communities
had difficulties with the idea of educating women, as one female
missionary disclosed: "[we] very often lose sight of [Indian
women] altogether. They frequently marry into families which are
opposed to the teaching of women" (291).

Despite an obvious resistance by the entrenched orthodoxies of
both communities, educating Indian women became an important
test for the "civilizing" policy of British rule. And as a corollary
to this task, if Indian women were to be "rescued" by liberalism,
they were to emulate the women of the rulers, even though the
natives were marked as subordinate. Thus, in the evidence before
the Provincial Committee, several witnesses pointed out that this
reform only took place under the controlling rein of European
women. The Reverend Banerjea testified that female Indian
teachers trained in missionary schools were working "under the
supervision of European ladies" (238). And Miss Good of the
Church of England and Mrs De Niceville, a school principal,
revealed in their testimonies a concern for the education of
Indian women and an understanding that such an education
would be modeled on their English experiences (261–71). Miss
A.M. Hoare, engaged in the supervision of female education in

Calcutta, also stated that "the upper classes of women in this country can never take their proper place in society without a knowledge of English" (282), and Miss Hook, superintendent of the American Mission, reinforced the Western influence when she declared: "Female education [in Bengal] owes its origin and present progress to European and American ladies" (289).

The general consensus in the transcription of these testimonies was that the colonial government had a clear commitment to promote the education of women, and its agents recognized both the "difficulties"—especially in the case of Muslim women—and the progress made. As one testimony pointed out (240):

> Fifty years ago . . . perhaps not a single girl of a respectable family could be found attending school, but I have now known persons of the highest position in society going to the Bethune School [in Calcutta] and therefore I say that it is developing itself daily and that old prejudices are disappearing.

Educators also had attendant concerns about responding, for example, to objections to male teachers. This led to some consideration about the status of Indian women who would train as teachers—whether they should be "married or widows" and "whether unmarried women and widows could be employed as schoolmistresses . . . without the risk of some grave scandal" (ibid.).

The story told by documents such as these mutes the cultural conflicts and contradictions. While revealing the details of practical policy considerations, these official accounts assert a broad consensus among the rulers and the elite Indians, co-opted as agents of empire. Thus, we learn that educating women was not aimed at re-ordering the social hierarchy but at inviting them benevolently into the cause of the "civilizing mission," as another testimony to the Provincial Committee states: "[women] are the first educators, and unless they are wise and good, no education is likely to be effective" (252). To map the ideological grid of the dissensions generated by this issue, one has to listen to some different voices in a non-official context.

Mrs Marianne Postans, wife of an English civil servant, writing in 1835, echoes the liberal call for saving Indian women from their disadvantaged conditions:

If, in a state of real ignorance, and apparently habitual apathy, the women of the East display at times so much natural capacity and mental energy, why, it may reasonably be asked, should they not be equally capable of receiving intellectual culture, and by consequent development of their faculties . . . be prepared for and permitted to take the part of real usefulness and responsibility in social life, which nature designed in the creation of women . . . fair and gentle women, who need only the fostering hand of civilization to render them in all other things, as they are now in feature and grace of form, the more than equals of their Western sisters.[15]

What was couched in the rhetoric of objectivity in the testimony before the Provincial Committee is more evident in Mrs Postans's account, namely, a natural hierarchy dividing the "state of real ignorance" and "habitual apathy" of the East from the "fostering hand of civilization" embodied by the West. Thus, she seems unaware of any contradiction in inviting Indian women to "develop" their faculties and aspire toward the Victorian ideal of "responsibility in social life," while also asserting the superiority of the West. Like other colonial women, Mrs Postans seems oblivious of the constraints of her own role in maintaining the requisite racial divisions, even while her narrative oscillates between a closeness and distance from her Indian "sisters." The position of the native patriarchy, also muted in the official documents, was often divided about bridging the distance between Indian and Western women. Annette Ackroyd (later Beveridge) who came to Calcutta to establish a Western-style, though secular, school for girls, met with much resistance in the local Indian press. In June 1873, she described some of these attacks: "'What improvement of Hindu women can be effected by an Englishwoman?' the newspapers asked. 'What does she know of our social customs that our women should be really elevated by her instructions?' Or, 'are our women really so degraded that there is no other object to which compassion can be extended?'" (quoted in Barr 1976: 164–5). Underlying these interrogations was a more serious concern about disrupting the native sexual ideologies, based on the segregation between men and women. As one Indian man pointed out: "We have seen that the wives of all Europeans who live here are utterly shameless. Where women cast off their modesty and associate with men, that which principally constitutes female virtue is destroyed" (ibid.: 165). While such attacks were frequently printed, Mrs Ackroyd also received an obsequious approval from "A Hundred and Ten Bengallee Gentlemen" who spoke for the more pliant colonial subjects. They thanked her for "the zealous interest always felt by [her] in the welfare of our local institutions, and for the benevolent objects of [her] sojourn in our country generally" (ibid.: 165).

Interestingly, both parties, the native patriarchy and their Western rulers, claimed their authority from their duty to protect women, and female virtue in particular, implicitly eliding the vulnerable roles of both Indian and British women; some Indian men, like the "Bengallee Gentlemen," obviously had faith in the "civilizing effects" of British institutions while others saw the colonial influence being extended into their personal authority over their women. Thus, women were clearly the counters in the larger power struggle, even though, ironically, the Victorian ideology of the family as the "women's sphere" remained uncontested by the native males. And the question that remained submerged was that if Indian women were to be liberated from their familial communities by British liberalism, were they to enter the seclusion of Victorian domesticity? Such an interplay of identity and difference becomes more complicated within the colonial discourses about *sati*, i.e. the practice of "self-immolation" among widows of a few Hindu communities.

Sati was prohibited by law in 1829 by a British governor, William Bentinck. This was among the series of legislative reforms subsequently enacted on behalf of women in India. Looking back with the hindsight of history, it is quite obvious that these laws also became part of the pretext and justification for British rule and intervention. During Mogul rule in the sixteenth century, the emperor Akbar also passed an ordinance to prevent such deaths by self-immolation, but as one critic points out, the Mogul prohibition of *sati* did not become a strategic political move and did not figure in their representations of themselves or their Hindu subjects.[16] The English discourse on *sati* was undoubtedly linked to the idea of freedom from "barbarism," though, as Lata Mani (1987) suggests in a seminal essay, it produced a complex version of the "rescue" fantasy. The colonial administrators did not, according to Mani, call for outlawing "Sati as a cruel and barbarous act," but went through a convoluted process of appeasing the Brahmins by looking for indigenous precedents distinguishing between legal or "voluntary" *sati* and the coerced or forced suicide. Thus, to establish the prohibition, English magistrates and other officials had to monitor actual *sati* to judge the validity of the woman's "motives" even as the colonizers circulated stereotypes of native barbarism at the hands of bloodthirsty Brahmins (Mani 1987: 128–9; Sharpe 1993: 51–2).

It is significant that this discourse on the abolition of *sati* was based on a construction of the native widow that did not record her voice, but rather required British and Indian men to speak for her.[17] She became the mute, yet central, "character" in a theatrical spectacle that seemed to both fascinate and repel the European agents of surveillance. Some administrators, such as the Marquess of Hastings, were drawn to the psychology of martyrdom, and one critic describes his somewhat curious response to this horrific act: "[Hastings] hits rightly on the elements of excitement and adventure, and the exhibition of the ego in the performance of the rite."[18] According to Hastings, *sati* was not an act of sublimation or self-sacrifice, but a release of a "vehemence of energy" in the widow's "saddened heart," and "the woman had been taught that it is praiseworthy to encourage herself in the intoxication, and she does so, enjoying too much the novel pleasure of it to look aside." In thus brutally re-casting her death by burning in terms of "pleasure," Hastings gets quite carried away:

> The husband's death is a revolution in their existence, which gives an opening for the mind's bursting out of the ordinary track of depression. . . . As is the case with all spirits that have been long held in restraint, the momentary emancipation is carried to extravagance. Working themselves up to a frenzy they pledge themselves to they know not what.
>
> (quoted in Dyson 1978: 104)

After describing the spectacle as a form of ecstasy, referring, it seems, as much to his own condition as to the woman's, who is supposedly transfixed by the "frenzy" and "extravagance," Hastings acknowledges that "[the widow's] own dread of disgrace, and still more, the instigations of her kin, will . . . prevent her from faltering." Then, retreating into the conventional position of the European moral agent, he castigates the Brahmins for their lack of reason:

The interest of the Brahmins in [*sati*] . . . is that it is a triumph over reason. The scene is an additional perplexity to that common sense, the growth of which they sedulously . . . endeavour to stunt in the lower classes. Subjugation of the intellect, that they may reign over the bodies of the multitudes is the unremitting object of that worthless and successful caste.

(ibid.)

While witnessing this spectacle of *sati*, Hastings represents the colonial machinery of surveillance by which this rite is to be "seen" and judged. However, his rhetoric of "pleasure" undermines his own position as a colonial agent of reason and civilization. Typically, as Sharpe (1993) and others have pointed out, the official discourse on *sati* casts the British official as the moral agent who sympathizes with the widow's plight, while relatives, such as her father, "with tearless eye [lead] forth a spectacle to the assembled multitude, who with barbarous cries demand the sacrifice . . . [of the] unconscious and unresisting victim."[19] In this version, it is only the colonial agent who recognizes her as a victim who must be saved.

While the construction of the Indian widow as a victim to be saved was intrinsic to the official position on *sati*, the British response to this cruel rite was by no means uniform. According to some British observers, one trait of Indian women that they found puzzling, and contradictory to their conventional expectations, was that they could be obstinately self-willed. Thus, at times they seemed genuinely baffled at the fierce determination of some women, even though today we may question the problematic nature of "choice." Colonel Sleeman offers a compelling record of a *sati* of a 65-year-old widow which he witnessed on November 29, 1829.

This was the first time in her long life that she had pronounced the name of her husband. . . . When the old lady named her husband, as she did with strong emphasis, and in a very deliberate manner, everyone present was satisfied that she had resolved to die. . . . She came on with a calm and cheerful countenance. . . . She then walked up deliberately and steadily to the brink, stepped into the centre of the flame, sat down, and leaning back . . . was consumed without uttering a shriek or betraying one sign of agony.

(Sleeman 1844: 20–3)

Whether it is Sleeman's admiring but restrained depiction of the old widow, or a British magistrate's account of barbaric horror, the sight of the woman committing *sati* did not constitute a static trope of otherness in the colonial imagination—one that was only applicable to the Indian woman. Rather the image had multiple and shifting dimensions applicable to different ideological agendas: for instance, while the woman who committed *sati* was denigrated as a victim of superstition, her chastity and fidelity could not be ignored, considering the importance of these virtues within the Victorian model of behavior constructed for Englishwomen, both at home and in the colonies. The distance between the nineteenth-century Englishwoman and her native "other" was not, after all, as wide and unfathomable as Jane Eyre suggested: "I had as good a right to die when my time came . . . and not be hurried away in suttee."[20]

The Victorian Englishwoman and the Indian widow, both mirror desirable qualities of virtue, fidelity, and subservience. Yet, within colonial discourse, one is symbolically rescued through the sacrifice and devaluation of the other. To get a sense of the sexual politics of colonial relations, particularly as they concern women and *sati*, let us turn to a well-known novel, *On the Face of the Waters* (1897), by Flora Annie Steel. Recent feminist studies have undertaken detailed analyses of this historical Mutiny novel, especially as a recapitulation of a colonial "rescue" plot.[21]

Within this scenario of deliverance, the novel temporarily erases the distance between the Indian woman, Tara, the Persian Zora, who has died, and Kate Erlton, the English heroine. Both literally and symbolically, the novelist brings the Indian and British women close to each other, and in fact, for fleeting moments she makes their identities seem interchangeable. But the conclusion of the novel, not unlike that of *Seeta*, blocks off any permanent cross-over of identities and cultures. The hero, Jim Douglas, alias James Greyman, an adventurer/spy and government agent, is the central character in this elaborate historical plot about the events surrounding the fall of Delhi during the Indian Mutiny against British rule in 1857. Interwoven within the political/military events are a series of escapes of women, arranged by the hero. When he finds Mrs Erlton, dressed as a native woman, in hiding from the rebels, he brings her to live with Tara Devi, a high-caste Rajput woman, whom he had rescued from her dead husband's funeral pyre eight years earlier. After his intervention, Tara, an outcast in her own community, became a servant to his former Persian mistress, Zora, whom he had bought from a house of prostitution.

Early in the novel, the young Zora lies dying "as so many secluded women do, of decline," though for Douglas, life with her had been "eight years of pure passion . . . a dream of absolute content" (Steel 1897: 28). He had paid for her, "not only because she was beautiful, but because he pitied the delicate-looking child. . . . Not that his pity would have led him to buy her if she had been ugly, or even dark. . . . Romance had perhaps had more to do with his purchase than passion" (28). At the time of her death, he has little regret for a still-born child and the lost possibility of other "half-caste children," or that she "had been but a small part of his life," while "the world held no more for her save her passion for him" (37–8). In terms of the plot, Zora is just a memory of an oriental idyl, and the novel focusses on the later rescue of Kate Erlton, the Englishwoman, who will appropriately be his wife at the end. Yet before the satisfactory conclusion, we see Kate Erlton also living in solitude and in native disguise, thus becoming a curious reincarnation of the dead Zora's loneliness on the same terrace. Douglas establishes the link when he gives Kate Zora's native ornaments to complete her disguise: "I should prefer [that you wear these ornaments]. These jewels belonged to a woman I loved very dearly, Mrs. Erlton. She was not my wife—but she was a good woman" (285). Later, such images intrude into Douglas's growing attraction for her when he sees her with the escaping English child in disguise (357):

> As he sat, . . . watching the pretty picture which Kate, in Zora's jewels, made with the be-tinseled, be-scented, bedecked child, he thought of his relief when years before he had looked at a still little morsel lying in Zora's veil. . . . Would that dead baby have grown into a Sonny? . . . because Sonny's skin was really white beneath the stain that he thought of him as something to be proud of possessing.

Such scenes pre-figure her union with Douglas beyond the novel's conclusion, though at this point Kate is in an ambiguous position, still bound in a loveless marriage to another man. And her role on the terrace further blurs the distinction between Victorian domesticity and an Eastern idyl, implicitly suggesting that perhaps the two modes of existence are not too far apart, even though the novel evades this issue at the end.

Tara Devi, the other woman in this dynamic, also inhabits a physical and psychic liminal space, as an outcast widow who has deferred her obligation to the rites of *sati*. Jenny Sharpe (1993), in her perceptive analysis of the novel, shows how Tara Devi is "a character out of the colonial intervention in Sati" (105). Her life as a woman who is and is not married reveals a human problem that neither the British nor the Indian supporters of the prohibition of *sati* addressed. How was the Hindu widow to deal with the ascetic conditions of her life of perpetual mourning and celibacy? Humanitarian feelings notwithstanding, reformers did not call for viable alternatives to a life of asceticism for widows. Thus, the re-marriage of widows was practically non-existent, even after it was made legally permissible (Sharpe 1993: 103–10; Sunder Rajan 1993: 48).

It is ironic that Steel illuminates these tragic contradictions embodied in Tara's role by, at least momentarily, displacing them on to Kate, in a curious interplay of identity and difference between the two women toward the end; feeling a sense of hopeless rivalry with Kate, Tara urges the English woman (the "mem") to disguise herself as a *sati* in order to make her escape: "The mem will be suttee too. . . . The mem will shave her head and put away her jewels! the mem will wear a widow's shroud and sweep the floor, saying she comes from Bengal to serve the saint" (398). While somewhat tantalized by the idea, Tara both welcomes and disbelieves such a possibility (399):

> The mems were never suttee. They married again many times. And then this mem was married to someone else. No! she would never shave her head for a strange man. She might take off her jewels, she might even sweep the floor. But shave her head? Never!
> But supposing she did?

Tara, Kate, and the novelist, it seems, all playfully point toward such a possibility only to defer it. For a brief moment, Kate also experiences the liminality, if only symbolically, of being/not being a "Suttee." As Douglas is called away, Kate arranges her final escape on her own; therefore for her, a disguise as a *sati* is part of "becoming interested in her own adventures, now that she had . . . control over them" (400). Finally, though, Tara snatches the razor from Kate and declares: "The mems cannot be suttees," and they settle for a disguise as a "screened woman . . . a Hindoo lady under a vow of silence . . . in the hope of securing a son . . . through the intercession of . . . the Swami" (401).

On the Face of the Waters ends like any other colonial romance, with the cross-over experiences of Kate and Douglas discursively contained as an adventure novel. The "dream" of the Indian rebels was over as they recognized that the "Huzoors were the true masters" (382). And Tara commits the obligatory *sati* in a wanton fire, witnessed by English officers who, predictably, express the horror of "civilized" people. While the cultural distance is re-established between the "mem" and the "suttee," and only the former escapes, the novel ends with an unease about this distinction as Tara pointedly remarks about Kate: "though the mem could not of course be suttee, still she did very well as a devoted and repentant wife" (403). Kate manages to escape her loveless marriage, but the novel does little to disrupt the Victorian ideal of domestic confinement for women. Overall, in this rather compelling interplay of identity and difference between "mems" and "suttees"—between Kate and Tara—we can see the ambiguous role of the British women within the erotics of imperial conquest. The Eastern idyl of domesticity on the terrace, with all its suggestions of a harem—in which Zora blends into the "native" Kate—evokes the familiar trope of feminized Eastern lands waiting to be *discovered*, *possessed*, and *mastered* by the colonizer, in this instance the attractive and brave Douglas. Zora, Kate, and even implicitly Tara, suggestively replay this erotic, colonial scenario, but of course, it has to be repressed at the end for the cause of civilization: Zora is dead, Tara a martyr as *sati*, and Kate is distanced from the Indian women to marry Douglas, implicitly in the service of empire.

III

While the British Raj tried to bring Indian women into the fold of the "civilizing mission" through education and social reforms, such as the abolition of *sati*, one native figure remained outside the imperial project of reform: the Indian courtesan. Images of Indian courtesans or *nautch* girls—generally both singers and dancers—figure prominently in English writings of the eighteenth and nineteenth centuries. Within the Indian society of the time, the courtesan inhabited a liminal space, outside the domestic sphere and yet close to the power centers of the aristocracy or the temple priests (in the case of some Hindus) who were their patrons. George Forster, who arrived at Madras in 1770, as a writer and clerk in the East India Company, distinguishes between illiterate family women and accomplished courtesans in his letters, stating that "acquired accomplishments" were not considered necessary for "the domestic classes of the female sex" (quoted in Dyson 1978: 146). The dancing girls, on the other hand, according to Forster and other observers, were not only educated but also received government protection. They were free from stigma, recognized as a distinct professional class, and taxed according to their income. Public or princely lands were allotted to them and those attached to temples received grants from the temple revenues (in certain regions). Those who did not have secure incomes were, according to Forster, "little less dissolute and abandoned" than women of "similar description in European countries" (ibid.: 147).

Dancing girls, or courtesans, were a feature of both Hindu and Muslim society, and this tradition continued well into the nineteenth and even twentieth centuries, till the last vestiges of the landed aristocracy were stamped out. In the mid-Victorian period, the *nawabs* of Oudh in central India were famous patrons of highly accomplished courtesans, until the forced exile of Nawab Wajid Ali Shah by the British in 1856, after which the tradition was gradually debased into prostitution. It is important to note that in aristocratic Indian culture, distinctions between talented courtesans and common prostitutes were clearly maintained, usually along class lines. A historical view of the famous, highly accomplished courtesans from Lucknow (in the court of Oudh) gives us a sense of their profession in the mid-nineteenth century:

> The world of the courtesans of Lucknow was as complex and hierarchical as the society of which it was a part. Under the patronage of the Nawabs [rulers] and the notables . . . the apartments in the Chowk Bazaar, where these women lived and entertained in decadent opulence, were centers for musical and cultural soirees. . . . A courtesan was usually part of a household established under a chief courtesan . . . [who] owned and maintained extra apartments, having acquired wealth and

fame through her beauty and musical and dancing abilities. . . .
Every reputable house maintained a team of skilled male musicians who were often connected to famous lineages or *gharanas*
of musicians thereby enhancing the prestige of the establishment . . . [the courtesans] were intensively trained from an
early age to dance, sing, converse, amuse, and excel in exagger-
ated politeness. . . . To acquire this social fastidiousness, the
young sons of gentry were sent to the salons of the courtesans
for lessons in etiquette and proper appreciation of . . . poetry.
(Talwar-Oldenburg 1984: 134–6)

Given the courtesans' role in the aristocratic native culture, it
was not unusual for the British to witness their performances.
For the colonizing imagination of nineteenth-century Anglo-
India, the figure of the *nautch* girl held an appeal that was both
tantalizing and threatening to the colonial social and sexual
arrangements. Images of courtesans performing appear frequently
in a variety of British journals and memoirs, revealing an interpretive and epistemological crisis in the viewers who witnessed a
spectacle of excessive availability, yet did not have the terms of
intelligibility to know the aesthetic, intellectual, or social codes of
the *nautch*. The otherness of the courtesans' world disoriented the
British because it eluded the colonial, "civilizing" codes and yet,
at the same time, it held out a promise of cultural and sexual intimacy with the rulers. What is apparent in British accounts of the
nautch girls is a collision between the ideal of Victorian domesticity and the erotics of imperial conquest, whereby the feminized,
sexual space of the *nautch* offered a sensual invitation, yet
prompted the colonial imperative for sexual and cultural boundaries between the rulers and the ruled. A Mrs Sherwood reveals
some of the strains within British responses to the courtesans:

The influence of these nautch girls over the other sex, even over
men who have been brought up in England, and who have
known, admired, and respected their own country-women, is
not to be accounted for. It is not only obtained in a very
peculiar way, but often kept up when beauty is passed.
It steals upon those who come within its charmed circle in a
way not unlike that of an intoxicating drug, being the more
dangerous to young Europeans because they seldom fear it;
for perhaps these very men who are so infatuated remember
some lovely face in their native land and fancy they are wholly

unapproachable by any attraction which can be used by a
tawny beauty.

(Sherwood 1910: 405–6)

In Mrs Sherwood's convoluted moral imagination, young
Englishmen's desire for Indian courtesans is "peculiar" and "dangerous" because, unlike her, they do not immediately realize that
a "tawny beauty" could outweigh the attractions of some "lovely
face" of an Englishwoman. Thus, using a curious logic, she seems
to suggest that the young men are trapped precisely because they
are unaware of and underestimate the erotic power of these
women. And ultimately, her disapproval of the courtesans goes
beyond a fear of their sexual power over the Anglo-Indian man
to an anxiety about a breakdown of racial and cultural boundaries, whereby the "natural" distinctions between English and
Indian beauty may be lost.

When the Europeans used the terms *nautch* or *nautch* girls, they
usually elided the courtesan's liminal social and sexual role with
her aesthetic function in keeping alive the traditions of Indian
classical music and dance. Thus, eye-witness accounts of the courtesans' performances—a frequent event in the Europeans' formal
interactions with elite Indians—reveal a link between the spectators' inability to interpret the complex aesthetic conventions of
the *nautch* and their alternating fascination and dislike for the
spectacle. Faced with proliferating cultural signifiers, in this
instance in the complex aesthetic vocabulary of the *nautch*, the
British, like their predecessors in the seventeenth century, elided
inscrutability with barbarism.

By most accounts, Europeans were often invited to these enter-
tainments, as Miss Roberts describes in 1835:

Moosulman gentlemen of rank frequently give parties to the
European visitants at Delhi in which ladies are included;
and at these the *nautch* or dancing girls are invariably introduced. . . . Sometimes five or six sets of . . . inharmonious
vocalists appear together, all singing at the same time . . . not
having an idea of making their voices accord with each other.
The dancing, though not equally barbarous, is exceedingly tire-
some, when, as in the presence of ladies, it is circumscribed
within the bounds of propriety; but there are some European
gentlemen who acquire the native taste for an exhibition

which, when addressed to male eyes alone, is said to be not particularly decorous.

(Roberts 1910: I, 248–53)

European responses to the courtesans' performances were not, of course, uniform, but notwithstanding the degrees of interest, they all point to an unbridgeable cultural divide. The Marquess of Hastings, writing in 1814, recalls a performance:

> The nautch girls then sang only two at a time, but without any attempt at a duet after our fashion . . . their highest elegance in winning airs appears to be slipping off and putting up again the part of the . . . veil which is thrown over the head. There is a perpetual repetition of this last gentility. The natives will sit for hours enjoying this exhibition. To us nothing can be more tiresomely monotonous.

(in Dyson 1978: 338)

Bishop Heber, in an 1828 journal, has a similar response:

> There was a good deal of Persian singing and instrumental music, the character of which does not seem a want of harmony, but dullness and languor . . . their exhibition as dull and insipid to an European taste as could well be conceived. In fact, nobody in the room seemed to pay them any attention.

(ibid.: 340)

Such disapproval of the performances extended to every aspect, including the elaborate costumes, which, according to some observers, seemed ridiculous because they did not conform to European standards of attractiveness. In various accounts the *nautch* girls are described as wearing "cumbrous trousers which entirely cover their feet . . . a profusion of petticoats," "huddled up in huge bundles of red petticoats," dressed in "some fashion passing . . . comprehension" with "blue muslin" at least 20 yards "rolled in every direction . . . the ends brought over the shoulders and hanging down . . . dressed in keeping with a mad woman."[22] Other descriptions of the costumes and choreography seem more open and appreciative, like Miss Roberts's: the "ladies present very picturesque figures, though somewhat encumbered by the voluminous folds of their drapery" (ibid.: 346).

Those European observers who were disoriented by the proliferation of signifiers in the production of the spectacle, often felt so because they could not read the stylized erotics of the *nautch*, which one observer aptly described as the "songs, and the motions of the dance [as they] combine to express love, hope, jealousy, despair, and the passions so well known to lovers" (ibid.: 337).

In contrast to the frequently cautious response of some European men, noted traveler, Richard Burton looked at the *nautch* as a counterpoint to Victorian decorum and prudery. An unabashed viewer of the courtesans' performances, his account, however, reflects another aspect of colonial discourse, namely the impulse to perpetuate an Orientalist fantasy in which the courtesan conformed to stereotypical Western expectations of "exotic, oriental women."[23] Despite his obsession with an Orientalist scenario, Burton's letters and memoirs record a struggle to make the experience of the *nautch* intelligible to himself and his compatriots: "At last, when a few years had thoroughly broken my taste to bear what you have just heard, I could listen to it not only without the horror you experience, but also with something more like gratification" (Burton 1851: II, 174–5). His journal vividly shows how his keen ear responded to the "erotic verses and mystical effusions" of their songs, and his eye read the defining feature of the courtesans' art, namely the ability to simulate a nuanced erotics within a seemingly repetitive repertoire. Addressing a stereotypically English "Mr Bull," Burton points to the subtleties of the dancer's role:

> I promised you a *Nautch*, Mr Bull, and Hari Chand has secured the services of a celebrated lady of pretty name, Mahtab— the Moonbeam. . . . The exact setting of every feature in that perfect oval of hers gives her as many lovely faces as there are varying positions for that one. . . . The expression of her countenance is strange . . . it is a settled melancholy, as if the owner had been a victim of a grande passion, which . . . is not the case. . . . The *Nautch* commences . . . the Moonbeam is going to engross every eye.
>
> (Burton 1851: II, 240–6)

Responses to the *nautch* differed widely, as we have seen, but we learn that the courtesans' performances also varied, some dances being "addressed to male eyes only," just as there were some "European gentlemen who acquire the native taste for an exhibition which . . . is said to be not particularly decorous" (Roberts 1910: 186–7). Because the courtesans were considered an erotic threat, they were constrained to perform "in a dull and decorous manner" in the presence of women. Thus, typically, in representations of the *nautch*, the European women represented Victorian standards of decency in danger of being transgressed, hence Captain Mundy's anxiety in their presence:

> there is some danger of [the courtesans'] carrying the suppleness of their body . . . beyond the graceful and even bordering on the disgusting. The situation of a gentleman in this case is irksome and uncomfortable . . . [sitting] in constant dread lest these fair liberales in morality should commit some, perhaps unintentional, solecism against decency.
>
> (1832, in Dyson 1978: 345)

If the edifice of the British Raj was based on an idealized Victorian domesticity, with the protection of women's virtue as its centerpiece, the figure of the native courtesan was obviously both tantalizing and threatening to the male agents of empire. Richard Burton vividly (and satirically) sums up this contradiction:

> "But stop Mr Bull [he addresses the stereotypical colonizer watching a *nautch*], at this rate you will be falling in love with the 'Moonbeam' [the dancer]: I tremble to think of the spirit in which your lapse would be ·received by the bonneted, well curled, be-mantled, straight-laced, be-petticoated partner of your bosom . . . say nothing of the scene when you return home: it would grieve me even to dream of 'minx' and 'savage' in connection with yonder masterpiece of prettiness."
>
> (Burton 1851: II, 240–2)

The courtesans' performances, however inscrutable to some, undoubtedly pointed to the limitations of the Victorian dichotomy between a "straight-laced" wife and the courtesan whose "languishing glances, wanton smiles, and attitudes . . . are so much admired" (Dyson 1978: 336). As an artistic form exploring a range of aesthetic and erotic constructions of "femininity" in gestures and words, the *nautch* could not easily be domesticated by the colonizing imagination. The elite Indian patriarchy, who were its patrons, considered the courtesans' performances an intrinsic part of cultural refinements not available in the domestic sphere, as Europeans testify: "Many *nautch* girls are extremely rich, those most in esteem being very highly paid for their performances" (Roberts 1910: 249). Others are "said to be women of

good character . . . [and] get large sums for their performances" (in
Dyson 1978: 355).

It is striking that the fate of the native courtesan did not figure
in the nineteenth-century colonial debates about the rescue of
women. While the education of wives (and daughters) and the
burning of widows became occasions for the struggle over the
divergent priorities of British officials and the indigenous male
elite, ironically, both positions represented women as embodiments
of tradition, virtue, and domesticity. What was at stake was not
women, but competing claims over a discourse of the salvation of
women—who were discursively constructed as victims or heroines.
And while the elite indigenous males provided the necessary
patronage for the courtesans, they, for obvious reasons, did not
see them in need of moral rescue, but rather accepted their quasi-
respectable status as purveyors of cultural refinements.

This native acceptance of the "respectability" of the courtesan
culture ran counter to the official British position on the "civilizing
mission." After all, the courtesans disseminated valuable training
in cultural appreciation among the aristocracy. Yet the story of
the courtesans of Lucknow, after the deposition of the local ruler
in 1856 (mentioned earlier), ironically reveals how the courtesans'
marginal position vis-à-vis marriage also gave them an independent status, unavailable to most women in colonial domesticity.
For instance, writing in 1859, P. Carnegie, a British civil servant
in Lucknow, testifies to the fact that the only women on the tax
register at the time were courtesans classified as "dancing girls."
According to him:

> Prostitution is not a "*lawful* trade," but in Oudh we are not
> bound by Regulations, while by custom and by oriental consent
> this trade is held in estimation, not only as not unlawful, but as
> a highly respectable one, and why therefore should this, the
> most profitable of all trades in Lucknow, not be taxed, when
> others, which we hold in much higher esteem are.
>
> (quoted in Talwar-Oldenburg 1984: 165)

While Carnegie acknowledges their "respectability" by "oriental
consent," his decision to tax their income also signals the colonial
transformation and decline of an accepted social institution by
the reduction of this practice to a purely pecuniary activity. With
the *nawab*, Wajid Ali Shah, in exile after 1856, the profession lost
its chief patron and gradually experienced a decline in its feudal

patronage. Among indigenous clients from the court society, there was a clear understanding of the distinction between accomplished courtesans catering to a selective aristocratic clientele and common prostitutes for ordinary citizens "incapable of cultural interludes" (Talwar-Oldenburg 1984: 136–7). During the *nawabi* (or the rule of the *nawab*) "until a person had association with courtesans he was not a polished man." The British did not see them as a cultural asset, but as a necessary evil; thus, after the exile of the *nawab*,

> the new patrons were the creatures of the new rulers, [among whom] were European soldiers roving in the city after dark. The soldiers understood little or none of the urbane Urdu speech used in the salons. They had neither taste, time, nor money to partake of the pleasures of the nautch [performances].
> (Talwar-Oldenburg 1984: 137–8)

Liaisons between Indian prostitutes and Europeans, especially soldiers, were a common practice since the early eighteenth century. And the East India Company nabobs were frequently known to have mistresses among Indian courtesans, especially prior to the arrival of white women. Ironically, these illegitimate interactions comprised the limited personal or intimate contact between the rulers and the ruled. However, it was the decline or takeover of Indian princely states that led to a loss of indigenous patronage for the courtesans, especially for their *nautch* performances.

It is also known that among eighteenth-century nabobs, and prior to the consolidation of colonial rule through a replication of Victorian domesticity, "the performances of the nautch-women, which included both singing and dancing, had a definite vogue among the British, at least during the first half of the period [between 1765 and 1856]" (Dyson 1978: 111). According to Captain Williamson, "between the years 1778 and 1785 . . . the prime sets of dancing girls quitted the cities, and repaired to several cantonments [British enclaves], where they met the most liberal encouragement" (ibid.). The arrival of British women on the scene and the attendant concerns about the morality of the empire changed attitudes.

One way of mapping the loss of interest in the *nautch* performances by the British is to examine the discursive construction of the courtesan within the official regulations by the mid-nineteenth century. Again, taking the instance of Lucknow, where the

famous houses of courtesans had begun their gradual decline
toward prostitution, the official definition of their roles jettisoned
their aesthetic accomplishments and function. Instead, they were
demonized as repositories of disease while being considered a
necessary evil for fulfilling the sexual needs of European soldiers.
The Cantonment Act of 1864 extended the registration and medi-
cal inspection of prostitutes from ports and garrison towns to the
colonial enclaves. The Indian members of the municipal committee
asserted a distinction between courtesans and prostitutes, and
disagreed on whether courtesans should be subjected to the same
clinical examinations as the latter. While they prevailed in having
about fifty "dancing girls of a higher class" exempted, the tide was
obviously turning against a cultural institution (Talwar-Oldenburg
1984: 140).

Regulations such as the 1864 Act implicitly marked the native
women as a source of contamination, while expressing a concern
for the health of the soldiers as sentinels of the empire. A hundred
women were selected as registered prostitutes within the colonial
military enclave in 1864, but these women had to go through rou-
tines of inspection of their homes and their bodies. By the 1880s,
government memos ensured a supply of "sufficiently attractive
women" while instructing the soldiers on disease prevention (Ballhatchet 1980: 15–20; Talwar-Oldenburg 1984: 142). By the end of
the century, official "patronage" supported prostitution, while
stories of English soldiers, by Kipling and others, regretted the
shameful liasions between men of the ruling race and the "fallen"
women of the subject people.

The colonial "rescue" fantasy implicitly came into play in these
official discourses, though with an ironic twist: while prostitution
was considered a necessary evil, the British male, especially the
soldier, was more generally considered in need of moral rescue
through marriage to a white woman. Yet again, the figure of
the European woman was mobilized to ideologically hold in place
the divisions between "civilized" Victorian values and native
"decadence." Administrators tacitly understood that more young
European men should be allowed to marry and take their wives
to colonial outposts, in order to escape temptations that may lead
to varied kinds of cultural contamination, ranging from disease to
illegitimate children. One colonial official sums up this position as
follows:

Both morally and medically, there can be little doubt of the desirability of a large number of married men among the rank and file. . . . Sir John Lawrence himself stated: "I believe a great deal of unhealthiness [among soldiers] arises from their being unmarried. . . . There can be no question that marriage poses a barrier to immorality of a certain nature and consequently to disease."

(Prichard 1869: 328)

Thus, in colonial discourse we inevitably return, full circle, to an ideal of a European marriage and its attendant domesticity, as the centerpiece of the nineteenth-century British Raj. The diverse figurations of the native woman in colonial narratives—the *sati*, the *nautch* girl, and the ascetic widow—are rhetorically caught up in structures of deferral and erasure. It is not coincidental that at a time of the debates on *sati*, the plots of the Mutiny novels call for the deaths of the native women, however virtuous or desirable, so that suitable British women may replace them. Thus, even while their roles uncannily replicate the constrictions of Victorian domesticity, the "logic" of colonial discourse ultimately keeps them apart from their Western "sisters."

IV

The gendering of the British Raj at the nexus of tradition/modernity is not simply a matter of history. In postcolonial India (as in other former colonies) elements of the earlier colonial discourse frame the re-constitution of female subjectivity within the contemporary problematic of Westernization versus tradition. When postcolonial feminists like Mani and Spivak expose the nineteenth-century collusion between the colonizers and the native patriarchy in calling for an end to *sati*, but not to ascetic widowhood, they point to the insidious effects of "tradition" when conflated with the category of "woman."[24] In such counter-narratives of colonial history, contemporary feminists challenge the liberal view that colonialism, with its project of "reform," brought with it a positive reappraisal of the rights of women. Undoubtedly, women were the focus of public discourse in the nineteenth century, but an ostensible concern for them also became an occasion for a moral and political power struggle between the rulers and the indigenous elites. And feminists often identify analogous situations in postcolonial India, exemplifying the continuing persistence of colonial discourse. For instance, the recent conflicts between Muslim scriptural edicts and the secular state laws in India recapitulate the nineteenth-century debate on *sati*, dramatizing the "woman/tradition/law/scripture nexus, now complicated by a [communal] political environment" (Mani 1987: 154).

Feminists have broken new ground in their critique of both imperialism and native patriarchy, but sometimes they view colonialism as a prototype for subsequent typologies of oppression. Of course, they rightly suggest that the emergence of communalism in India, in a certain sense, is "inextricably linked with colonialism."[25] However, such an analogy, based on an irrecoverable past, can also prove more convenient than useful. For instance, when a "third world" nation-state promotes "tradition," some groups may recuperate it as a colonial trope, while deploying it as an alibi for communal and misogynist politics. Such an indigenous appropriation of "tradition" was powerfully evident during the horrifying *sati* that took place in India in 1987. The conservative defendants of this *sati*, like some nineteenth-century nationalists, were after all, simply "discovering" their ancient Indian traditions of "pure" womanhood.[26]

Today, feminists in postcolonial societies, in India and elsewhere, are faced with choices in resisting specific Western edicts of "reform," as young Islamic women do in wearing the veil, while also attempting to "discover what might make intervention possible," mediating between essentialist labels of "victim" and "agent" (Sunder Rajan 1993: 35). A knowledge of the gendering of nineteenth-century colonial discourse is useful in tracing its effects on our contemporary understanding of Indian culture and its complex and shifting notions of tradition. But in doing so, we also run a risk of unequivocally reading the present in terms of a particular construction of the past. For instance, when we consider how the Brahmins of the nineteenth century harkened to a "golden age" of Hinduism as a static frame by which to judge the practice of *sati*, we are cautioned against judging contemporary politics of communalism entirely in the context of colonial discourse, even though the rhetoric may sound familiar. Thus, feminist politics in postcolonial societies face a challenge in negotiating the thickets of "tradition," while resisting Western interventions that re-enact the old colonial "rescue."

NOTES

1 I am indebted to Macheray (1978) for my formulation of a "symptomatic reading."
2 This is a compelling story that reveals Kipling's ambivalence toward the taboo against marrying native women. Dunmaya, the hill woman, who marries Phil Garron, the British planter, is portrayed sympathetically, but the planter is described as "weak" and "not worth thinking of twice" (Kipling 1987: 34).
3 For a fuller account of *Seeta*, see Patrick Brantlinger 1988: 212–16.
4 My definition of "colonial discourse," used here and elsewhere, is specifically indebted to Peter Hulme's use of the term as a "set of language-based practices, unified by their common deployment in the management of colonial relationships" (1986: 2–3); it is also informed by David Spurr's (1994) definition of the "rhetoric of colonization."
5 Several feminist critics identify the rescue scenario as a crucial aspect of the gendering of colonial discourse. Among these are Jenny Sharpe 1993: 27–68, and Lata Mani 1987: 143–56.
6 Anne McClintock (1995: 4–9) makes a useful case for viewing "gender dynamics . . . [as] fundamental to the securing and maintenance of the imperial enterprise" (7).
7 For a fuller discussion of the relationship between çolonialism and utilitarian liberalism, see Parekh 1994: 11–12. Also see Stokes 1989: 287–322.
8 Quoted from Sunder Rajan 1993: 42–3, who discusses the trope of chivalry in the context of British colonial administrators.
9 Chris Bongie (1991) describes the rhetoric of "imperialist exoticism" as implying a quest rather than an adventure. According to him, "there is a path for experience and this path leads through the extraordinary and the exotic (as opposed to the familiar and the common). By contrast, this positing of a 'way out' is not at issue in the world of the [quest] where it is a given that the object one desires can never be fully experienced" (21–2). The death of the native woman at the end of colonial romance novels enacts such a deferral of interracial desire. For a discussion of colonial romances/adventures, also see Pratt 1992: 90–102.
10 The connection between the condition of Indian women and the justification of colonialism became a central issue among the rulers and the ruled at the height of the British Raj.
11 Mary Poovey's study of domesticity in relation to colonialism is useful in this context (1988: 164–98). Also see Suleri 1992: 76–82, and Sharpe 1993: 89–97.
12 Althusser 1971: 127–35.
13 Sen's speech is discussed by Barr 1976: 163–4.
14 Gauri Vishwanathan (1989) makes a persuasive case for the role of English education in the production of pliant colonial subjects.
15 This passage is a composite of quotations from two accounts by Mrs Marianne Postans, *Cutch: or Random Sketches* (1839) and *The Muslim Noble* (1857). Mrs Postans arrived in India as the wife of

Captain Postans, and after her husband died in 1846, she married William Henry Young, a surgeon, in 1848. Her three collections of writings about India show a deepening sense of romance with India combined with autobiographical self-revelation. For a fuller discussion of Postans's narratives about India, see Dyson 1978: 261–72.

16 See Sunder Rajan's outline of the history of *sati* during Mogul rule (1993: 60, n. 8).

17 Several postcolonial feminists point to the lack of women's voices in the historical record on *sati* and its prohibition. These include Spivak 1985: 122; Mani 1987: 152; and Sharpe 1993: 49–51.

18 Dyson (1978: 103–4) discusses Hastings's responses to *sati*, as expressed in his journal, in some detail.

19 *Parliamentary Papers on Hindu Widows* (1825: xxiv, 243), cited by Sharpe 1992: 51.

20 For a comparative analysis of the discourses on *sati* and the references to the practice in *Jane Eyre*—enacted in the death by burning of Bertha Mason—see Sharpe 1993: 33–55.

21 Sharpe 1993: 97–110; Sunder Rajan 1993: 47–8. I am indebted to Sharpe's detailed analysis of the novel's treatment of *sati*, though I focus more broadly on constructions of female identity in the context of colonial binaries in the novel.

22 See Dyson 1978: 338–44, for several descriptions of the dresses of *nautch* girls.

23 Richard Burton, as a translator of the *Arabian Nights* and the *Kama-sutra*, had an obvious interest in the psychological and sexual aspects of Oriental cultures (Dyson 1978: 295–7). However, his Introduction to the *Arabian Nights* is packed with Oriental clichés about harems, princesses, slaves, veils, and dancing girls, which combine to produce a sentimentalized prurience that passed off as "knowledge." I am also indebted to Ryan Bishop's ideas on the genealogies of sexual "others" in *Nightmarket: Thailand in Postcolonial Sexual Carto-graphies* (Bishop and Robinson, forthcoming).

24 A subtle analysis of the contemporary feminist interpretations of the nineteenth-century debates on *sati* can be found in Sunder Rajan 1993: 53–5.

25 Mani (1987: 154) links contemporary communalism in India to coloni-alism. Of course, colonial rule in India and elsewhere depended on and exploited internal religious and ethnic divisions, but when feminists attach their critique of contemporary politics almost entirely to an irrecoverable past, they may face a conceptual impasse.

26 The sensational Roop Kanwar *sati* in 1987 generated a controversial debate about the role of Indian women within the problematic of tradition and modernity. An attack on Westernization was the basis of most defenses of this horrifying self-immolation, which was seen as a return to tradition. For a detailed history of this event and the debate surrounding it, see Hawley 1994: 101–86.

WORKS CITED IN CHAPTER 3

Althusser, Louis. "Ideology and Ideological State Apparatuses." In *Lenin and Philosophy and Other Essays*. Trans. Ben Brewster. New York: Monthly Review Press, 1971: 127–86.

Ballhatchet, Kenneth. *Race, Sex, and Class under the Raj: Imperial Attitudes and their Policies and their Critics, 1793–1905*. London: Weidenfeld & Nicolson, 1980.

Barr, Pat. *The Memsahibs: In Praise of the Women of Victorian India*. London: Secker & Warburg, 1976.

Bishop, Ryan and Lillian Robinson. *Nightmarket: Thailand in Postcolonial Cartographies*. New York: Routledge (forthcoming).

Bongie, Chris. *Exotic Memories: Literature, Colonialism, Fin de Siècle*. Stanford: Stanford University Press, 1991.

Brantlinger, Patrick. *Rule of Darkness: British Literature and Imperialism, 1830–1914*. Ithaca: Cornell University Press, 1988.

Burton, Sir Richard Francis. *Scinde; or the Unhappy Valley*. 2 vols. London: n.p., 1851.

Chatterjee, Partha. *The Nation and its Fragments: Colonial Postcolonial Histories*. Princeton, N.J.: Princeton University Press, 1993.

Dyson, Ketaki Kushari. *A Various Universe: A Study of the Journals and Memoirs of British Men and Women in the Indian Subcontinent, 1765–1856*. New Delhi: Oxford University Press, 1978.

Evidence taken before the Bengal Provincial Committee (1884). Selections from the Records of the Government of India, Home Office, No. lxvii.

Hawley, John Stratton. Ed. *Sati, the Blessing and the Curse: The Burning of Wives in India*. Oxford and New York: Oxford University Press, 1994.

Hulme, Peter. *Colonial Encounters: Europe and the Native Caribbean, 1492–1797*. London: Routledge & Kegan Paul, 1986.

Kipling, Rudyard. "Yoked with an Unbeliever" (1886). In *Plain Tales from the Hills*. Oxford: Oxford University Press, 1987: 30–41.

Loomba, Ania. *Gender, Race, Renaissance Drama*. Manchester: Manchester University Press, 1989.

McClintock, Anne. *Imperial Leather: Race, Gender and Sexuality in the Colonial Contest*. London: Routledge, 1995.

Macheray, Peter. *The Theory of Literary Production*. London: Kegan Paul, 1978.

Mani, Lata. "Contentious Traditions: The Debate on Sati in Colonial India." In *Cultural Critique*, 7, 1987: 119–56.

Mills, Sara. *Discourses of Difference: An Analysis of Women's Travel Writing and Colonialism*. London: Routledge, 1991.

Parekh, Bhikhu. "Superior People: The Narrowness of Liberalism from Mill to Rawls." In *Times Literary Supplement*, February 25, 1994: 11–13.

Poovey, Mary. *Uneven Developments: The Ideological Work of Gender in Mid-Victorian England*. Chicago: University of Chicago Press, 1988.

Postans, Marianne. *Cutch: or Random Sketches taken during a Residence in One of the Northern Provinces of Western India*. London: n.p., 1839.

—— *The Muslim Noble: His Land and People*. London: n.p., 1857.

Pratt, Mary Louise. *Imperial Eyes: Travel Writing and Transculturation*. London: Routledge, 1992.

Prichard, Iltdus T. *The Administration of India: 1859 to 1869*. 2 vols. London: Macmillan, 1869.

Roberts, Emma. *Scenes and Characteristics of Hindostan, with Sketches of Anglo-Indian Society* (1835). 3 vols. London: n.p., 1910.

Scott, Joan W. "Gender: A Useful Category of Historical Analysis." In *Coming to Terms: Feminism, Theory, Politics*. Ed. Elizabeth Weed. London: Routledge, 1989: 81–100.

Sharar, Abdul Halim. *Lucknow: The Last Phase of an Oriental Culture*. Trans. and ed. F.S. Harcourt and Fakhir Hussain. London: Paul Elek, 1975.

Sharpe, Jenny. *Allegories of Empire: The Figure of the Woman in the Colonial Text*. Minneapolis: University of Minnesota Press, 1993.

Sherwood, Mrs Mary Martha. *The Life of Mrs. Sherwood* (chiefly autobiographical). Ed. Sophia Kelly. London: n.p., 1854.

—— *The Life and Times of Mrs. Sherwood*. Ed. F.J. Harvey Darton. London: n.p., 1910.

Sleeman, Sir William Henry. *Rambles and Recollections of an Indian Official* (1844). Ed. Vincent A. Smith. London: 1915.

Spivak, Gayatri Chakravorty. "Can the Subaltern Speak? Speculations on Widow Sacrifices." In *Wedge*, 7–8, 1985: 120–30.

—— "The Rani of Sirmur: An Essay in reading the Archives." In *History and Theory*, 24, 3, 1987: 247–72.

Spurr, David. *The Rhetoric of Empire: Colonial Discourse in Journalism, Travel Writing, and Imperial Administration*. Durham, N.C.: Duke University Press, 1994.

Steel, Flora Annie. *On the Face of the Waters: A Tale of the Mutiny*. New York: Macmillan, 1897.

Stokes, Eric. *The English Utilitarians and India*. Delhi: Oxford University Press, 1989.

Suleri, Sara. *The Rhetoric of English India*. Chicago: University of Chicago Press, 1992.

Sunder Rajan, Rajeswari. *Real and Imagined Women: Gender, Culture, and Postcolonialism*. London: Routledge, 1993.

Talwar-Oldenburg, Veena. *The Making of Colonial Lucknow: 1856–1877*. Princeton: Princeton University Press, 1984.

Taylor, Meadows. *Seeta*. London: Kegan Paul, 1872.

Vishwanathan, Gauri. *Masks of Conquest: Literary Study and British Rule in India*. New York: Columbia University Press, 1989.

Williamson, Capt. Thomas. *The East-India Vade-Mecum; or Complete Guide to Gentlemen intended for the Civil, Military, or Naval Service*. 2 vols. London: 1810.

Chapter 4

Shakespeare and the "civilizing mission"

I

Quantities of baboos [Bengalis] were applauding on the back of their books . . . [at a performance of *Macbeth*]. The native generation who have been brought up at Hindu College are perfectly mad about Shakespeare. What a triumph it is for him, dear creature!

(Emily Eden, *Letters from India, 1837–40*, II: 264–5)

Indian Empire, or no Indian Empire; we cannot do without Shakespeare! Indian Empire will go, at any rate, some day, but this Shakespeare does not go, he lasts forever with us.

(Thomas Carlyle 1840: 109)

Imagine the social scene of nineteenth-century Calcutta where the agents of the British Raj had established a society in a faithful imitation of the "mother" country. Numerous impressions left by the journals and memoirs of the rulers testify to the gaiety, splendor, and extravagance of life in British Calcutta, which one writer later recalled as "happy days, more than half a century ago" (Taylor 1882: 92). Among the round of social activities, theater-going was a popular pastime, and one that reflected the expatriates' anxiety to imitate the cultural practices of London, as Fanny Parkes describes in *Wanderings of a Pilgrim*:

Chowringhee Theatre was in the height of its celebrity. This was an institution established and kept up by private parties, but which in the excellent acting it exhibited, and the admirable management by which it was conducted, was equal to many of the minor theatres in London and superior to most provincial theatres. Seldom or ever was there so efficient a body of amateur actors as those who were in Calcutta assembled in 1829.

Horace Hayman . . . James Barwell, Henry Parker . . . and last but not the least, William Palmer, the "Calcutta Kean," as he was called.

(quoted in Taylor 1882: 90)

While this scene would be somewhat commonplace and innocuous in eighteenth-century London, it marks an important historical moment in colonial India. Such a re-creation of London's theatrical scene in Calcutta signaled the transportation of British civilization and culture from the metropolis to the new colony. Starting in 1775, when the Calcutta Theatre or the New Playhouse opened under the patronage of the then Governor General, Warren Hastings, and continuing for a period of about a hundred years, English theaters in Calcutta entertained a largely British audience of officers, merchants, clerks, and "adventurers" associated with the East India Company and later with the civil service. The repertoire of plays performed here included *Hamlet*, *Richard III*, *The School for Scandal*, and a medley of lesser-known plays such as *The Comedy of Beaux Strategem*, and *She Would and Would Not*. Most theater historians note that the model for the playhouse in the colonies, including the popular proscenium stage, came from the architecture of London theaters such as Covent Garden and Drury Lane. Other theaters followed, notably the Chowringhee, which opened in 1813, and the Sans Souci, inaugurated on August 21, 1839, the year the former was gutted by a fire.[1]

These different playhouses drew on a fairly similar repertoire: the Chowringhee, often a venue for musical comedies and farces, was also popular for its Shakespearean performances, such as *Henry IV* in 1814, *Richard III* in 1815, and *The Merry Wives of Windsor* in 1818. And the Sans Souci was also long remembered for its Shakespearean productions: Esther Leach, a prominent actress who moved there from the Chowringhee, arranged for a few artists to be brought from London, among whom was a James Vining. Having acted in Drury Lane and Covent Garden, Vining gave some important performances at the Sans Souci, among which was his appearance in *The Merchant of Venice* in 1843, playing Shylock, with Mrs Leach as Jessica and Mrs Deacle as Portia. However, the Sans Souci production that remains the most memorable is that with Baishnav Charan Adhya as Othello and Mrs Anderson (the daughter of Esther Leach) as Desdemona, as one account reported: "a Bengali youth in an English play in an English theatre catering to a [large] English audience in . . . the nineteenth century is certainly a memorable event in the history of Calcutta's theatres."[2]

In their early years, these were exclusive playhouses, determined to insulate themselves from the natives, so that even the ushers and doorkeepers at the Calcutta Playhouse were English. Given these conditions, an Indian actor's identification with the role of Othello certainly created a stir in the local community, as is evident in one letter to the *Calcutta Star*, which described the actor as "a real, unpainted nigger Othello" (quoted in Raha 1978: 10). The anxiety of this reader was probably shared by others, considering how the Indian actor's donning of a "black face" must have displaced and complicated the dichotomy between the colonizers and the colonized. This interracial casting was an exception to the casting of Europeans rather than Indians in what was exclusively a European repertory. However, the theaters gradually opened their doors to elite, aristocratic Indians, some of whom were associated with the later productions. Among the founders of the Chowringhee theater was a leading member of the Bengali aristocracy, D.N. Tagore, who later joined other Indian contributors in also subscribing to the relocation of the Sans Souci.

That the range of theatrical activity in and around Calcutta prominently included the plays of Shakespeare was not unusual, since productions of Shakespeare's works enjoyed great popularity in Britain from the late eighteenth to the end of the nineteenth centuries. And by the mid-Victorian period, the grand-scale pictorial realism of the London productions, combined with the trend of canonizing individual characters, had left a strong impression on the popular imagination. Shakespeare's characters and plots had become both commonplace and sources of inspiration for artists and writers. Thus, the Victorian colonists in India, while apishly promoting Shakespeare's works in colonial Calcutta, were, in effect, reproducing the metropolitan culture as a part of the "civilizing mission" of the British Raj. And not only were the Calcutta productions popular, but visiting troupes from overseas increased the local exposure to dramatic "classics" such as Shakespeare, as for instance, the Bandmann's Company, which staged *Hamlet*, *Macbeth*, and *Richard III* in 1882. Later, in 1909, on another tour, well-known Shakespearean actors Matheson Lang and Charles Vane accompanied the troupe.[3]

By the mid-Victorian period, according to one theater historian, the "English-educated Bengali middle class as well as the property owning and trading rich had been exposed to English theatrical ideas and conventions and to Shakespeare fairly extensively" (Raha c. 1965: 23). Such an interest in Western drama coincided with the official colonial policy of promoting the English language and literature in India. As the British consolidated their presence in India, the impulse to educate the natives gained a wide consensus because it was based on an awareness that the rulers could only rule by co-opting a native elite as a "conduit of Western thought and ideas."[4] While there was intense debate about whether Indians should receive an education in English or in classical Indian languages, such as Sanskrit or Arabic, the cause of English literature won the day, with the passage of the Indian Education Act 1835. Several recent studies, most notably by Gauri Vishwanathan, have persuasively argued that both the Anglicists and the English Orientalists partook of the notion that cultural values moved *downward* from a position of power.[5] Thus, in introducing English literature to the elite Indians—or in allowing them access to Calcutta theaters—the colonial rulers were not being egalitarian, but rather engaging in a "hegemonic activity" by which, in Gramsci's terms, "the consent of the governed is secured through intellectual and moral manipulation rather than through military force."[6]

II

A history of theatrical activity in Calcutta, from the late eighteenth through the nineteenth centuries, gives us a sense of the social and cultural arrangements within colonial society. And an important aspect of these arrangements was the complex relationship between the colonists and elite Bengalis—the objects of the British "civilizing mission" and the "conduits" for Western ideas, who, ironically, were in search of a cultural identity that would put them on a par with the rulers. Thus, an interest in Calcutta theaters and in English literary figures like Shakespeare became important markers for Indians/Bengalis seeking validation as civilized and refined natives.

In this context, it is not surprising that Shakespeare's works were treated with considerable reverence in colonial society. This was apparent in the way the name "Shakespeare" functioned as a key signifier within colonial discourse, while demarcating the familiar binaries: barbarism and civilization, tradition and modernity. To get a fuller sense of this process, I will examine how the material and discursive production of Shakespeare's plays in nineteenth- and early twentieth-century Calcutta intersected with the "civilizing mission," especially as it manifested itself in English liberal education, and more obliquely, in the ideals of the Bengal Renaissance. This influence, I argue, led to a cultural struggle extending into the postcolonial era, producing hybrid forms of theater, ranging from the early company *nataks* in Bengal to the indigenous versions in contemporary India. By hybridity I mean a specific form of *transculturation*, or a process whereby marginal or subordinate groups select and create new cultural forms from materials of the dominant culture.[7]

Yet, this hybrid, theatrical idiom is only one aspect of the complex cultural phenomenon known as "Shakespeare in India."[8] On the one hand, Shakespeare has become an accommodating ideal, a means of reconciling disparities of race and class not unlike the ideology of nationalism. On the other hand, his works have also been appropriated within indigenous theatrical modes— stirring debates about the problematics of translation—and often in ways that question the Bard's canonical Western status. Thus, overall, this chapter explores the formation of India's colonial and nationalist cultural identity, from the nineteenth century to the present, by charting the reception of Shakespeare's works. Taking this somewhat circuitous route, I examine how Shakespeare became a means of contextualizing and prescribing perceptions and expectations about the British "civilizing mission," as well as its postcolonial manifestations and revisions.

In order to understand the ideological underpinnings of the British "civilizing mission," with its related educational policies and cultural practices, let us turn to the ideas of Charles Trevelyan. A civil servant and the brother-in-law of Macaulay, he was a strong advocate of the Anglicist position of promoting an English education among the natives. In his important study entitled *On the Education of the People of India* (1838), Trevelyan does not view the official policy as an arbitrary fiat of the colonial rulers. Rather, he argues for the cultural superiority of the British in the context of a historicized "theory" of intercultural exchange. "The past history of the world," he believes, "authorizes us to believe that the movement [in English education] taking place in

India, if properly directed . . . , will end in bringing . . . a decided change for the better in the character of the people" (36). Trevelyan draws on the broad sweep of Western history to show how the "superior civilization of one country has taken deepest root and fructified most abundantly in other countries" (36):

> Every scholar knows to what a great extent the Romans culti-
> vated Grecian literature, and adopted Grecian models of taste.
> It was only after the national mind was impregnated from this
> source, that they began to have a literature of their own. . . .
> Virgil was a mere imitator, however noble . . . Roman literature
> is only an echo of the Greek literature. . . . the Roman language
> and literature, thus enriched and improved, was destined to still
> prouder triumphs. The inhabitants of the greatest part of
> Europe and of the North of Africa, educated in every respect
> like the Romans, became in every respect equal to them . . .
> [and] . . . Latin to this day forms the basis of the tongues of
> France and southern Europe. . . . After this came the great
> revival of learning at the close of the fifteenth and sixteenth
> centuries . . . [when] all the modern languages were in a state
> extremely barbarous . . . [thus the spirit of the time] was excited
> chiefly by the admiration of the ancients. . . . Not only the
> manner of the ancients were imitated, but their language
> [Latin] was adopted. . . . [From this] mental stimulus . . . arose
> . . . the vernacular literature of Europe.
>
> (Trevelyan 1838: 36–41)

Giving this example of such a cultural transformation from "barbarism" to "civilization," Trevelyan then discusses Russia, "a nation which had previously been in a state as barbarous as that in which our ancestors were before the crusades." Now Russia is taking its place among "civilized communities" (43), only because the Tsar was taught "those foreign languages in which the greatest mass of information has been laid up" (44). The Russian example serves the English official's purpose when he points to an analogy with India: *"The languages of Western Europe civilized Russia. I cannot doubt that they will do for the Hindoo what they have done for the Tartar"* (44; my emphasis).

Trevelyan's "theory" has an undoubtedly Eurocentric basis, as he does not account for the history of Arabic, Persian, and Sanskrit, and their culturally enriching cross-fertilizations with one another. Yet, one can also detect a conceptual break in his formulation, typical of nineteenth-century liberals: while emphasizing imitation or emulation of a superior culture (such as the Indian imitation of the English), he seems to create a model of intercultural exchange that is not based on the principle of cultural purity or exclusiveness; yet later, he defines English as "preeminent even among the languages of the West" (86). The logic of this "theory" of emulation is played out more fully when he discusses the supposedly unscientific, 'and therefore fluid, nature of Indian languages:

> in Bengalee and Hindustanee nothing is fixed; everything is yet to be done, and a new literature is to be formed . . . to speak of the delicate sensibility of a Bengalee or Hindustanee being offended by the introduction of new words to express new ideas is to transfer to a poor and unformed tongue the feelings which are connected only with a rich and cultivated one. It will be time enough after their scientific vocabulary is settled, and they have masterpieces of their own, to think of keeping their language pure. When they have a native Milton or Shakespeare, they will not require us to guide them in this respect.
>
> (ibid.: 123)

Finally Trevelyan's goal for the empire is one in which the "languages of India will be assimilated to the languages of Europe, as far as the arts and sciences and general literature are concerned; and the introduction of further improvements will be facilitated" (124). According to him, because the English language and literature will facilitate "progress" and "civilization," for the Indians, the latter will "become more English than Hindu . . . [while] daily convers[ing] with the best and wisest Englishmen through the higher medium of their works" (190). Ideally, according to Trevelyan, colonial subjects would aspire "to *resemble* [Europeans]" (192), while repudiating their own religion and culture. Speaking in the voice of colonial liberalism, he beckons the Indian subjects into its fold, while also designating them as inferior.

Thus, not surprisingly, the attendant social and psychic dislocations of such a mission of acculturation, critiqued by Fanon a century later in *Black Skin, White Masks* (1967), completely escaped the Englishman's colonial logic here. Referring to the Antillean black more than a century later, Fanon describes his dilemma in a way that retrospectively reveals the limitations of Trevelyan's call to emulation: the source of the "antillean Negro's inferiority complex," according to Fanon, is born when he adopts a "language [and culture] different from that of the group into which he was born" and mimics "European forms of social intercourse . . . adorning the Native language with European expressions" (25). Thus, the "black man" in a colonial society has two dimensions: "one with his fellows and the other with the white man" (17). While Fanon identifies the psychologically negative aspects of imitation, Homi Bhabha, more recently, captures the way in which the native subjects could undermine colonial authority through "simultaneous mimicry and resistance."[9]

Trevelyan, writing a century earlier, seems to have no consciousness of the effects of Anglicization on the Indian subjects. But in pointing to an interplay between identity and difference, Trevelyan also reveals the characteristic paradoxes of nineteenth-century colonial liberalism. His formula for "reform" evokes both benevolence and mastery, cultural interaction and domination, and an affinity and a difference between the rulers and their subjects. Through mimicry and emulation, Indians could attain English "identities" as long as they accepted the rulers as their "natural protectors and benefactors" (192). Trevelyan's views echo the ideas of another prominent Victorian liberal, John Stuart Mill, who also welcomed the "blending" or "admixture of nationalities" but only if the "superior group remained the dominant partner" (quoted in Parekh 1994: 11). To gain the consent of their subjects for this philosophy, they promoted English literature as a source of Christian social virtues, giving moral credibility to the empire.

Finally, Trevelyan's colonizing imagination in *On the Education of the People of India* is not static: he sees English education in terms of an indistinct future of a "happy independence." "The natives will have Independence, after first learning [through their Anglicization] how to make a good use of it . . . and we shall long continue to reap in the affectionate attachment of the people, and in a great commercial intercourse with her splendid country" (194–5). Thus, ironically, as Trevelyan projects a future of enlightenment for the Indians, when "native activity will be fully . . . employed in acquiring and diffusing European knowledge," he looks ahead to the legacy of the "colonial book" only to defer the end of empire.

III

Many accounts suggest that Shakespeare's works functioned as the "colonial book" in the British Raj, though not without some ambivalence in terms of its authority. At the time when the Shakespearean productions in Calcutta were drawing in elite Indians, educational institutions in the city were promoting Shakespeare as part of the new English literary curriculum. As Sushil Mukherjee recapitulates:

> When the English came to Calcutta they brought with them the plays of Shakespeare. Early in the nineteenth century, Shakespeare was a subject of study in the Hindu College [in Calcutta]. Much before that Shakespeare's plays had begun to be staged in the theatres that local Englishmen had set up in the city for their entertainment and relaxation. The names of David Garrick, the great eighteenth-century Shakespearean actor and Garrick's Drury Lane theatre . . . were familiar in Calcutta among the readers of Shakespeare and lovers of the theatre.
>
> (Mukherjee 1982: 1–2)

Here we can get an idea not only of how "Shakespeare" functioned as a privileged signifier within colonial discourse, but how his works in turn contextualized and shaped the curricular and theatrical practices of the time. In order to examine why the Bard's works figured prominently in the new English curriculum following the Education Act of 1835, let us turn to the educational concerns of the time. The English literary pedagogy that evolved out of an interest in the enlightenment of the natives was not entirely uniform, given the differences between missionary and secular institutions. But all institutions shared the basic principles of an Arnoldian curriculum which "was a course of studies with a heavy stress on classical languages and literatures . . . [combined] with the poetry of the Romantics to teach . . . the deeper relations between nature and the human soul." Its goal was the "inculcation of a code of Christian values by which men of culture were to live" (Vishwanathan 1989: 55–6).

This emphasis on English literature as a vast repository of Christian values helped the administrators to represent literary texts as transcendental and timeless. Thus, they found an ally in literature in promoting the superiority of the British/Christian culture under the guise of a liberal education. While the missionaries questioned whether literature could replace the Bible, they could not do much to alter the government's restrictions on an explicitly religious education. As an alternative, the missionaries focussed on the shared features of literature and Christianity. For instance, a Reverend William Keane described the proselytizing powers of English literature in a testimony before officials:

> Shakespeare, though by no means a good standard, is full of religion; it is full of the commonsense principles which none but Christian men can recognize. Sound Protestant Bible principles, though not actually told in words, are there set out to advantage, and the opposite often condemned. So with Goldsmith . . . and many other books which are taught in the schools . . . [which] have undoubtedly sometimes a favourable effect in actually bringing them to us missionaries.
>
> (quoted in Vishwanathan 1989: 80)

While there was some disagreement among missionaries as to whether Shakespeare's language reflected a pagan rather than a Protestant morality, the playwright's cultural stature and relevance to colonial discourse under the auspices of Christianity cannot be undervalued. A lively exchange in the *Bengal Magazine* in 1876 reveals some curious twists in the Shakespearean mission of the empire. A devout Indian Christian establishes a moral distinction between "Shakespeareans" and "Christians," arguing as follows:

> Shakespeare is of the earth . . . but the Bible is of the heaven heavenly. The one says—Be ye like the heroes of the world who never pocketed an insult and never forgave an enemy! The other says—Be like your Father in heaven who causeth His sun to rise both on the just and the unjust.
>
> (Anonymous 1876: 232)

The editors of the *Bengal Magazine* refute this charge in the same issue: "The division of the whole English nation into Shakespeareans and Christians . . . seems to us to be entirely fanciful. Many . . . Christians . . . intensely admire Shakespeare not only as an artist, but also as a moral teacher" (237). Notwithstanding some quibbling about the Christian aspects of Shakespeare's works, the more pervasive assumption is of the playwright being a repository of Christian beliefs. Thus, despite the divisions among missionaries, Shakespeare became one viable means of contextualizing and prescribing a desirable Christian morality—an important justification of the nineteenth-century British Raj as a harbinger of civilization.

Given the general social, cultural, and moral investment in Shakespeare, the literary curriculum in government schools in nineteenth-century India inevitably included several tragedies, often *Hamlet*, *Othello*, and *Macbeth*.[10] As the secular policy ensured a classical approach to the study of language and literature, literary texts were understood as objects of study in and for themselves. In this context, students of Shakespeare were taught through an emphasis on the language and rhetoric of the plays. Memorization and recitation of particular scenes were popular methods of learning. One critic offers a vivid description of how a knowledge of Shakespeare was disseminated in educational institutions in Calcutta:

> While the English playhouses by their production of English, especially Shakespeare's plays, created an appetite for theatrical performances, the foundation of the Hindu College in 1816, and the teaching of Shakespeare by eminent teachers like Richardson [who was also a founder of the Chowringhee Theatre] created in the minds of the students—the intelligentsia of modern Bengal—a literary taste for drama as such, and taught them, not only to appreciate Shakespeare criticism, but also to recite and act scenes from his plays. This fashion spread to every academic institution.
>
> (S.K. Bhattacharya 1964: 29)

This fashionable veneration of Shakespearean language and rhetoric undoubtedly surfaced in the numerous literary societies and other such institutions that sprung up with the spread of English education. Mostly imitative in their structure, these societies produced Macaulay's Anglicized subjects who were known, among other things, for their ability to quote from "Hume, Gibbon . . . Shakespeare and Milton, to reveal . . . beauties in Milton . . . and [undetected] archaisms in Shakespeare," or to write "essays on Shakespeare's tragedies" (quoted in Vishwanathan 1989: 160). Such a mimicry of British cultural values on the part of Indians had complex dimensions: what seemed an anxious pedantry on the part of a new Bengali male elite was also their way of finding a place for themselves in the new socioeconomic terrain opened by the British.[11] Overall, it is arguable whether the Indians' "love" of the Shakespearean text (and of other English literary works), sometimes emerging in pedantic veneration, was really a benign practice of "appreciation."

One way of looking at the colonial manipulation of literary reception would be to note how literature functions as an ideological apparatus (in an Althusserian context) in perpetuating dominant power relations. When the English text was yoked to the notion of the "civilizing mission", it produced inevitable contradictions, as evident in the relationship between the Indian reader and the English text: this was based on what one critic defines as the "inclusion/exclusion principle," whereby the Indian was encouraged to become a surrogate Englishman while also being reminded of his inability to fully comprehend the "truths" enshrined in the Western texts. Thus, as the colonial ideology projected its viewpoint as transcendental and ahistorical, it was able to claim to represent "human nature" and to define those whom it considered to be *outside* the bounds of humanity—who then became its "others."[12]

IV

Several reasons explain why this ideology of the universal English text, with its quasi New Critical focus, took hold in nineteenth-century India. Once the Indian Education Act, 1835, produced teaching and critical practices that focussed on English rather than indigenous literatures, such an education translated into employment within the colonial administration. For the eager "baboos . . . applauding" at Shakespearean performances, described by Emily Eden, the Bard's works undoubtedly constituted a form of "cultural capital" with an exchange value in terms of job opportunities. The belief in the transcendent humanism of English literature also created a new native elite culture, as it "offered a programme of building a new man who would feel himself a citizen of the world while the very face of the world was being constructed in the mirror of the dominant culture of the West" (Loomba 1989: 21). If English literature played a crucial role in the self-definition of a new class of Indian male elites, it was not entirely the "colonizer's plant on the Indian consciousness to gag it into the torpor of slavery" (Bagchi 1991: 146). Jasodhara Bagchi persuasively argues for a "dialectical relationship" between English studies and the "new class of Bengalis that was emerging within the colonial apparatus" (148). For them "English literature was not merely a literature of the masters, but it was *literature*, a source of non-denominational spirituality, a harbinger of a secular outlet," an extension of enlightenment reason that occupied the grey area between the state and religion (Bagchi 1991: 149–50).

Thus, this liberal legacy of English literary studies opposed to Sanskrit obscurantism maps the terrain from which an Indian nationalist ethos grew in the late nineteenth century. English literature was idealized by elite Indian nationalists, imbued with a liberalism that saw the "Bengal Renaissance" in the late nineteenth century as a rebirth or rediscovery of a heroic Hindu age under the progressive wings of English literature. Major literary figures in Bengal like Ishwarchandra Vidyasagar and Michael Madhusudan Dutt imitated English models such as Milton's vernacular epic to produce the genre of a nationalist epic in a Miltonic cast, Dutt's *Ramayana* being representative of this genre. Some introduced Bacon and Hume to Indian students or translated Shakespeare. Thus, as Bagchi notes, "through the solid institutional backing provided mostly by the indigenous elite, English literature became the *Mantra* for the New India in its fight against obscurantist traditionalism" (151).

It is both ironic and telling that Western literature, and specifically Shakespeare, offer useful *contexts* for understanding the particular form of hybridity that constituted the Bengal Renaissance. Proponents of this movement were "a new class of Bengalis" who not only emerged from the "colonial apparatus," as Bagchi suggests, but were specifically shaped by the assumptions of the "civilizing mission." Sudipto Chatterjee explains this curious acculturation very aptly:

> The Bengal Renaissance was the outgrowth of the grafting of a foreign culture onto a more-than-willing native culture. For the Bengalis their response to what was imposed by the British was a search for a cultural identity that could, at some level, set them on a par with their European overlords. It is in the wake of this endeavour to assume/regain a respectful self-identity that, in the 1840s, several theatres [among other institutions] were spawned in the native quarters of Calcutta.
>
> (Chatterjee 1995: 20)

Thus, not surprisingly, within the colonial dichotomy between tradition and modernity, both the British and the Bengali elites placed English studies on the side of progress and civilization (even though they included traditional canonical works in this formulation). Ironically, while the native elites aimed at inventing or discovering a new nationalist identity for themselves they were attempting to do so in terms set by English liberalism, and by its corollary, English literary studies. In this context, Charles Trevelyan's remark in 1838, suggesting that "when [the Indians] have a native Milton or Shakespeare, they will not require us to guide them in this respect" (122–3), seemed to be validated by nineteenth-century Bengali intellectuals like Bankim Chandra. The latter frequently designated Shakespeare as the literary model par excellence. For instance, in his essay entitled, "Shakuntala, Miranda, Desdemona," Bankim Chandra deems "*The Tempest* comparable to [the Indian epic] *Shakuntala* for its narrative skill, [but] the tragic mode of Shakespeare's *Othello* is given the final word for its portrayal of the nobility of human nature" (quoted in Bagchi 1991: 156). By the late nineteenth century, Trevelyan's teleology began to ring hollow, given that English literature was naturalized and domesticated in Indian, and particularly Bengali, culture.

Given the nineteenth-century consensus between the rulers and the elite Indians about the role of English studies in building a civic society, the passage of the Shakespearean text from the British Raj to postcolonial education in India has been a relatively smooth one. A crucial aspect of this civic society was that it held in place both the empire and the new Indian social hierarchies. This explains the persistence of the colonial trope of universalism after independence, no longer deployed in the service of a "civilizing mission," but used instead as an accommodating ideal for the continuing class and linguistic divisions within the new nation-state. Commemorating the quatercentenary of Shakespeare's birth in 1963, noted critic C.D. Narasimhaiah blithely remarks:

> to us educated Indians, the coming of the British . . . meant among other things, the coming of Shakespeare, of noble speech and brave deeds and so Shakespeare must have a special significance for us in India. Until recently, for hundred and fifty years or so [since 1835], we have learnt English through Shakespeare, and thanks to him the learning has been so pleasant and profitable. Indeed to most of us, English educated Indians, Shakespeare's characters, the situations in his plays, and those memorable lines of his have become almost as intimate a part

of our lives as those of the best of our own writers. Shakespeare, more than the English monarch, seems to be the true and vital link between India and England (iii).

The Indian critic's reading of colonial history, sixteen years after independence, is rhetorically not far removed from Carlyle's look into the future, when, the latter believed, the loss of Britain's political empire would be compensated by the continuing presence of Shakespeare ("This Shakespeare . . . lasts forever with us"). In Narasimhaiah's vision too, the implicit relationship between Shakespeare and empire is also entirely beneficent, naturalizing a bond between the British and the Indians in a way that occludes colonial history. The critic's investment in a close reading of the plays—implying a transcultural intimacy with the characters, their language, and their experience—is explained by his own position as an "English educated Indian," an elite minority in India. While he implicitly reveals that those who are not "English educated" may not experience a natural love of the Bard, he does not dwell upon this divide. Instead, his idealization of Shakespeare, a conceptual move framed by colonialism, functions precisely to erase continuing social and linguistic divisions in independent India.

Narasimhaiah's idealizing gesture imagines and constitutes all students, including the un-Anglicized majority, as admirers of the universal Bard. More recently, however, critics, writing from a historical perspective of postcoloniality, question the dominance of English as the language used by the bourgeoisie for political and social control.[13]

However, their interventions into the "intimacy" of the supposed East–West encounter have not, as yet, changed the curricular practices to accurately reflect the socio-economic factors of Indian society. Most Indian students in university must study English literature for at least one year.[14] In these classrooms, it seems, Shakespeare still reigns as an autonomous artifact, and as in the case of New Criticism in America, it provides a useful pedagogical strategy for coping with a large, diverse student population in a changing industrialized society (Eagleton 1983: 50–1). The anxiety of one critic (in 1963) explains why teachers/critics continue to reproduce the Shakespearean text as an accommodating ideal: "In our technological world where the humanities are crumbling . . . how shall we salvage Shakespeare?" In his view, the Bard is worth salvaging because his works "prepare us for the new world of industrial and scientific changes" (Muliyil 1963: 82–5). But he does not explain how this can be achieved; what he promotes is an ideology of literary transcendence.

V

The Shakespearean text in postcolonial India (in large part) continues to be reproduced as a "classic," discursively removed from colonial history, yet aligned to the class and linguistic hierarchies established or reinforced by colonialism. And this legacy of the nineteenth-century classic Shakespeare—of the fetishized text—not only suggests a problem for postcolonial societies, struggling to free themselves from the cultural hegemony of the Europeans. Writing in the 1930s, Bertolt Brecht also pointed to the limitations of "classic" nineteenth-century representations of Shakespeare's plays in Europe. He attacked "the traditional style of performance [of Shakespeare's works] which is automatically counted as part of our cultural heritage" on the grounds that "what gets lost is the classic's original freshness . . . [and] the lessons taught the audience are tame and cosy" (quoted in Heinemann 1985: 212).

Brecht's methodology of historicizing dramatic texts works, not by eliding the past and present in a timeless aestheticism, but by dialectically setting one against the other. A similar dialectical pattern is evident in the *performance history* of Shakespeare's plays in India. Most theater historians agree that contemporary Indian theater originated in Bengal in the mid-nineteenth century. There had been no direct evolution of ancient classical Sanskrit drama to contemporary forms, and Indian theater needed some fresh impetus. Thus, when the English-educated Bengalis were exposed to Shakespeare and other "classic" European dramatists in the mid-nineteenth century, they sought to emulate these productions while affecting a distaste for the indigenous folk plays.[15] Box sets, footlights, and proscenium stages were novelties for the Calcutta elite who took their cue from English productions. An ironic aspect of this emulation is that it revealed the Indian gentry's desire for a stronger cultural presence and identity in the city. Again, Sudipto Chatterjee explains the reasons for this native investment in theatrical activity:

Concentration of wealth in the hands of the *babus* [the bour-
geoisie] and the rise of a Western-style educated middle class
[Macaulay's subjects] provided the right moment of pollination
for the budding of a Bengali theatre. . . . Close contact with
the British inspired both classes to create their own theatre in
the European mould. With the coming of economic, political,
and social stability [for these classes]—with a mean being
struck between traditional Bengali culture and the . . . British
cultural imports—a system of patronage was born that was to
keep Bengali theatre alive for some time.

(Chatterjee 1995: 20)

And in keeping with this impulse toward a peculiarly hybrid
cultural autonomy, the first Bengali playhouse, called the Hindu
Theatre, opened on December 28, 1831 in a private residence
with a performance of excerpts from *Julius Caesar* and an English
translation of a classical Sanskrit play.

It is not within the scope of this chapter to give a comprehensive
account of individual Shakespearean productions or to trace a
detailed stage history. Rather, it offers a selective overview of
some local stage versions of his works in Bengali, and later in the
national theaters, from the mid-nineteenth century to the present.
Within this historical span, the Shakespearean canon has under-
gone a constant metamorphosis on the Indian stage. On the stage,
in contrast to the debate in educational institutions, the plays
have taken many divergent forms, ranging from English adaptations to unrecognizable indigenous translations. As a result, the
grip of the colonial "civilizing mission" has been considerably
loosened. A striking aspect of this process has been the adaptation
of Shakespearean dramaturgy to native theatrical traditions drawn
from folk drama like *Yakshagana* and the classical dance forms of
Kathakali. Such a rich, though uneven, diversity of interpretations
on the stage has given the lie to the notion of a "timeless" text,
while implicitly undermining Trevelyan's mocking challenge to
produce a "native Shakespeare."

In mapping these Indian theatrical appropriations of the past
hundred years, one can note multifaceted and contingent responses
to the canonical, "classic" Shakespeare, in contrast to the diligent
veneration of his works found in standard Indian literary criticism
and pedagogy. These stage versions show us that when Shakespeare is produced in a theatrical, as opposed to a discursive,

idiom, endless possibilities of interpretation open up, as German director Fritz Bennewitz (working in India) recently suggested: "what happens when a live body like Shakespeare meets a live body like Indian theatre? The meeting can never happen in the universities, only in the streets, in the theatres" (quoted in Gahlot 1991: 8).

Given the Indian theater's innovative and sometimes eclectic re-interpretations of Shakespeare, it would be appropriate to suggest that in their methods, the original works go through a process of *transculturation*, a term used by ethnographers to define a process whereby marginal or subordinate groups "select and invent from materials transmitted to them by a dominant culture" (Pratt 1992: 6). Within nineteenth-century educational policy, Shake-speare's works constituted the "colonial book," aligned to specific cultural and pedagogical practices. However, the emerging theater community at the time, particularly in Calcutta, transformed the Shakespearean texts through various strategies of translation and adaptation, thereby undermining their canonical association with European or metropolitan culture. This process of transculturation has continued to influence the politics of interculturalism through the postcolonial era.

Let us now examine this process of *transculturation* of Shake-speare's works from the mid-nineteenth century to the early twentieth century in Bengal. As I have suggested earlier, these works were fairly popular in amateur theatrical activities involving elite Bengali students, especially with the founding of Hindu College in 1816. The influence of teachers such as D.L. Richardson, who was also the founder of the Chowringhee theater, led to the wide-spread practice of reciting or acting scenes from the plays: "In 1837 Bengali students staged the Court Scene from *The Merchant of Venice* in the Governor's House, in 1852 and 1853 the students of the Metropolitan Academy and David Hare Academy staged Shakespeare's Plays" (S.K. Bhattacharya 1964: 29).

In 1853 former students of the Oriental Academy together with current students raised funds to found the Oriental Theatre, which staged *Othello* in 1853 and *Henry IV* in 1855. While such commitments to productions of Shakespeare in English are well known, evidence also suggests an awareness, both in the Oriental Theatre and in Indian culture, of the *hybrid* nature of this venture. An advertisement in *The Citizen*, March 2, 1854, for *The Merchant of Venice* suggests that this was not a professional theater of

the English or Indians, but a production by "Hindu Amateurs."
Or, in 1855, *The Hindu Patriot*, while praising a performance of
Henry IV at the same theater, bemoaned the lack of public
response and advised the staging of Bengali plays.[16]

Nineteenth-century productions of Shakespeare in Calcutta
coincided with the development of a vigorous Bengali theater.
But there is some debate regarding the influence of the Bard
beyond the period of the English theaters in Calcutta, which
lasted till the end of the last century. Most theater historians
agree that contact with vigorous theatrical activity among the
English produced a "Renaissance" in the Bengali theater, which
coincided with the larger movement of cultural consciousness
among elite Bengalis. The loose plot-constructions of Shakespeare's plays provided popular models for indigenous playwrights, who found little of use in the classical plot structures of
Greek dramas with their unities or in neoclassical French plays.
The romantic story lines of Bengali plays also seem closer to
Shakespearean multiple plots and their free use of space and time
dimensions than to classical Sanskrit five-act dramas.

Poet and dramatist Rabindranath Tagore testifies to this interest: "Shakespeare's plays have always been our ideal of drama.
Their complexity due to multiple branches of plot . . . clash and
conflict have attracted our mind from the very beginning"
(quoted in S.K. Bhattacharya 1964: 33). By all accounts, critics
and dramatists used Shakespearean criteria to judge other plays,
sometimes even via a critique of the model, as one dramatist
chided another:

> I wish you had not thought of Shakespeare so much as you
> appear to have done, when you sat down to peruse poor
> *Kissen Kumari*. Some of the defects you point out are defects
> indeed, but it does not fall to the lot of every one to rise super-
> ior to them, and even Shakespeare himself does not do so often.
>
> (ibid.: 32)

Others followed Shakespeare's practice of mixing comic elements
in tragic plays, as the famous poet–dramatist Madhusudan Dutt
recommends to a colleague:

> The only piece of criticism I shall venture upon is . . . never
> strive to be comic in a tragedy, but if an opportunity presents

itself . . . do not neglect it in the less important scenes, so as to have an agreeable variety. This I believe to be Shakespeare's plan. You will not find many scenes in his higher tragedies in which he is studiously comic.

(ibid.: 33)

Overall, however, the Bard's influence cannot be measured by the number of productions of his plays translated or adapted for the Bengali public or commercial stage—as these numbers gradually declined between the years 1874 and 1920. In part, language became the deciding factor in the decline of the English plays (among Bengalis) and the emergence of a Bengali repertoire of plays, as well as Sanskrit plays. However, Shakespeare's effect on this native movement cannot be underestimated in that the budding playwrights and critics of Bengal drew on his concept of tragedy, his tragi-comic dramaturgy, and his multi-faceted characters. The actual products of this influence, the Bengali adaptations of Shakespeare of the late nineteenth and early twentieth centuries, were striking in terms of their cultural hybridity. Popularly known as company *nataks* (or company productions), these Bengali adaptations reproduced Shakespeare's plays in the context of the pictorial realism of Victorian theater (touched up by nineteenth-century French melodramas) quite removed from the stylized conventions of their Elizabethan origins.

The efforts that went into them offered clear evidence of the processes of *transculturation* as these playwrights, like *bricoleurs*, freely improvised on the elements of the colonial texts. Translating them into another idiom, they could choose "what aspect of the Western form [to] use and what [to] absorb into it" (Pratt 1992: 5–7). In 1893, Girish Chandra Ghosh, noted stage figure in Bengal, translated and produced *Macbeth* with painstaking care at the Minerva Theatre in Calcutta. The production proudly announced its indigenous influences in an advertisement in the newspaper, *Amrita Bazar Patrika*, on January 28, 1893: the headline promises the audiences "Shakespeare in Bengal" with a Bengali version of *Macbeth*. While the set, the announcement declares, was "mounted by European artists," the performance had its own distinctive character. According to a contemporary issue of *The Englishman*, "a Bengali Thane of Cawdor is a living suggestion of incongruity, but the reality is an astonishing reproduction" (quoted in Mukherjee 1982: 81–2).

Many other Bengali adaptations of Shakespeare, reflecting varying degrees of transformation of the originals, also made their
appearance on the Calcutta stage, as the following examples
show: on June 21, 1897, a popular and somewhat carefree adaptation of *Hamlet*, entitled *Hariraja*, was produced by Nagendra
Chaudhry in the Classic Theatre; on December 4, 1915, *Saudagar*,
an adaptation of *The Merchant of Venice*, was staged by Bhupen-
dra Bandhopadhya; and on March 18, 1919, *Othello*, translated
by Devendra Nath Basu, was also performed at the Star Theatre.
Productions such as these often re-created Shakespeare's works in
ways that were superficial and formulaic, focussing on dramatic
devices, often with inaccuracies in the primary materials, in order
to make them more appealing to the audiences of a commercial
theater (Raha c. 1965: 25-6; S.K. Bhattacharya 1964: 30–1). While
these productions in themselves did not achieve great heights,
cumulatively they invigorated the Bengali dramatic Renaissance,
in the way, as one critic describes, Girish Chandra Ghosh absorbed
Shakespeare:

> Ghosh . . . studied Shakespeare as none had done before
> him, from the combined viewpoints of avid student, an actor,
> director, producer, and playwright. . . . One can detect the influ-
> ence in the . . . contrivances of plot, and more importantly, in
> his adoption of the external devices of Shakespeare's plays,
> like cruel murders, ghosts, sudden deaths, transvestite decep-
> tions. . . . Resemblances can be found in many of the characters
> he created [in his own works] . . . Falstaff, the Fool, Lady
> Macbeth, and Queen Margaret.
>
> (Raha c. 1965: 24)

Such cultural encounters with Shakespeare on the commercial
Bengali stage (after the theater moved out of the households of
the aristocracy) was accompanied by the production of plays
depicting the glory of Hindu heroism and national regeneration.
In this process, evocations of a new golden age of India, aiming
at independence, emerged in conjunction with English literary
values (Bagchi 1991: 155). Thus, ironically, Shakespeare, among
other Western writers, became an important context for the
Bengalis' rediscovery of their own cultural identity as well as of a
burgeoning nationalism.

Today, theater historians do not recall these productions as
artistic achievements, but as contemporary playwright Girish

Karnad notes: "[Shakespeare] comes to us through [these] Company Nataks . . . [a] tradition which was influenced by the 19th Century Victorian theatre, which in turn is derivative of Shakespeare . . . ultimately a reduction to absurdum of Shakespeare's plotting" (quoted in Sondhi and Nadkarni c. 1980: 14). From 1920 to the 1940s Shakespeare's plays disappeared from the Calcutta stage, as the repertoire of original Bengali plays grew. But one can still infer that their influence pervaded the intellectual and imaginative lives of students, scholars, and theatrical figures from the mid-nineteenth century onwards. This is evident from the fact that Shakespeare has been translated into Bengali far more than any other foreign author.[17]

VI

While the company *nataks* were indebted to English theatrical traditions, even while adapting the originals to local tastes, the Shakespeare revivals on the Bengali stage after Indian independence were markedly different from the earlier colonial versions. Prior to independence, the discourse about Shakespeare was framed within a colonial trope of civilization, the assumptions of which were eagerly accepted by the native elites. In contrast, postcolonial Shakespearean theater, in most instances, self-consciously attempted to acquire an indigenous identity, free from the British criteria of cultural value. One aspect of these hybrid productions of Shakespeare meant that they undermined the colonial binaries of tradition and modernity. As Indian directors and translators re-cast canonical Western plays within indigenous dramaturgical traditions, while often commenting on contemporary postcolonial social realities, they forced their audiences to re-examine their historical bearings in the past, present, and future—as well as among colonial and native cultural forms and their differing social functions.

The new, postcolonial drama movement of the mid-1940s had a two-fold purpose: of introducing the plays of famous dramatists, ancient and modern, to Bengal, and of making drama more responsive to the social and political realities of the Indian masses. And Shakespeare figured prominently in this hybrid endeavor of applying contemporary concerns to Western canonical texts. The name most associated with such a revival of Shakespeare is that of Utpal Dutt, noted actor/director and revolutionary. Starting his theatrical training with Geoffrey Kendall's Shakespeareana company in 1947, Dutt started his own Little Theatre Group in Calcutta to produce Shakespeare's plays in English.

By 1951, members of Dutt's group had begun to share his revolutionary zeal in producing a political theater. Hence, they "realized that they could not presume to be radical so long as they continued to perform Shakespeare's [plays in English], exclusively for a minority audience, the Westernized intellectuals of Calcutta" (quoted in Bharucha 1983). Dutt's revolutionary theater was close to Brecht's epic theater in its instructive goals. According to Dutt, "the political theatre must ceaselessly assail the thinking habits of its players, the grooves and patterns in which they find themselves and are quite content in" (ibid.: 30). Like Brecht, he wanted drama to challenge conventions of realism, wrestling with notions of "falsehood" and "truth" variously applied to the dramatic effects, but he felt that "Brecht's historicizing . . . seemed to be too intellectual, too cerebral an exercise for an audience nurtured on the violence and mimesis of folk theatre" (2).

While the theoretical underpinnings of Dutt's theory were diffuse and sometimes contradictory, it was motivated by the idea of bringing Shakespeare to the masses. According to him, "the classics were not a prerogative of an elite. They would cease to exist unless they were brought to the people."[18] In his Bengali translation of *Macbeth*, which toured several villages, he immersed the Western play in the ritual world of *Jatra*, the vigorous folk theater of Bengal. By thus transforming Shakespeare's language into a bold, declamatory form of incantation, typical of *Jatra*, Dutt's company brought Shakespeare to the rural masses who had never figured in the colonial project of edification. The rural audience responded to the *Jatra Macbeth* as a mythic spectacle, which Dutt believed to be important to a non-elitist revolutionary theater. Describing his staging techniques for the production, Dutt stated that his purpose was to "try to shake the audience out of its unthinking stupor by sensation, visual surprise, songs, dances, and color on stage."[19]

Bringing Shakespeare to the villages meant rejecting the conventions of the Victorian proscenium stage and working with indigenous theatrical traditions. Ironically, as critics have noted, Dutt's rural production of *Macbeth* was probably closer to the blood and guts of the Elizabethan theater than many recent European revivals. In fact, according to one review, the early performances in the villages were far more successful in re-creating a sense of the original Elizabethan popular theater than his later proscenium production in Calcutta, in which the play was transformed into a nineteenth-century melodrama (Bharucha 1983: 242–3). Dutt's method of merging Western and Indian theatrical traditions in the productions was not unique. In fact, such intercultural experiments in reproducing Shakespeare (and to a lesser degree Brecht) have continued to preoccupy India's theater professionals—in private companies such as the Little Theatre Group and in the National School of Drama in New Delhi.

The overarching assumption of this interest in intercultural improvisation does not presuppose an easily appropriable Shakespearean text. Rather, it takes into account language, education, and class, among others, as constituent factors in any mode of cultural production. The issue of Shakespearean language has often engaged theater intellectuals as a difficult obstacle in translation, as contemporary poet Raghuvir Sahay explains:

> There are just two of us [the poet Bacchan and Sahay himself] who have translated Shakespeare in verse and both of us are a generation apart. But Shakespeare has been translated a number of times, the same play at a different period of time in the same language. There is a significance of repeating the translation every twenty years. The target language grows— the meaning of the original text grows . . . the quality of the dramatics changes. The medium changes. This need for a Shakespeare translation after every generation emphasizes both the eternal Shakespeare and the evergrowing Shakespeare. That is Shakespeare's challenge. I met the challenge. . . . A translator's job is not to find an easier way. It is to find *the* way. And there are more difficult things to cope with. A whole culture is transferred when a translation is attempted.
>
> (quoted in Sondhi and Nadkarni c. 1980: 10)

This encounter between a Shakespearean text and its Indian translator denotes a cultural struggle separate from the thrall of a colonial or neocolonial hierarchy. In fact Sahay discusses translation in terms of the "donor language" (English) and the "recipient language," with a mediation taking place between "the quality of writing of the donor language" and the "heritage of the recipient language" (10). He seems to idealize this process of cultural exchange, especially when he describes his Hindi version of

Macbeth in the production at the National School of Drama in 1982: he argues that his translation was "independent of any form" and that he was doing it "for the love of Shakespeare," simply bridging the divide between the "place of Shakespeare" in the history of English literature and his "own relationship as a poet with [his] own language" (ibid.: 12).

For Sahay, then, translation ultimately involves subjective choices rather than a sense of a confrontation between two different cultures—a tendency that reflects his own ease with the two languages. Other theatrical experiments (like Dutt's) reflect a keener sense of the linguistic and class divisions between the Westernized urban audiences and the rural viewers. Indian director Habib Tanvir vividly describes these cultural divisions in his improvisations from *A Midsummer Night's Dream* with his troupe of folk actors from an area called Chattisgarh. These are a community of tribals, mostly peasants, belonging to an ethnic minority in India. As members of Tanvir's company, they have performed in a variety of productions that use tribal/folk theatrical traditions. Tanvir describes his experiment in using the "mechanicals' play" as an exercise in improvisation:

> I did two little improvisations with my Chattisgarhi folk actors. . . . One episode was from *A Midsummer Night's Dream*, where the weaver, the Tinker, the Tailor etc. act out the tragedy of "Pyramus and Thisby." I assembled the scene in a few days as a demonstration of sorts. I chose it for the obvious reason that Shakespeare goes rural here and deals with rustic actors. Even this little episode, with my illiterate rural actors, had problems. This wasn't because they couldn't capture the vitality, the robustness and the apparent coarseness of those very funny rustics of Shakespeare's play. The problem was the scene in its totality. Its depth and dimension are experienced only through the comments and asides of the Duke and Duchess and the genteel people who are watching the folk performance . . . with comments and asides. . . . I didn't have the actors to convey all this. Strangely, even to portray Shakespeare's rustics, there has to be somewhere a very refined actor . . . the important point is that the urban refinement in the actor is an essential prerequisite for any attempt at Shakespeare.
>
> (ibid.: 13)

While Tanvir points out the difficulties of cultural translation and the need for refined actors, he also reminds us, via his use of tribals, of the popular and non-elitist aspects of Shakespeare's works. Perhaps the most significant aspect of this production was its conception as a bi-lingual or multi-lingual adaptation, as described in a recent review:

> Ultimately Tanvir came back to the . . . *Dream* because it offered him the best strategy of bilingualism. The Duke and his entourage would speak English; the people of the woods would converse in Urdu and the artisans would opt for their [Chattisgarhi] dialect. The harassment of the artisans by Puck on a physical level would get reinforced by the use of a foreign tongue and that could be fun.
>
> (Padmanabhan 1994: 11)

In the end, Tanvir had to produce a somewhat truncated production with only two strands of the plot and without the English actors, but hopes to mount his original idea in the future.[20] The point of this production was not only to show linguistic and class divisions between the English and the Indians, but also between the Indians and the ethnic tribals, as Tanvir explains: "the ethnic community is alienated from both the English and Indian culture" (S. Bhattacharya 1994: 2).

Such experiments in mixing traditions have been the concern of many Indian directors adapting Shakespeare (as they have been in other cultures). For instance, when *King Lear* was presented as a Kathakali dance drama at the Edinburgh Festival in 1990, Western critics had mixed responses. Their reviews went under such headings as "Cultural hodge podge" and "Empty gestures." Audiences in India, including Kerala, the home of the Kathakali, also found the performance "bizarre" (Awasthi 1993: 172). This failed effort, according to Awasthi and other critics, reveals the importance of a thorough understanding of performance traditions before application to another culture. By refashioning a script into an idiomatic non-poetic language aligned to Kathakali's largely non-verbal tradition, the production rendered Shakespeare's text, with its dense narrative and complex interweaving of plot and sub-plots, thin and greatly reduced in dramatic power (ibid.). More importantly, the

type-denoting Kathakali make-up easily transformed Shakespeare's characters into stereotypes, all either absolutely virtuous or . . . evil. Cordelia and the King of France represented
absolute virtue and Goneril and Regan absolute evil, thus
destroying the moral complexity of the play and the equally
complex psychological interplay within and between the
characters.

(ibid.)

Thus, this intercultural experiment stifled aspects of both traditions, while diffusing the subtleties of *King Lear* into gestural
theatrics.

But this example does not mean that such mergers between the
two performance cultures are impossible. In 1982, B.V. Karanth
overcame some of these problems in his production of *Macbeth*
called *Barnam Vana* (Birnam Wood). Presenting Sahay's new
verse translation in Hindi at the National School of Drama (mentioned earlier), he drew on the stylized form, and not the structure,
of the Indian folk tradition, *Yakshagana*. By form, I mean the
method of acting, lighting, and music, which Karanth adapted,
while keeping close to the Shakespearean language (verbatim) and
plot. In the case of costumes, he found the following solution:

[Karanth] . . . stated that *Yakshagana* characters, who are from
Indian mythology, have fixed dresses. In fact they are recognized from the headgear they wear. So, in order not to replicate
those costumes and confuse the audience, he has had to base
them on the traditional theatre costumes of Asian countries
like Bali, Japan, Cambodia, Burma and Indonesia.

(Sahay, quoted in Sondhi and Nadkarni c. 1980: 13)

This production kept intact the language and psychological
complexity of the Renaissance text, while enriching it with a
stylized indigenous idiom. The result was not merely decorative,
as Oriental tradition often becomes when used in the West.
Rather, a process of *transculturation* took place, whereby *Macbeth*
was transposed into a familiar idiom, making Shakespeare, as one
critic remarked, truly "our contemporary."

Alongside these various examples of cross-cultural Shakespeare,
we must not forget that in India the Bard's plays are regu-
larly staged in English before elite, Anglicized audiences. A 1990

production of *Othello* in Bombay testifies to a new kind of commodification of the English Shakespeare—one not based on a colonial reverence, but on a growing urban population looking for novel modes of entertainment. Directed by noted stage director, Alyque Padamsee, who "knows how to market anything from Shakespeare to Strindberg," this glamorous version drew large audiences. Reviewers testified to its popularity, in part because of its cast of well-known film stars. From all accounts the production lacked cultural specificity and most reviewers described *Othello* in Bombay as a tragedy of "jealousy" and "misunderstanding" (Bharvani 1991: 9). Except for one scene of Othello's self-flagellation, which some saw in Islamic terms, Padamsee's "magnificent" version did not engage with the racial politics that have a particular resonance in the West, but evoke little interest in India.

Culturally neutral English productions such as Padamsee's are commonplace in urban centers in contemporary India. But they do not conform to the standards of politically conscious critics trying to mediate between Western and Eastern traditions—as well as between "high" and "low" culture—especially as these socio-economic divisions are held in place by the English language. Even the English Shakespeare Company, touring India in 1991, followed their English productions with a "Land Rover Tour," in which they performed Shakespeare to audiences with no access to conventional theater, using performance skills rather than linguistic ones to communicate (McGill 1991). These concerns of the British company, dividing its time between urban stage productions and grassroots versions, characterize the complex performance history of Shakespeare in colonial and postcolonial India—a history that foregrounds India's divisions between colonial and native cultures, and between differing visions of "tradition" and "modernity."

VII

Postcolonial theorists, most notably Bharucha, have drawn our attention to Western appropriations of Indian and other Eastern theatrical traditions. Theater practitioners in the West such as Grotowski, Craig, Schechner, and Brook, they argue, have appropriated and decontextualized Indian conventions in ways that range from the ethnocentric to the eclectic. Rustom Bharucha, particularly, views this interculturalism as an ethical travesty. He argues on the ground that these Western appropriations represent Indian "tradition" as static and as immutable, without any regard for its present "socio-cultural condition." Thus, he makes a persuasive case connecting these contemporary forms of "cultural tourism" to colonial hierarchies and their residual manifestations (Bharucha 1993: 3–4). Bharucha's argument is useful in making us aware of the "performative realities" of drama and of Western appropriations which "fail to contextualize Indian performance traditions within the minutiae of their ever-changing histories" (4). But it is arguable whether one can set precise standards for theatrical adaptations. Shall we, for instance, demand "accurate" reproductions of Elizabethan stage conditions? And more importantly, the issue of Indian appropriations of Western texts such as Shakespeare is largely excluded from the scope of Bharucha's inquiry.

Thus, in mapping the East–West cultural struggle in the aftermath of colonialism, one has to consider this interculturalism as a two-way process, one in which native cultural forms often undergo a complex process of *transculturation*, as I have demonstrated. In this interaction, Shakespeare's works, for instance, constitute what Bharucha defines as the "source culture" which is "transformed, 'restored,' broken up, reconstituted and placed in an altogether different *mise-en-scène* intelligible to an audience of the target [Indian] culture."[21] In this context, an Indian assimilation or *transculturation* of colonial models such as Shakespeare, via the proscenium stage of the nineteenth century, tells us a different story of interculturalism. It is a story of a developing theatrical idiom that undermines the binary opposition between the colonizer and colonized, thus offering a counterpoint to the revered Shakespeare of the nineteenth-century colonial "civilizing mission" and the mainstay of postcolonial criticism and pedagogy. On the Indian stage, multi-lingual, hybrid Shakespearean productions have consistently countered the univocal authority of the colonial book. As a result they have enabled native directors to re-discover indigenous cultural forms via the revered Shakespearean canon. Thus no longer a mouthpiece for the "civilizing mission," Shakespeare "speaks" in many voices on the contemporary Indian stage.

NOTES

1 For a full account of the rise and development of the English theaters in the social milieu of colonial Calcutta, refer to my earlier essay, "Different Shakespeares: The Bard in Colonial/Postcolonial India" (Singh 1989). Also see Mukherjee 1982: 1–7; Guha-Thakurta 1930: 40–8; Bharucha 1983: 7–9; and Raha 1978: 8–12.

2 A discussion of this performance and the public response to it can be found in Mukherjee 1982: 7.

3 Shakespeare's popularity in Britain during the eighteenth and nineteenth centuries was reflected in the conventions of pictorial realism and literal historicism. These in turn led to an interest in the lives of the characters, which extended to contriving imaginary biographies. The infusion of a romanticized realism into Shakespeare's plays, when transported to the colonial stage, influenced the shape of Bengali drama or company *nataks*, which originated at the time. For an account of the nineteenth-century popularity of Shakespeare, see Oakley 1986: especially 8–20.

4 I base my discussion of the production of English literary studies on Vishwanathan's study (1989), especially 1–45. Also see my earlier essay (Singh 1989).

5 See Vishwanathan's filtration theory (1989: 57–80, 116–17). Also note Loomba's obervations (1989: 22–3).

6 My reference to Gramsci draws on G. Vishwanathan's application of his notion of hegemony (1989: 1–3).

7 My use of the term *transculturation* derives from Pratt 1992: 5–6, and I discuss it at length later in this chapter.

8 I take this term from the collection of essays entitled *Shakespeare in India*, which assumes the "universal" appeal of the Bard in India (Nagarajan and Vishwanathan 1987).

9 Reading Fanon's *Black Skin, White Masks*, especially 1–80, one can see the effects of colonial liberalism such as Trevelyan's, which created a disjunction within the black psyche. The colonized subjects wanted to become like the rulers, via their culture and language, but the results were not positive. Thus Fanon gives the lie to Trevelyan's vision of the future. Homi Bhabha's essay, "Signs taken for Wonders" (1985), is also useful in identifying native responses to the "colonial book," through strategies that are "at once a mode of appropriation and resistance" (162).

10 See Vishwanathan's discussion of the nineteenth-century English curriculum (1989: 54), as a representative example of the debates of the time.

11 For the background to the fashion of literary societies, see *Calcutta Review* (1852): 18, vii, and (1855): 24, i–iii. Also see Bagchi's departure (1991: 146–58) from Vishwanathan's focus on the designs of colonial masters. She examines the "initiative of the Bengali elite in the introduction of English studies in Bengal" (147), and in the creation of a "new class of a Hindu male elite" (152).

12 This description of the post-imperial ideology of English literature is taken from Loomba 1989: 19–23, especially her discussion of an earlier version (1988) of Jashodhara Bagchi's essay, "Shakespeare in Loin Cloths."

13 A detailed analysis of the continuing dominance of the English language can be found in Whittey 1971: 4–6. Also see Loomba 1989: 31.

14 These figures for Delhi University students are from the years 1983–4 and have probably increased by now. See Loomba 1989: 28–9.

15 Some qualifying factors must be noted here, namely that an interest in Western drama was accompanied by the revival of classical Sanskrit drama—as a part of the Renaissance of Indian cultural forms. According to Sudipto Chatterjee (1995), "when the tenets and principles of Western drama started influencing Bengali theatre more palpably, this strong inclination for both Sanskrit texts and subjects continued to thrive . . . even in the midst of the Western style theatre that was adopted by the Bengalis" (23).

16 For a more detailed account of the stage history of this period, see Singh 1989: 44–5.

17 According to Farley Richmond, "nearly two thousand adaptations and translations [of Shakespeare] have been created in Indian languages" (Richmond et al. 1990: 438). Because of more flexible copyright laws, it is difficult to trace the exact number of adaptations in the different languages. According to Raha (c. 1965), Bengali adaptations or translations seem most popular.

18 A detailed discussion of Dutt's views on Shakespeare and popular culture can be found in his interview in *Sunday* (1985: 2–3).

19 A good account of his views on the social function of drama can be found in Dutt 1982: 15–27. Also see Bharucha 1983: 56–63.

20 British actors of the English Shakespeare Company were supposed to join Tanvir's cast as the courtiers, but the British Council did not have the funds to support them. See Santwana Bhattacharya 1994: 2.

21 While Bharucha's concluding analysis and critique of theories of interculturism do not consider Eastern borrowing of Western traditions, his assumptions about the colonial underpinnings of interculturalism are useful. Especially see, Bharucha 1993: 240–50.

WORKS CITED IN CHAPTER 4

Anonymous ("A Hindustani"). "The Bible and Shakespeare." In *Bengal Magazine*, Vol. 5, December 1876: 228–35.

Awasthi, Suresh. "Plays for the Proletariat." In *The Economic Times*, June 14, 1993: 10.

—— "The Intercultural Experience and the Kathakali *King Lear*." In *New Theatre Quarterly*, 34, 1993: 172–8.

Bagchi, Jasodhara. "Shakespeare in Loin Cloths: English Literature and the Early Nationalist Consciousness in Bengal." In *Rethinking English: Essays in Literature, Language, History*. Ed. Svati Joshi. New Delhi: Trianka Press, 1991: 146–59.

Bhabha, Homi. "Signs taken for Wonders: Questions of Ambivalence and Authority under a Tree outside New Delhi—May 1817." In *Critical Inquiry*, 12, 1, 1985: 143–65.

Bharucha, Rustom. *Rehearsals of Revolution: The Political Theatre of Bengal*. Honolulu: University of Hawaii Press, 1983.

—— *Theatre and the World: Performance and the Politics of Culture*. London: Routledge, 1993.

Bharvani, Shakuntala. Review of Padamsee's production of *Othello*. In *Afternoon Despatch and Courier*, February 4, 1991: 9.

Bhattacharya, Santwana. Review of Tanvir's *A Midsummer Night's Dream*. In *Indian Express*, March, 1994: 2–3.

Bhattacharya, S.K. "Shakespeare and the Bengali Theatre." In *Indian Literature*, 7, 1964: 27–40.

Calcutta Review. vols 18 (1852) and 24 (1855).

Carey, Eustace. Ed. *Memoirs of William Carey, D.D.* Boston: Gould, Kendall & Lincoln, 1836.

Carlyle, Thomas. "The Hero as Poet. Dante; Shakespeare." (1840). In *On Heroes, Hero-Worship, and the Heroic in History*. Chicago and New York: Rand McNally, n.d.

Chatterjee, Sudipto. "*Mise-En-(Colonial)-Scène*: The Theatre of the Bengal Renaissance." In *Imperialism and Theatre*. Ed. J. Ellen Gainor. London: Routledge, 1995: 19–37.

Dutt, Utpal. *Towards a Revolutionary Theatre*. Calcutta: M.C. Sarker & Sons, 1982.

—— "Interview: A Weapon of Change." In *Sunday*, November 3, 1985: 2–3.

Eagleton, Terry. *Literary Theory: An Introduction*. Minneapolis: University of Minnesota Press, 1983.

Eden, Emily. *Letters From India, 1837–40*. London: n.p., 1872.

Fanon, Frantz. *Black Skin, White Masks*. Trans. Charles Lamm. New York: Grove Press, 1967.

Gahlot, Deepa. "India's Shakespeare Connection." In *The Times of India*, September 22, 1991: 8.

Guha-Thakurta, P. *The Bengali Drama: Its Origin and Development*. London: Kegan Paul, 1930.

Heinemann, Margot. "How Brecht read Shakespeare." In *Political Shakespeare: New Essays in Cultural Materialism*. Ed. Jonathan Dollimore and Alan Sinfield. Ithaca: Cornell University Press, 1985.

Loomba, Ania. *Gender, Race, Renaissance Drama*. Manchester: University of Manchester Press, 1989.

McGill, Stewart. "The Shakespearewallahs: Review of the 'English Shakespeare Company.'" In *Indian Express*, February 17, 1991: 11.

Mukherjee, Sushil K. *The Story of the Calcutta Theatres 1753–1980*. Calcutta: K.P Bagchi, 1982.

Muliyil, G. "Why Shakespeare for Us?" In *The Literary Criterion*, Vol. VI, 1963: 79–85.

Nagarajan, S. and S. Vishwanathan. Eds. *Shakespeare in India*. Oxford: Oxford University Press, 1987.

Narasimhaiah, C.D. "Foreword." In *The Literary Criterion*, VI, 1963: iii–vi (special number on Shakespeare).

Oakley, Lucy. "Words into Pictures: Shakespeare in British Art, 1760–1900." In *A Brush with Shakespeare: The Bard in Painting, 1780–1910*. Montgomery: Montgomery Museum of Fine Arts, 1986: 3–20.

Padmanabhan, Chitra. "The Playful Rites of Spring: Review of *A Midsummer Night's Dream*." In *The Economic Times*, March 8, 1994: 10–11.

Parekh, Bhikhu. "Superior People: The Narrowness of Liberalism from Mill to Rawls." In *Times Literary Supplement*, February 25, 1994: 11–13.

Parliamentary Papers: Second Report from the Select Committee of the House of Lords, together with the Minutes of the Evidence, Vol. 32, 1852–3.

Pratt, Mary Louise. *Imperial Eyes: Travel Writing and Transculturation*. London: Routledge, 1992.

Raha, Kironmoy. *Bengali Theatre*. New Delhi: National Book Trust, 1978.

—— "Shakespeare and the Bengali Theater." New Delhi: n.p., c. 1965: 22–6.

Richmond, Farley P., Darius L. Swann, and Phillip B. Zarrilli. Eds. *Indian Theatre: Traditions of Performance*. Honolulu: University of Hawaii Press, 1990.

Singh, Jyotsna. "Different Shakespeares: The Bard in Colonial/Postcolonial India." In *Theatre Journal*, 14, 4, 1989: 445–58.

Singh, Nanda. "The Selling of Shakespeare." Review of *Othello*. In *Free Press Journal*, December 2, 1990: 1–2.

Sondhi, Reeta and Dnyaneshwar Nadkarni. "Interviews: The Relevance of Shakespeare in India." New Delhi: n.p., c. 1980: 9–15.

Taylor, William. *Thirty-Eight Years in India*, Vols I and II. London: W.H. Allen, 1882.

Trevelyan, Charles. *On the Education of the People of India*. London: Orient Longman, 1838.

Vishwanathan, Gauri. *Masks of Conquest: Literary Study and British Rule in India*. New York: Columbia University Press, 1989.

Whittey, Steve. "English Language as a Tool of British Neocolonialism." In *East Africa Journal*, 8, 1971: 2–6.

Yajnik, R.K. *The Indian Theatre: Its Origins and its Later Developments under European Influence*. London: George Allen & Unwin, 1933.

Chapter 5

The Blind Age: discovering a postcolonial nation

I

Often as I wandered from meeting to meeting, I spoke to my audience of this India of ours, of Hindustan and of Bharata, the old
Sanskrit name derived from the mythical founder of the race. . . .
  Sometimes as I reached a gathering [of peasants], a great roar of
welcome would greet me: *Bharat Mata Ki Jai*—Victory to Mother
India! . . . I would [then] endeavour to . . . explain that India was
all this that they had thought, but it was much more. The mountains and the rivers of India, and the forests and the broad fields,
which gave us food, were all dear to us, but what counted ultimately
were the people of India, people like them and me, who were spread
out all over this vast land. *Bharat Mata*, Mother India, was essentially these millions of people and victory to her meant victory to
these people. You are parts of this *Bharat Mata*, I told them, you
are in a manner yourselves, *Bharat Mata*, and as this idea slowly
soaked into their brains, their eyes would light up as if they had
made a great discovery.

(Nehru 1959: 28–30)

In this episode from Jawaharlal Nehru's *The Discovery of India*,
first published in 1945, the new nation-state emerges from the
trope of discovery. For Nehru, it seems, India has mythical and
romantic associations, much as the notion of a fabled "India/
Indies" had for the seventeenth-century travel writers and the
golden age of Hinduism had for the eighteenth-century colonial
Orientalists. Countering the peasants' experiential understanding
of geography, Nehru (India's first Prime Minister) struggles to
define the concept of a nation to which they all belonged. Discrete
images of nature—the "mountains and rivers . . . the forests and
broad fields"—coalesce in his abstract personification of "Mother
India." While the narrator transforms the new nation-state into

an embodiment of beneficence and plenitude, ironically, he invokes an old myth of origin to give it a coherent, unifying identity, harking back to Bharata, "the mythical founder of the race."

Such invocations of a past in India's common "spirit" and shared myth of origins appear frequently in his book, paradoxically representing the modernity of Indian *swaraj* or self-rule through a recuperation of its ancient culture. However, more importantly, the focus of Nehru's ideological construction of India's national identity is in the image of a *unified* national state. In the opening chapter of *The Discovery of India*, Nehru explains that his search for India is not for an "anthropomorphic entity," given the "diversities and divisions of Indian life, of classes, castes, religions, races, different degrees of cultural development" (27–8). However, while acknowledging difference, he nonetheless asserts that a "country with a long cultural background and a common outlook on life develops a spirit that is peculiar to it and is impressed on its children" (28). To build a home for India's future, the author argues, "we would have to dig deep for foundations" (28). Thus, in Nehru's characteristically liberal vision, India becomes an accommodating ideal, one which seamlessly binds together the pre-colonial past with the moment of independence as it brings together different "classes, castes, religions, races" (28). At times, Nehru even resorts to essentialist, Oriental clichés to evoke a unified India with an inscrutable, feminized identity (27):

> India with all her infinite charm and variety began to grow upon me more and more, and yet the more I saw of her, the more I realized how very difficult it was for me or for anyone else to grasp the ideas she had embodied. . . . She [India] was like some ancient palimpsest on which layer upon layer of thought and revery had been inscribed. . . . All of these existed together in our conscious or subconscious selves, . . . and they had gone to build up the complex and mysterious personality of India. That sphinxlike face with its elusive and sometimes mocking smile was to be seen throughout the length and breadth of the land.

Such essentializing moves enable his narrative to rhetorically elide all divisive forces into a lyrical unity, as he states: "Though outwardly, there was diversity and infinite variety among our people, everywhere there was that tremendous impress of oneness, which has held all of us together for ages past . . . the unity of

India was no longer merely an intellectual conception for me; it was an emotional experience which overpowered me" (27). Here, Nehru's premise seems to suggest that people should not intellectually consider existing divisions, but should, instead, give themselves over to the emotional sway of a romanticized, unifying abstraction of common origins.

In the dominant Indian nationalist discourse, articulated by Nehru here, the unifying figure of the nation—of *Hindustan*, of *Bharat Mata*—symbolically bridges the social, regional, and economic differences among its subjects or "children" within a teleology of progress and modernity.[1] Insofar as this nationalist discourse was anti-colonial, it was strengthened by positioning itself in stark opposition to the singular hegemony of the British Raj against which all Indians had fought and won. Therefore, ironically, while colonial discourse enabled the "discovery" of a new India through *swaraj* or self-rule, it also refurbished the role of a centralized nation, with its extended regime of power. There is much evidence to argue that what most postcolonial nations have in common is a centralized state, which holds in check the pulls between nationalism and regionalism as well as new versions of tradition and reform (Sunder Rajan 1993: 6). While these tensions and pulls in the fabric of the Indian state are more apparent now, Nehru's emotional evocations did not acknowledge any strains or even foresee them. Instead, he creates a benign picture of unity and continuity by discursively eliding India's future of modernity with a shared myth of origins, of its common "spirit" or *Geist*, in the romantic sense.

Underwriting Nehru's lyrical vision of a unified India is a European nationalist discourse echoing the nineteenth-century colonial liberalism in which differences were harnessed to produce the idea of the nation as Homi Bhabha describes it: "a continuous narrative of national progress."[2] Such a rational, positivist narrative, combining past and future in a shared glory, was characteristic of the post-enlightenment age of nationalism in Europe, which coincided with the ebbing of religious belief. As Benedict Anderson explains, while nation-states were "widely conceded to be 'new' and 'historical,' the nations to which they give political expression always loom out of an immemorial past, and glide into a limitless future. It is the magic of nationalism to change chance into destiny" (1983: 19). Such a sense of predestination was clearly evoked by Ernest Renan in his 1882 lecture, "What is a nation?"

> A nation is a soul, a spiritual principle. Two things, which in truth are but one, constitute this soul or spiritual principle. One lies in the past, one in the present. One is possession in common of a rich legacy of memories; the other is present-day consent, the desire to live together, the will to perpetuate the value of the heritage that one has received in an undivided form.
>
> (Renan 1990: 19)

Such a mystification of nineteenth-century nationalism was underpinned by an acceptance of a universal standard of "progress" by which the development of a particular national culture is measured (Chatterjee 1986: 1). Thus, according to Partha Chatterjee, the liberal rationalist European (from the nineteenth through the twentieth century) "can first identify in positive terms, and then 'sympathetically' understand, the difficult conditions under which the poor and oppressed [colonized] nations of the world have to strive to attain those universal values of reason, liberty, and progress" so crucial to the enlightenment concept of the nation (ibid.: 6). Eastern nationalism, in this formulation, supposedly appeared among "peoples recently drawn into a civilization" (2), who were called upon to shed their supposed backwardness and embrace a nationalism that went hand in hand with reason, liberty, and progress.

Thus, as Indian nationalists called for an end to colonial rule, their rhetoric embodied a paradox: on the one hand, it denied the alleged inferiority of the colonized people by asserting that a "backward" nation could modernize itself while keeping its culture; while at the same time, it accepted the intellectual premises of modernity on which colonialism was based. In doing so, it could not escape the thrall of the colonial binaries: tradition and modernity, backwardness and progress. Furthermore, while the premise of this new age was the modern framework of knowledge, Eastern nationalist discourses such as Nehru's did not reflect on how the masses would know or "discover" the new, independent India—or more broadly, on how knowledge could be independent of culture and of power (Chatterjee 1986: 1–35).

Some aspects of this paradox are summed up by Nehru in *The Discovery of India* when he reflects that at the time when Britain conquered India, there were "two Englands": one was the

England of Shakespeare and Milton, of noble speech and writing and brave deeds, of political revolution and the struggle
for freedom, of science and technical progress . . . [the other
England was the one] of the savage penal code and brutal behavior, of entrenched feudalism and reaction. . . . Which of these
two Englands came to India? It was inevitable that the wrong
England . . . should come in contact with and encourage the
wrong India in the process.

(Nehru 1959: 196–7)

As a response to this recognition, Nehru's goal, as stated in *The
Discovery of India*, is to create the right kind of modernized
India, by replacing the colonial state by a centralized nation-state
as the main agency of power. This state would be the driving
force behind economic production in postcolonial India: "no
country can be politically and economically independent . . .
unless it is highly industrialized . . . [and the economy], based on
the latest technical achievements of the day, must necessarily be a
dominating one" (144).

To sum up, the ideological premise underpinning Nehru's
nationalist thought achieves several things: it places the nation-
state at its very heart, it reinforces a colonial teleology of progress
and modernity, and more problematically, it claims a spurious
ideological unity among all citizens, irrespective of caste, religion,
sex, wealth or education—the natural entity called "Mother
India" whose "mountains . . . rivers . . . and fields . . . were all
dear to us." It is this idealized vision of a unified nation that
enables Nehru to press on with his unrelenting faith in development and modernity. While he suggests that a society must be
both "stable and progressive" (384), Nehru repeatedly reminds
his readers of India's backwardness. In his concluding meditations
on the future of the nation, he declares (393):

we [in India] have too much of the past about us and have
ignored the present. We have to get rid of that narrowing
religious outlook, that obsession with the supernatural and
metaphysical speculations, that loosening of the mind's discipline in religious, ceremonial, and mystical emotionalism. . . .
We have to come to grips with the present, this life, this world.
Some Hindus talk about going back to the Vedas; some Mos-
lems dream of an Islamic theocracy. Idle fancies, for there is

no going back to the past; there is no turning back. . . . There is
only one-way Traffic in time.

Nehru's promotion of a secular modernism, in contrast to the
"narrowing religious outlook" drawn from Hinduism or Islam,
echoes the nineteenth-century colonial project of civilizing the
natives and rescuing them from their traditions. Yet the author
seems oblivious of any similarity between the goals of the colonists
and the nationalists, and instead, puts all his faith in an abstract
idea of the future buttressed by an equally vague notion of the
"spirit of the age" (393–5). In taking his bearings between India's
past and future, Nehru basically straddles a paradox: while suggesting that "nationalism is essentially group memory of past . . .
traditions" (391), he also selectively repudiates a variety of Indian
traditions as forms of "superstition." All through the work, however, he never confronts this dichotomy while representing India
as an accommodating ideal—as Mother India.

While the nationalists like Nehru offered the Indian masses such
seamless visions of progress and unity in 1947, why has the
category of the "nation" not proved to be an entirely stable and
harmonizing ideal in postcolonial India—as well as in numerous
other countries in Africa and in South Asia? Several factors come
into play that explain the political and discursive instability of the
Indian nation. Some of these were foreseen by Rabindranath
Tagore. Although he was considered a patriot and nationalist, he
pointed out the limitations of the idea of the nation as far back
as 1917:

> Even from childhood I had been taught that the idolatry of the
> Nation is almost better than reverence for God and humanity.
> I believe I have outgrown that teaching, and it is my conviction
> that my countrymen will truly gain their India by fighting
> against the education which teaches them that a country is
> greater than the ideals of humanity.
>
> (Tagore 1917: 83)

Thus, while rejecting nationalism as a "great menace" in its
emphasis on India's *political* destiny, Tagore calls for the need for
better socialization within Indian society.[3] Political nationalism,
according to Tagore, should be secondary to and preceded by
social changes:

The thing we in India have to think of is this: to remove those social customs and ideals which have generated a want of self-respect and a complete dependence on those above us—a state of affairs which has been brought about entirely by the domination in India of the caste system, and the blind and lazy habit of relying upon the authority of traditions that are incongruous anachronisms in our present age.

(ibid.: 88)

Tagore's cautionary argument foresaw the limitations of the concept of nationhood in blindly eliding past and present as well as in ignoring the social forces pulling the country apart. Since independence, for instance, there has been a continuing split between the politics of the elite and the politics of the subaltern classes described in nationalist thought as a split between rationality and unreason and between science and faith. In this vein Nehru often mentions the "peasant, with his limited outlook" and is troubled by "the growth of this religious element in our politics" (1959: 387). Furthermore, within contemporary cultural politics in India, challenges to the centralized power of the nation-state—as envisioned by the early nationalists including Tagore—have come from other sources precisely because the dominant nationalist discourse could not harness the new forms of social populism.

Most common and dangerous among these are the threats posed by essentialist indigenisms, which in their fundamentalist and communal aspects recall imaginary entities such as "Hindu India" or call for a pure Islam in opposition to a corrupt West.[4] Yet these are precisely the institutions and practices—of both Hinduism and Islam—that Nehru and other nationalists dismissed as relics of the past. In declaring that for India, there is "no going back to the past," the nationalists blocked off any consideration of the appeal of religious ideology in the formation of a coherent identity. The demolition in 1992 of the mosque at Ayodhya, also a venerated site for Hindus, and the widespread Muslim support for the *fatwa* against Salman Rushdie are two instances of such fundamentalist attempts to define national identity. Ironically, these communal versions of national identity also set out to "discover" the real India in a mythical view of its origins in *Ram Rajya* or Hindu rule, not unlike Nehru's Mother India. However, these fundamentalist, chauvinist projects turn their backs on liberal visions of unity and instead, call for regressive social practices, such as widow-immolation, to define national culture and identity along narrow, exclusionary religious lines.[5]

Such competing versions of nationalism in postcolonial India and elsewhere, whatever their qualitative differences, point to a fractured discursive field of the "nation" rather than to Nehru's seamless vision of unity. Furthermore, they also reveal the *invention* of nations in myths, allegories, and abstractions.[6] As Ernest Gellner put it: "Nationalism is not the awakening of nations to self-consciousness: it invents nations where they do not exist" (quoted in Anderson 1983: 15). The idea that nations are invented or imagined has become a critical commonplace in the post-Foucauldian era. As Timothy Brennan explains: "Nations . . . are imaginary constructs that depend for their existence on an apparatus of cultural fictions in which imaginative literature plays a decisive role" (1990: 49).

Drawing on this relation between the nation and fiction, one can explore India's coming into being as a system of cultural signification within a complex and fragmented discursive field of the "nation." Numerous instances of ties between literature and the nation can be found in the rise of the modern nation-states of Europe, and postcolonial states are no exception. Of course, given the multi-lingual terrain of India, varied literary narratives have not cohered to create a singular national identity in the way that English literature has for Britain, one example being the mobilization of Shakespeare as the national icon of Britain and its empire, and another being the colonial novels by Kipling, Forster, and Conrad, among others, which buttressed Britain's national identity as an imperial power (Said 1993).

Nonetheless, since independence, Indian literatures have played a crucial role in shaping the cultural and political struggles within the state. In this context, the relation of literature and the formation of the Indian national identity will be discussed in this chapter from three perspectives: the Indo-Anglian realist novel; the magic-realist, postmodern vision of Salman Rushdie; and the critical reception of *The Blind Age* (*Andha Yug*), a play by Dharamvir Bharati, expressing a postmodern skepticism about grand narratives regarding India's mythic identity. In thus exploring the varied fictions that go into the making of the concept of the nation itself, one can get a sense of the competing and often ambivalent definitions of Indian nationality. For instance, while the realist novel in English draws on the dominant nationalist assumption (akin to Nehru's formulations in *The Discovery of India*), about the essence of a single Indian nation, Bharati's play implicitly echoes Tagore by dramatizing the futility of such imaginings of unity and coherence in the nation.

II

Let us first turn to the phenomenon of the Indo-Anglian realist novel. Since India's independence, numerous English-language novels, among other cultural forms, have determined the images and style of the national imagination. It is not coincidental that realism has been the predominant mode of most of these Indo-Anglian fictions, apparently modeled on nineteenth-century European novels. With skillful strokes of verisimilitude, writers such as R.K. Narayan, Anita Desai, and most recently Vikram Seth, among many others, have given a sociological solidity to disparate actors and actions. In relatively seamless narratives, they have naturalistically woven together or elided the material disparities and discursive instabilities of a nation-in-formation. In fact, these works illustrate the concept, developed by Anderson (1983) and others, of the nation as an "imagined community." In this formulation, then, a nation's symbolic structure works like the plot of an old-fashioned realist novel. The movement of calendrical time gives the imagined world of the nation a sociological solidity, as Anderson notes: "The idea of a sociological organism moving calendrically through homogenous, empty time is a precise analogue of the idea of the nation, which is also conceived as a solid community moving steadily down or up history."[7] In thus conceptualizing the nation as a narrative, the critic offers a useful paradigm for the process of nation-formation.[8]

Specifically, the analogy between a nation and a realist novel shows how a particular construction of an imagined community can seem *natural* and inevitable. In postcolonial India, for instance, while the nationalist narratives of the Indian nation-state, as I have outlined, encompass competing cultural definitions of nationality based on secular liberalism, on religious populism, or on a skepticism of both, novels can easily weave these strands into timeless and/or universal pictures of "progress" or transition, among other things.

In this context, Indian realist novels written in English, from the 1950s to the present, frequently depict cleverly constructed, familiar landscapes, naturalizing social and economic structures, as well as racial, gender, and religious divisions, that in reality are hardly timeless and static. As this novel has developed within the ideology of Indian nationalism, a sense of "Indianness" suffuses diverse works, and because the Indian reality is mediated in English, it evokes a national "imagined community." Nowhere are readers reminded of the status of fiction as *fiction*, and that varied fictions go into the making of national and cultural identities.

For instance, whether it is R.K. Narayan's Malgudi, a fictional small town in South India in *The Guide* (and other works), or Anita Desai's Old Delhi in *The Clear Light of Day*, references to the events surrounding Indian independence create an impression of shared experiences of *all* Indians, however removed by geographical and cultural differences. In this context, R.K. Narayan's *The Guide* (1958) creates a vivid picture of Malgudi, the imaginary town, as a site of India's arrival into modernity and progress. A particularly crucial image in the novel is that of the expanding railway line. Raju, the novel's story-teller, and the local guide of Malgudi, is our enthusiastic witness to this moment:

> One fine day, beyond the tamarind tree the station building was ready. The steel tracks gleamed in the sun; the signal posts stood with their red and green stripes and their colourful lamps; and our world was neatly divided into this side of the railway line and that side. Everything was ready. All our spare hours were spent in walking along the railway track up the culvert half a mile away. . . .
>
> One day we were all given a holiday. "The train comes to our town today," people said excitedly.[9]

Later, Raju gives the readers a picture of Malgudi's link to the larger world of recognizable Indian cities (36):

> As soon as a certain bridge of Malgudi was ready, regular service began on our rails; it was thrilling to watch the activities of the station master and the blue-shirted porter as they "received" and "line-cleared" two whole trains each day.

Such naturalistic vignettes of India proliferate in numerous Indo-Anglian novels. Another example from Anita Desai's *The Clear Light of Day* casts the same spell of Indian reality over the reader. Published in 1980, this novel is set in Delhi during and after independence, and focusses on this period of transition: on how it affected one family as well as the larger community around it. This transition is repeatedly evoked, sometimes from an historical perspective:

> Old Delhi does not change. It only decays. . . . Now New Delhi they say is different. That is where things happen . . . the British built New Delhi and moved everything out. . . . Anyone who isn't dull and grey goes away—to New Delhi, to England, to Canada.[10]

In pointing to such vignettes, and thereby to Indo-Anglian fiction's investment in the realist mode, my purpose is not to question its aesthetic value, but rather to reflect on its political function. First, we must recognize that in emulating and privileging the English novel as a genre, with its strong tradition of realism, Indian writers choose to contextualize the diversities and divisions of India within British literary and intellectual conventions, and via the English language that can cut across these divisions, while domesticating them through shared knowledge. Some Indian literary critics have grappled with the problem of representation in a language that is not of Indian origin, and furthermore, is the legacy of colonialism. Meenakshi Mukherjee appropriately uses the label of "twice-born fiction" to define the Indo-Anglian novel as the "product of two parent traditions" and suggests that "a recognition of this fact is the first step towards granting the Indo-Anglian novel its proper place in modern Indian literature."[11] Mukherjee's aim is to evaluate Indian novels in terms of their techniques and themes, and she disagrees with critics who consider the English language unsuitable for Indian writers (10).

English, Mukherjee argues, has a broad, unifying scope: "The English language cuts across diverse ethnic, religious, and cultural backgrounds . . . [getting] a wider audience in India" (1971: 25). The critic acknowledges that English depicts Indian urban culture more realistically, yet some writers in English can also depict provincial life very convincingly and, in fact, achieve a "universal vision through [English]" (25).

It is precisely this "universal vision" that seems to be the aim of Vikram Seth's recent, highly acclaimed realist novel, *A Suitable Boy*. In this, the author uses a quasi-historical structure to re-live the early years after Indian independence in a story of four extended families, which is also the "story of India, newly independent and struggling through times of great crisis—when the landed estates of the gentry are being appropriated by land reform, when courtesans and musicians are losing their patronage, when hunger besets the peasantry, and when [the country] faces its first General Elections" (dust-jacket blurb). With a broad and sweeping scope, the novelist re-creates multiple lives: of wretched tannery workers, of courtesans, politicians, and *zamindars* or feudal landowners, among numerous others. Confronted by these disparate, though solid realities, the omniscient reader can place them together within the "imagined community" that she/he recognizes as "India."

The chronological structure of *A Suitable Boy* represents both the passing of events and of simultaneity in "homogenous empty time." In the novel, this concept translates into proliferating scenes with a huge cast of characters, some of whom interconnect directly or tangentially, while others remain largely unaware of one another; yet all their actions occur in the same "clocked, calendrical time" (Anderson 1983: 31). One effect of this strategy of a simultaneity of action, is that it creates the impression of a large national community that easily coalesces in the reader's mind as the nation. The novelist's skill is apparent in imparting a density and plenitude to the imagined world of India, while following the destinies of the individual families, the Khans, Mehras, Chatterjees, and Kapoors, interwoven with the personal love story of Lata, the daughter of the Kapoors.

One convention of realism used in the novel is the use of direct references to historical conditions or events by the characters themselves, as for instance when L.N. Agarwal, the fictional Home Minister, ponders the impending historical elections in the face of communal riots between Hindus and Muslims: "What will the effect of this be on the jatav (Hindu) vote and the Muslim vote? The general elections are just a few months away. Will these vote banks swing away from the Congress? If so, in what numbers?" (242). In the legislative discussion of the Bill to end *zamindari* (or feudal landownership), the novelist reveals the different class positions via representative characters. Begum Abida, a legislator representing the aristocracy, offers historical justification for the elite classes: "The class of people [the aristocratic *zamindars*] who preserved the culture, the music, the etiquette of this province is to be dispossessed, is to be driven through the lanes, . . . to beg its bread" (281). To which the socialist member, Dewakinandan Rai responds: "If I had my way, she would not beg for her bread, but she and those of her class would certainly have to work for it. This is what simple justice requires" (281).

Whether it is the *zamindari* system, the courtesans' milieu, marriage ceremonies, English departments, or religious riots, Vikram Seth invokes images that would constitute a shared knowledge among Indians, thereby offering a chronicle with many intimate or at least historically familiar points of reference for most Indian readers who read English. Published in 1993, *A Suitable Boy* retrospectively enacts the creation of the Indian national identity caught between the opposing pull of colonial customs and institutions, such as the *zamindari* system and marital constraints on women, and the new explorations of an uneven democracy. As the characters struggle to discover and define what it means to be an Indian in an independent nation, their definitions of tradition and modernity are inextricably, and somewhat confusedly caught between indigenous and colonial traditions, as the nation-in-formation itself.

The complex struggle comes to life in a somewhat comic scene set in an English department (in fictional Brahmpur) engaged in a discussion about a suitable curriculum of English literature for Indian students. At issue is whether some of James Joyce's works should be considered essential reading for undergraduate students. Pran, the junior faculty member, promotes Joyce's works on the grounds that he is "a great writer. This is now universally acknowledged. He is the subject of increasing academic study in America. I do think he should be on our syllabus too" (51). To rebut Pran, the chairman of the department interprets his advocacy of Joyce as a threat to Indian nationalism: "We in India pride ourselves on our Independence—an Independence won at great expense by the best men of several generations. We should hesitate before we blindly allow the American dissertation mill to order our priorities. . . . Let us step to the music we hear . . . in India" (51). Later in the debate, the chairman declares that "India is a democracy and we can speak our minds," but soon afterwards invokes the pre-independence days and the "tradition [that] the Modern British Literature paper does not include writers who were living at the time of the Second World War" (55). When reminded that T.S. Eliot remains in the curriculum, the chairman invokes the cultural authority of F.R. Leavis, the influential British critic: "But Eliot . . . surely—we have objective criteria enough in this case—why even Dr. Leavis [would agree]—" (56). That this discussion about English literary studies extends to issues of nationality and colonial tradition—and whether to "appraise the dead over the living" writers—illustrates how India's colonial past casts a long shadow over the new nation's struggles for identity.

Even though *A Suitable Boy* has as its *theme* the strains and pressures pulling apart the new nation, it is aligned to the official nationalism in its assumption of a unified India—an all-encompassing entity into which the multiple narratives that comprise the novel are subsumed. Most importantly, by assuming an unmediated transparency of the English language, the author does not question the *constructed* nature of both the writing of the novel and of the history it purports to represent. Instead, Seth offers his readers a powerful illusion of a coherent national consciousness, very much like Nehru's accommodating ideal of Mother India. It is quite notable that three generations after Nehru, Seth also sets out to "discover" India in a narrative structured by Western expectations of teleology and a coherent myth of origins. In effect, Seth tells a story of Indian nationalism as an omniscient narrator, while seemingly oblivious to its multiple variants as well as to the myths and fictions upon which it is based.

Overall Vikram Seth's work is in keeping with the realist tradition of most Indo-Anglian novelists since independence. Here Seth does what is most often ascribed to many of his compatriot writers, namely, he "summons up the everyday reality of India" (blurb), though his forte is the comedy of manners rather than a wrenching psychological realism. In creating an illusion of a bustling world of India, with its teeming diversity of peoples and locales, realist Indian writers such as Seth impart a sociological stability to a country marked by deep political, economic, and cultural divisions. Thus, within the naturalized space of their novels, they evoke an "imagined community" of disparate peoples, recognized by readers as the nation. While such novels in English have a limited readership in India, the realist mode nonetheless performs a crucial role in ideologically securing the idea of India as a single *nation*, as well as in building a consensus around this idea among the Anglicized bourgeois readers who are the ruling elite of the postcolonial era.

Given that most English narratives of the nation are mimetic, it is not surprising that they lack a self-consciousness of the class-divided relationships between the Indians and the English language. Therefore, even a quasi-historical novel like *A Suitable Boy* does not reveal or question the making of "Indianness" within the colonial language and in this sense can be considered a variant of the colonial novel. Ironically, while the Indo-Anglian novel has been labeled "the twice-born fiction," it does not acknowledge its genealogy within colonial cultural forms; instead, most Indian novels in the English language use the conventions of realism to create largely a transparent picture of postcolonial conditions.

Salman Rushdie's novels are among a few notable exceptions to the realist narratives of the nation. And it is to him that one must look for insights into the fictive quality of the Indian state. Rushdie acknowledges the dilemma of producing a "twice-born fiction" by "re-making English as an Indian vernacular."[12] This process is apparent in his *Midnight's Children*, for instance, which traces the genealogy of India-qua-nation from the moment of its inception in 1947. Writing in a non-mimetic mode, drawn in part from indigenous, oral narrative styles, he maps the social formation of the Indian subcontinent in multiple stories, presenting the narrator's choice of story as one of several possibilities. The novelist uses a mock-allegorical structure to set up the narrator as both a child and a representative of the fate of independent India. "Saleem Sinai is to be at once the voice of the individual and of a collectivity, to be spectator and participant" (Sangari 1987: 179). The opening lines of the novel clearly establish this analogy:

> I was born in the city of Bombay . . . once upon a time. No that won't do, there's no getting away from the date: I was born in Doctor Narlikar's Nursing Home on August 15th, 1947. And the time? The time matters, too. . . . On the stroke of midnight, as a matter of fact. Clock hands joined palms in respectful greeting as I came . . . at the precise moment of India's arrival at independence, I tumbled forth into the world.[13]

This is a world of jumbled genealogies, and Saleem Sinai, the somewhat ineffectual narrator, wants to present himself as a historian as well as an agent of history. This narrative reveals both his bravado and anxiety about the authenticity of his account. "Family history, of course, has its proper dietary laws. One is supposed to swallow and digest the permitted parts [of the meat]," he tells the readers at the outset, while viewing himself as the "first and only member of the family to flout the law" (59). Yet, a bit later, he confesses, "whenever my narration becomes self-conscious, . . . like a puppeteer, I reveal the hands holding the strings" (65). Struggling to put down the facts, Sinai fails to get an empirical grasp on history—a jumbled mass of facts, sometimes difficult to sort out—about which he worries: "Re-reading my work, I have discovered an error in chronology. The assassination of Mahatma Gandhi occurs in these pages on the wrong date. But I cannot say now what the actual sequence of events might have been; in my India, Gandhi will continue to die at the wrong time" (164).

The poignant irony of this observation is inescapable; Gandhi was assassinated at an inopportune moment in India's birth as a nation. Yet the narrator represents history, like all narratives, as improvisational and contingent. In his account, then, Saleem Sinai, as "character" and historian, repeatedly ponders the status of fiction versus "reality," both in the making of the self and the nation: "the illusion dissolves—or rather, it becomes clear the illusion itself is the reality" (164).

The world of *Midnight's Children* is not ordered by an omniscient narrator (as that of *A Suitable Boy*), or by a psychologically coherent protagonist of nineteenth-century realist fiction. What it offers, instead, is a parody of Saleem Sinai's attempts at self-aggrandizement, especially in wanting to become an agent of history. As he reflects (164):

> Am I so far gone in my desperate need for meaning, that I am prepared to distort everything—to re-write the whole history of my times purely in order to place myself in a central role? Today, in my confusion I cannot judge. I'll have to leave it to others. For me . . . I must finish what I have started, even if, inevitably, what I finish turns out not to be what I begin.

If the narrator has little control over the outcome of his story/history, it is because he must negotiate a fragmented terrain of his inner and outer worlds. The landscapes of the novel comprise diffuse, atomized locales, yet they reveal the narrator's alignments within the specificity of colonial and contemporary representations of the Indian subcontinent. His description of Bombay, for instance, takes shape through jumbled fragments of its genealogy (92):

> The fishermen were here first. Before Mountbatten's ticktock . . . and back, back, beyond Dalhousie and Elphinstone, before the East India Company built its fort . . . at the dawn of time, when Bombay was a dumb-bell shaped island tapering, at the centre, to a narrow shining strand. . . . In this primeval world, the fishermen . . . sailed in Arab dhows. . . . There were also coconuts and rice. And above it all, the benign presiding influence of the goddess Mumbadevi may well have become the city's. But then the Portuguese named the place Bom Bahia for its harbour, and not for the goddess of the Pomfret folk . . . the Portuguese were the first invaders, using the harbour to shelter their merchant ships.

This narrative of the city typifies Saleem Sinai's rhetorical strategy as a historian and story-teller: not only does he embrace the multiple myths of Bombay's origins here, but throughout the novel his fragmentary mode of story-telling activates *multiple* conceptions of India and Indianness. Thus, the "reality" of the independent nation is imbricated in textual fragments of non-chronological, linear time, in which the colonial (and pre-colonial) past elides with the postcolonial present. And as readers, we share Saleem's inability to locate any essence or "truth" about the nation, or to distinguish between the "real" and imagined India.

By representing Saleem Sinai's "India" in a constant state of metamorphosis and flux, Rushdie demonstrates that the category of the nation, far from being a stable entity, takes shape within a provisional idiom, emerging within multiple, and often competing "realities." Missing in the novelist's self-conscious play of textuality is any certainty about the "spirit of India," as articulated by Nehru in *The Discovery of India* or a cohesive vision of the disparate elements comprising a nation depicted by Vikram Seth in *A Suitable Boy*. In contrast to Rushdie's reading of the nation as a fiction, Seth's transparent rendering of Indian society seems a form of willed naiveté.

Salman Rushdie's most recent novel, *The Moor's Last Sigh*, further demonstrates his preoccupation with the postcolonial Indian nation-in-formation. Once again, his vision of a shifting, hybrid landscape goes against the grain of totalizing narratives of *both* colonialism and nationalism. The novel spans four generations of an Indian family, the De Gamas, from the last decades of the nineteenth century until the present. At its center stands the narrator, Moraes Zogoiby, the "Moor," a creature with a deformed hand and afflicted with a body which ages twice as fast as a normal human being's. He inherits a diverse mixture of races and creeds that are a part of India, though they comprise minority communities in a nation mainly divided between Muslims and Hindus. "Moor's" mother, Aurora, a celebrated painter, is a distant descendant of India's Portuguese invaders and a follower of their Catholicism. His father, Abraham Zogoiby, is one of the last Jews of Cochin in South India, and what is more a late descendant of Boabdil, the last Moorish ruler of Spain who gave up the Alhambra to Isabella and Ferdinand. Thus, there are two "Moors" and two mothers in this multi-layered story of exile, loss, and dispossession; the fifteenth-century Sultan Boabdil and his mother, the "terrifying Ayxa the Virtuous" (80), who mocked him for being less than a man and their fictional descendants, Aurora De Gama Zogoiby and her son Moraes, "Moor" Zogoiby, to whom, as to her other children, the sharp-tongued artist shows "no mercy" (125).

Opening in Cochin and ending in southern Spain, the novel is primarily set in the Bombay of Rushdie's birth. As an allegory of Indian colonial and postcolonial history, the novel expands on the chronology of *Midnight's Children* to include the rise of Hindu fundamentalism since 1989 and its aftermath. Furthermore, while the "India" of *The Moor's Last Sigh*, as of *Midnight's Children*, is in a constant state of metamorphosis, it more sweepingly cuts across boundaries of space and history—focussing not on the Hindu and Muslim majorities, but on the tiny minorities of Catholics with their ties to the Portuguese discoverers of India and of the Jews with their links to Moorish Spain. While living in accelerated time, the narrator vividly captures the flux of multiple, and often competing "realities" within which his and, in a sense, our "India" takes shape. As one critic remarks, "in Rushdie's dizzying, inclusive universe, the dispossessed, the exiled, the colonizers and the colonized clash, multiply, and miscegenate" (Hagedorn 1996: 26).

The author's rich, ironic, and often parodic characterizations of India are not simply aesthetic celebrations of hybridity and metamorphosis. Rather, by deliberately foregrounding the more marginal cultures and histories and doing so in textual fragments of metamorphic, non-chronological time, Rushdie's narrator provocatively interrogates the category of the nation itself. And it is apparent that these interrogations are aimed at the more purist, fundamentalist slogans of nationalism that continue to produce the Hindu–Muslim divisions in the country today. At one point, for instance, before the narrator recounts the impending partition of India, he playfully poses a serious question: "Christians, Portuguese, and Jews; Chinese tiles promoting godless views; pushy ladies, skirts-not-saris, Spanish shenanigans, Moorish crowns . . . can this really be India? *Bharata Mata* [Mother India], *Hindustan Hamara*, is this the place?" (87). The answer is, of course, it is. Rushdie's India is unequivocally protean and multi-faceted, resisting any unifying impulses.

Thus, as the narrator recounts the actual break-up of the subcontinent into two entities, "one Hindu, the other Mussulman," he suggests that his story takes us beyond the categories of a majority and minority dividing the nation into two: "Majority, that mighty elephant, and her sidekick, Major-Minority will not crush my tale beneath her feet. Are not my personages Indian, every one? Well then: this too is an Indian yarn. . . . To hell with high affairs of state! I have a love story to tell" (87).

The love story, of course, is that of his parents, the Catholic Aurora and the Jewish Abraham, whose cultural histories constitute the mix of Rushdie's polyglot India. In fact, throughout the novel, "Moor's" history of the De Gamas, and to a lesser extent the Zogoibys, allegorizes the formation of a nation, as it takes shape via multiple perspectives—dominant and marginal—on what constitutes India and Indianness. A recurring theme in Rushdie's often bitingly satiric allegory of emerging nationalism focusses on the conception of the nation as a mythical Mother India or *Bharata Mata*. In Jawaharlal Nehru's *The Discovery of India*, his nationalist view of a single, unified India is ideologically held in place by the image of a benevolent Mother India, who "essentially [encompassed] . . . millions of [Indians]" (Nehru 1959: 29). In contrast, Rushdie's novel harshly exposes both the naiveté and the spuriousness of this myth. In fact, at strategic moments in the novel, the narrator evokes the image of Mother India, not as a unifying, accommodating ideal, but as a protean and often deadly entity, and cast in the more ambivalent image of the erratic and unreliable mothers in the story: Epifania, Belle, Flory, and more centrally, "Moor's" overpowering mother,

Aurora. This analogy between Mother India and an unpredictable, devouring mother is introduced early in the story, when the young Aurora, after her mother's death, paints a huge fresco of India in proliferating images of precisely such a Mother India, which her father recognizes (61):

> And it [the painting] was set in a landscape that made [her father] tremble to see it, for it was Mother India herself, Mother India with her garishness and her inexhaustible motion, Mother India who loved and betrayed and ate and destroyed and again loved her children . . . Mother India with her oceans and coco-palms and rice fields and bullocks at the water-well . . . a protean Mother India who could turn monstrous, who could be a worm rising from the sea with Epifania's face at the top . . . dancing cross-eyed and Kali-tongued while thousands died . . . and above all, converged Mother India with Belle's face. Queen Isabella was the only mother goddess here, and she was dead; at the heart of this first immense outpouring of Aurora's art was . . . the pain of becoming a motherless child.

If Aurora re-creates her dead mother into a protean, often threatening, Mother India, "Moor," as the narrator, develops this allegory further by revealing its ideological grip over the Indian consciousness, reminiscent of his own mother's power over him. Thus, as he expresses his desire to break free from the "prison of the past," namely from the influence of his parents, he explains his dilemma in terms of the cultural myth of Mother India: "Motherness—excuse me if I underline the point—is a big idea in India: the land as mother, the mother as land, as the firm ground beneath our feet. Ladies-O, gents-O: I am talking *major* mother country" (137).

To stress the fictionality of the ideal of the nation as a benevolent Mother India, Rushdie's self-conscious narrator rather cynically reveals the *construction* of this myth in the famous Indian film of the 1950s entitled, *Mother India* (137):

> The year I was born, Mehboob Productions' all-conquering movie, *Mother India*—three years in the making . . . in the top three all-time megagrossing Bollywood flicks—hit the nation's screens. Nobody who saw it ever forgot the glutinous saga of peasant heroinism, the super-slushy ode to the uncrushability

of village India made by the most cynical urbanites in the world. And as for its leading lady—O Nargis [the actual actress] with your shovel over your shoulder and your strand of black hair tumbling . . . over your brow!—she became . . . the living mother goddess of us all.

Rushdie's narrator pointedly reveals the use of the myth of Mother India to idealize rural life, thereby eliding the class disparities between urbanites and Nehru's peasant masses—disparities that continue in contemporary India. In perhaps the most strikingly comic/parodic scene of the novel, Rushdie inserts the character of the real Nargis, a famous Indian actress, into a fictional scene of a social soirée at Aurora's Bombay residence. On this occasion, in an extended discussion of the film, *Mother India*, Rushdie further deconstructs the myth. While the actress praises the idealism of the film in depicting the "Courage of the masses" in the building of "dams," the symbols of modernity, Aurora and her friends reflect on the "incestuous" aspects of Nargis's real-life marriage to her "bad" screen son. As Aurora's artist-friend, Vasco Miranda, remarks, "*Mother India* [has] the subsidiary theme of forbidden [incestuous] love added to it" (138). While Nargis dismisses such speculations of "this godless anti-national gang," the narrator offers a scathing exposé of both the political agenda and the psychological impact of the film—and implicitly of the ideal of Mother India itself (138–9):

In *Mother India*, a piece of Hindu myth-making directed by a Muslim socialist, Mehboob Khan, the Indian peasant woman is idealised as bride, mother, and producer of sons; as long-suffering . . . and conservatively wedded to the maintenance of the social status quo. But for [the bad son], cast out from his mother's love, she becomes . . . that image of an aggressive . . . annihilating mother who haunts the fantasy life of Indian males.

When Moraes Zogoiby, the betrayed son of the novel, obsesses on the betrayal of all mothers—in life and in fiction—he also shows how the "reality" of the nation is imbricated in the textualized/cinematic constructions of the so-called traditional mother myths. Thus, in these scenes Rushdie skillfully draws on his narrator's responses to his mother to allegorize the inadequacies of the narrative of the nation as Mother India.

Ultimately, *The Moor's Last Sigh* represents the postcolonial Indian nation as *unrepresentable*, especially via the certitude of simple mimesis, the hallmark of post-independence Indian literature and film. As an artist trying to represent the changing India, Aurora confronts a crisis of representation, which the narrator defines as follows: "In the decade after Independence, Aurora fell into a deep, creative confusion, a semi-paralysis born of an uncertainty not merely about realism, but about the nature of the real itself" (173). And Rushdie, via his narrator, locates Aurora's dilemma within the historical popularity of realist art in the post-independence period, "when so many thinkers believed that the poignancy and passion of the country's immense life could only be represented by a kind of selfless, dedicated—even patriotic—mimesis" (173).

Salman Rushdie's *The Moor's Last Sigh*, like his earlier works, rejects the postcolonial trend of realism in representing the Indian national identity. Countering fundamentalist narratives of the Hindu nation or the Islamic state, Rushdie offers an irreverent "discovery" of India via jumbled genealogies and histories. Intimating his parodic historical method at the outset of the novel, the author gives the lie to certitudes of all myths of India's history as he reflects on the Portuguese arrival to the country (5):

Pepper is what brought Vasco De Gama's tall ships across the ocean . . . in the period called Discovery-of-India—but how could we be discovered when we were not covered before?— "we were not so much sub-continent as sub-condiment," as my distinguished mother had it. "From the beginning, what the world wanted from bloody mother-India was day-light clear," she'd say. "They came for the hot stuff, just like any man calling on a tart."

In such blasphemings of Mother India, Rushdie lays to rest all the comforting myths of postcolonial Indian nationalism.

III

Rushdie's works are not the only sources of non-essentialist, provisional representations of India as a nation in formation. Since independence, the Indian stage (especially in the vernacular languages) has frequently also been a site for the cultural explorations of national identity. While the analogy between the stage and a kingdom is an old one, the modern, centralized nation-state (both in its colonial and postcolonial manifestations) generally takes shape as an essentialist *narrative* by which boundaries of identity and power are established. In contrast, the performance and critical histories of an Indian theatrical masterpiece, *Andha Yug* (translated as *The Blind Age*), show how the play offers a dramatic counterpoint, if you will, to the standard story of Indian nationalism. It explores the more complex and wrenching aspects of the cultural struggles as they have shaped the Indian national consciousness since independence. Written in Hindi by the well-known romantic poet and novelist, Dharamvir Bharati, the play was published in 1955 and first staged nationally in 1962–3 in Bombay and Delhi (in separate productions). Since then it has been frequently staged—with notable productions in 1967, 1970, and 1986, and several in 1993, among many others. Translated into English and several Indian languages, it has also figured in student theatricals and classrooms as well as on the radio. Perhaps the most obvious reason for its appeal is the source on which it is based, the ancient Indian epic, *The Mahabharata*.[14]

Variously described as the "grand epic" or the "founding text" of Indian culture, *The Mahabharata*, together with its sister epic, *The Ramayana*, is passed on in oral narratives through generations of Hindu families. It would not be a generalization to suggest that in some form "every Hindu child receives it, and knows its genealogy by heart" (Mishra 1991: 201). In distinguishing between the two epics, one finds that *The Ramayana*, read allegorically, affirms Hindu genealogy, order, and sanctity of the family and constructs the Indian ideals of man and woman; in contrast *The Mahabharata* is about power and politics, about national disintegration and schisms: the Indian here confronts the forces of history. Thus, not surprisingly, Indians see the former epic as "life-atoning" whereas they never recite *The Mahabharata* in full for fear that it would lead to disharmony and chaos (Mishra 1991: 196).

It is these darker aspects of political conflict that Dharamvir Bharati brings to the foreground in his interpretation of the epic in *Andha Yug*, and which, undoubtedly, have touched a raw nerve in the national consciousness. And his tragic treatment of the traditional story stands out in marked contrast to the more populist television series on both Indian epics (the *Ramayana* and the *Mahabharata*), characterized by a jingoistic Hindu nationalism, as well as by Peter Brook's universalizing international production (which I discuss later). Most often, *Andha Yug* is described as an anti-war play—"about the consequences of war, [and] the physical and moral devastation it brings" (Jain 1978: 2–3). Critics also agree that while the warring clans of the Kauravas and the Pandavas in *The Mahabharata* provided the context for the anti-war theme, the playwright also drew directly on the experience of the Second World War, fresh in human memory in 1955 (Jain 1978: 2–3).

These readings of the play imply a universalist validity, namely that *The Mahabharata* can serve as a cautionary tale for all ages and cultures, an allegory about the dangerous consequences of war. I want to argue for a greater historical and cultural specificity in Bharati's play in which he confronts the conditions set by the twentieth century in India. Ironically, Bharati's vision of this impending modernity is *not* predicated on either colonial or nationalist assumptions of a progressive teleology. Instead, in a chilling interrogation of the ideals of "progress," *Andha Yug* brings modernity to life as *Kalyug* (the Age of Kali) or the debased age predicted in the epic. Thus, what Bharati does, in effect, is relocate the Indian national consciousness, via the revered *Mahabharata*, squarely within the postwar, postmodern world. In part the subject of *Andha Yug* is as much a search for historical bearings as it is the consequences of war. If the postcolonial nation must choose its bearings between its past and future, Bharati implies, it must approach with skepticism any transcendent, grand narrative, be it that of the nation, family, God, or tradition. For Bharati, then, India's mythic past cannot be recovered or rediscovered as a static golden age, but can only be enacted in terms of the exigencies of the present. In this resistance to an idealized past, Bharati's "discovery of India" differs radically from the vision of the British Orientalists in the eighteenth century as well as of the postcolonial Indian nationalists—both fundamentalist and secular—who share an idealist view of imaginary entities such as an "Aryan India" or a "Hindu India" in an ancient golden age, or in Nehru's *Geist*.

The action of *Andha Yug* takes place on the evening of the eighteenth day of the Great War between the Kauravas and the Pandavas in *The Mahabharata*. Dhritarashtara, the blind Kaurava king, is anxiously awaiting news from the front, and Sanjay, gifted with divine vision, reports the happenings of war to the king. Thus, when the play begins, the major action has already taken place, and what follows are horrific consequences. The moment of its discovery as it were is past and its effects constitute the outcome (as in the case of India-qua-nation). Drawing on narrative conventions of the Western epic form, Bharati uses several pairs of narrators and listeners to describe the action. The characters' speeches are frequently in the form of direct statements, as monologues, soliloquies, and semi-soliloquies (Awasthi 1978: 6).

As a result, the play creates a form of Brechtian alienation among the audience, repeatedly forcing them to reflect on the *effects* of the actions, rather than being lulled by an emotional identification or empathy toward the characters. However, unlike Brecht's sustained cerebral forms of epic drama, *Andha Yug* also resonates with powerful emotions evoked by death, physical pain, and moral confusion. What gives these tragic moments a coherence is Bharati's lyrical poetic form, especially his use of complex image patterns. In fact, Ibrahim Alkazi, who first directed the play, remarked that "the total impact of sound and visual images" created an "ultimate theatrical form" (1978: 5).

The actions of *Andha Yug* resonate around the images of blindness. Bharati explores different levels of this condition—blindness in its various physical, mental, moral, and spiritual manifestations. Between the two extremes of the physical blindness of the king, Dhritarashtara, and the beastly blind hatred of his grandson, Aswatthama, the play depicts many forms and shades of the human inability to see the face of reality. The familiar conflict between the Kauravas and the Pandavas is projected here between Aswatthama and Krishna, the presiding deity of Hinduism, but instead of representing this as a more traditional encounter between the forces of good and evil and darkness and light, the playwright depicts it as a brutal struggle for survival between different shades of darkness itself (Jain 1978: 2). The chorus in the opening scene of the play sets forth the theme of blindness:

> The stream of blood
> nears its end almost
> It would be strange if no one won
> or both sides lost
> On the throne of ages
> a blind man is seated
> and blindness wins on both sides

reason defeated
Blind with fear, blind with desire
The blindness of rulers conquered
the beautiful and good expire
the age of the gods is squandered.[15]

The king's guards echo the same sentiments in images of blindness and disease:

There was nothing to guard
in the civilization of the blind and the old
whose children
joined battle
and in their blindness, honour
was like a diseased harlot
diseasing the people
That blind culture
that sick honour
is what we have guarded
for seventeen days.

(ibid.)

In Bharati's play, the heroic battle of the revered epic, *The Mahabharata*, has been reduced to a nihilistic "end game." In it one can also find echoes of Shakespeare's travesty of the *Iliad* in *Troilus and Cressida*. However, crucially, while the playwright does not depend entirely on absurdity or satire to signal a fallen, godless world, even when he hints at the possibility of individual agency "to salvage the future of man" in the face of emptiness (21), he undermines this hope by the death of Krishna.

While *Andha Yug* explores fundamental questions about the nature of humanity—or, what makes us human—it also points to the political dimensions of these concerns. Specifically, in intervening in the mythic genealogy of Indian culture, it draws attention to the makings of a national consciousness. By re-enacting the story of the nation's origins as a drama about the difficulty in forging community and family, Bharati makes visible the divisive forces of competing loyalties. Several directors who have brought this play to the stage view it not only as an ironic commentary on India's myth of origins, but more on how this myth has been mobilized in contemporary struggles over India's "real" traditional culture. Ibrahim Alkazi, for instance, interprets *Andha Yug* via a reading of *The Mahabharata* as a record of India's ancient history, though not as a static golden age but as a protocolonial struggle between different tribes:

> *The Mahabharata* suggests to me a "new" people in a "new" land. The first terrible onslaughts had already been accomplished in the *Ramayana* (in which "new" people established their supremacy over the local tribes), and the first attempts at achieving settled kingdoms in which the principles, concepts, ideas contained in the early Shastras (doctrinal texts) could find concrete expression. No wonder that the aftermath of that crisis-on-the-brink was the stultifying centuries of Brahmanical tradition. . . . The whole poem posing the questions of evil, corruption, destruction, formulates questions that were the first cornerstones of a culture that would then through the ages be petrified into civilization.
>
> (Alkazi 1978: 4)

Alkazi's historicized reading of the origin myth reveals the dangers of falling back on stultifying tradition as a response to a crisis of identity. In Alkazi's response to Bharati's complex reading of history, the "new" Indians in the "new" India must confront (via the *new* version of the *old* text) the lingering questions about "corruption" and "destruction" as they define their postcolonial nationality. Furthermore, although Alkazi views the characters as "archetypes" and "symbolic representations," serious productions such as his do not depict them as instruments of Hindu xenophobia found in the Indian television series dramatizing the epic; rather, although we experience some alienation from the characters as individuals, we are drawn in by the profound, poetic exchanges between them.

Another stage director, Satyadev Dubey, who was the first to accept the challenge of directing *Andha Yug* in 1962, views the play as an instance of "a dynamic, language-oriented [Hindi] theatre having a personal meaning for us [Indians] as far as our confused national growth [is concerned]" (1978: 5). As this production was staged immediately after the Chinese attack on India, the meaning of the play, for Dubey, "acquired an added dimension" (5). In fact, he adds, "the play had on a personal level the same impact which the creation of Bangla Desh had on a national level" (5). In establishing this analogy between the creation/performance of the play and the birth of a nation out of bloodshed, Dubey interprets *Andha Yug* as a means of giving clarity and strength to "our confused national growth." Thus, through this production, the Indians and later Bangladeshis could claim their national identities with pride.

Both Alkazi and Dubey are interested in how the play mediates the national consciousness about the past and future, but they mainly emphasize their own directorial choices. Let us turn to Dharamvir Bharati's reflections on the formation of a national identity as they are developed *within Andha Yug*. In tracing the genealogy of India's national identity, the play, as stated earlier, depicts the aftermath of a bloody battle between two related clans. A crucial aspect of battle is the agonizing conflict the characters face between familial bonds and political affiliations with a larger cause, represented here in the abstract notion of "truth."

One character who strongly expresses these divisions in the play is Yuyutsu, whose small role in *The Mahabharata* (as religious text) is enhanced by Bharati to express the central dilemma of the play, namely the clash of disparate loyalties. He is a Kaurava who chooses to fight against his brothers and with the opposing side. Yuyutsu explains his choice as the defense of truth (8):

> My crime was simply that
> I was committed to the truth
> . . . and all the great [Kaurava] men
> dared not pit themselves
> against Durodhana [their leader].
> Even so I said
> I couldn't espouse untruth
> I too am a Kaurava:
> But truth is bigger than dynasty.

When Yuyutsu is faced with familial rejection and jeering crowds on his return to the defeated camp, a sympathetic Kaurava comforts him:

> A man who departs from
> familiar customs
> and determines his own actions . . .
> must expect such a reception
> from ignorant, terror-stricken
> commoners.

(ibid.)

In fact, he is told by the same sympathizer, "In all the dark history of the Kauravas/there's only you/who can hold his head high" (8).

What is the nature of the "truth" that Yuyutsu defends in the bloody battle? For Bharati, the ideal of a larger good, a communal, as opposed to familial, cause is suspect when it becomes a call to arms and destruction of another community. The issue emerging from this episode is whether Yuyutsu's choice "determines his own actions" or leads him blindly to a false faith in Krishna. Victory of goodness as an abstract ideal, as Yuyutsu learns in the aftermath of the war, is meaningless before a shrieking, wounded man: "My fire-tipped arrows/burnt away his knees/ How can he accept [comfort]/at the hands of one/who destroyed him?" (9). From Bharati's perspective, then, whatever it is that calls mankind to such destruction—be it the ideal of goodness or the cause of loyalty to a Nation, or a Clan—is meaningless and unjustified.

If Bharati warns Indians of the destructive potential of nationalism in the aftermath of the Second World War, his play echoes another prophetic Indian voice, namely that of Rabindranath Tagore, who argued that European nationalism produced the first Great War. Tagore decried the "European war of Nations" as a "war of retribution" and in "this frightful war the West has stood face to face with her own creation, to which she had offered her soul" (quoted in Thompson 1992: 9). Like Tagore, Bharati expresses deep skepticism about blindly accepting the premises of cultural and national myths. Thus, while the received tradition about *The Mahabharata* unproblematically posits the battle as one of good over evil, Bharati debunks this premise through the voice of Yuyutsu in the play. Yuyutsu challenges Vyasa, the original author of the great epic, to provide him with a justification of the war (9):

Vyasa said
to me
that where Krishna was
there would be victory.
This is Krishna's victory
that I am a murderer
forsaken by my mother
and an object of hate.

It is significant that Dharamvir Bharati does *not* re-create the world of *The Mahabharata* as an irrecoverable, static golden age against which the contemporary Indian realities are to be measured. In this he resists the Orientalizing impulse to "discover" *The Mahabharata* as a record of a glorious Hindu past evident in William Jones's Sanskrit translations, in Nehru's evocations of an ancient *Ram Rajya,* or in the Hindu fundamentalists' xenophobic aspirations to restore India's "pure" Hindu identity by reviving ancient epics like *The Mahabharata.*

Thus, *Andha Yug* does not offer the religious fundamentalists or other nationalists a model of an ancient society that they can recuperate in an essentialist vision of a new Hindu golden age. Bharati's irreverent use of received tradition is most apparent in his characterization of the God Krishna, the presiding deity of Hinduism, who is represented in the play as a disembodied voice. As the plot unfolds from the point of view of the Kauravas, the losers of the battle, Krishna is presented as a divine antagonist, who enables the Pandavas victory, not as an omnipotent God, but as an astute diplomat and opportunist. Aswatthama, the crazed revenger for the Kaurava defeat, accuses Krishna of treachery (12):

> "Aswatthama"
> he said,
> "you'll prevail
> where all the
> Pandava
> piety
> and privilege
> languish."
> My protection
> of them
> for love of Krishna
> gave them
> new courage
> and victory.
> But they killed
> by trickery.

Another, more faithful follower of the God Krishna questions his power:

I . . . follower of Krishna, devout, righteous
and now my voice is full of doubt
for it seems that my Lord
is like a useless axle
from which every wheel is detached
and which cannot turn by itself
But to doubt is to sin.

(ibid.)

While Krishna's powers seem limited, and his motives suspect, the play nonetheless suggests his lingering presence beyond his mortal death. Thus, if he is the presiding deity of the Hindu national imagination, his identity and presence lack certitude. He is killed by a hunter's arrow, a result of the Kaurava Queen Gandhari's curse: "Hear me Krishna/You could have stopped the war if you willed. . . . Whether you are the Lord/or whether you are omnipotent,/. . . your entire dynasty also will, like mad dogs,/tear each other up/And when you have seen them destroyed/yourself/shall die in a dense jungle/at the hands of a common hunter" (16). Krishna's acceptance of this curse is marked by a complex description of his double role as both human and divine: "Mother," he tells Gandhari, "Whether the Lord or the Omnipotent, I am your son, . . . /In these eighteen days of fearful strife/ It was none but I who died a million times/ . . . I am life, but I am also death, mother" (16).

While here Krishna seems to suggest an ability to assume the suffering of others, we also witness his human foibles by which he debunks the myth of a superhuman God who controls the destiny of mankind. Such an ambivalence about Krishna's role as a savior marks the play's conclusion, as the Hunter recalls the God's dying voice: "The future of man I kept alive till now./ But in this blind age/a part of me/will remain inactive, self-destructive/and disfigured" (21). Thus, Krishna bestows responsibility on humans for their own salvation: "others shall take all other responsibility," and yet looks to a renewed future when "new life will be built on old destruction . . . [and] I will live again and act again" (21).

Krishna's split identity—as both human and divine—brings home the dilemma of human faith. The characters are caught in a spiral of violence and revenge because they lead a blind existence, submitting their powers of discrimination to him. While one follower states that to "doubt [Krishna] is to sin," a foe describes faith as "Krishna's ability" to make "his people drunk [to commit] wide-spread murder" (19). Yet, finally the darkness of the play is lifted by intimations of cyclicality, whereby the "birth of the blind age/is repeated over and over," but countered by a "seed in the mind/of courage, freedom, and creation/that grows in the light of day" (21). Almost all the characters in the play reflect on how "in this blind age/the human future can be saved," and the playwright tentatively leaves us with some hope in human agency in the midst of skepticism.

Has *Andha Yug* been widely and frequently staged since 1962 because it has struck a familiar chord in a nation struggling with communal strife and divisions? While shedding its colonial yoke, is free India caught in a "Blind Age" of a loss of faith in tradition? In following the history of this play, one is inevitably faced with such questions regarding its mediations in the formation of Indian nationalism. Dominant strains in nationalist discourses, ranging from the views of liberals like Nehru to Hindu fundamentalists, have looked to India's mythic past for a "pure" national identity. In Dharamvir Bharati's vision in *Andha Yug*, ancient tradition offers no certitude or solace, but only a symbolic framework for enacting and enabling the contemporary conditions of communal violence and moral ambiguity.

Thus, Indian audiences watching their revered epic come to life on the stage are confronted, not with a mythic golden age, but with modernity as a condition of skepticism. However, while the playwright dramatizes the death of their God Krishna, he also gives them some hope of agency and identity, *without* resorting to any essentialist revivals of tradition and national glory, while highlighting that such essentialism simply allows the return to a Blind Age yet again.

IV

Indian critics generally emphasize the broad universalist dimensions of *Andha Yug* by describing it as an "epic story dealing with the fundamental problem of conflict between the forces of good and evil" (Awasthi 1978: 6). Others view it as an anti-war play. As N.C. Jain explains: "[it] is a play about the consequences of war, the physical and moral devastation it brings, destroying both the victor and the vanquished by its debasing and dehumanizing effect on the individual and society" (1978: 2). In historical terms, its anti-war stance is seen as a specific response to the Second World War and its aftermath. Undoubtedly, the historical memory of the European war must have informed the playwright's pessimism about the effects of bloody conflict. But, I believe, there is another dimension to *Andha Yug*'s cultural significance. This is evident in the way the play forces the postcolonial nation to confront its divisive present by taking its historical bearings between the idealist myths of its ancient past and the ambiguities and chaos of modernity. Thus, Bharati re-casts the familiar colonial and nationalist binaries of tradition and modernity into a wrenching vision of a cyclical, blind history, as the chorus reminds us at the end: "The birth of that blind age/is repeated over and over" (21). The teleology of progress, so central to Nehru's nationalism, is missing from Bharati's vision of India's future.

While Bharati's play resonates, both aesthetically and culturally, before indigenous audiences, it remains virtually unknown in the West, where Orientalist perspectives on classical India hold sway. It is telling that most Western audiences unfamiliar with Bharati's version of *The Mahabharata* would know the epic via the famed Western (and quasi-international) production by Peter Brook. Despite some controversy and criticism (mostly in India, though), Brook's *Mahabharata* has had world-wide exposure as a theatrical landmark since 1988 (and later as a film and television serial). While Brook deserves particular credit for revolutionizing the form of the theater itself—as an ultimate spectacle—some of the theatrical power is lost in the film versions. But where Brook's production is more problematic is in the playwright's interpretation of *The Mahabharata* as a vehicle of *universalist humanism*.[16] Brook explicitly read *The Mahabharata* as a vehicle for timeless and universal truths, as he states in an interview: "*The Mahabharata* is about conflict at all levels . . . meaning that something that, in human terms, is considered right and necessary against something, in human terms, that's unnecessary and destructive, and yet all within a universal meaning" (1991: 54). Some Indian critics, such as Vijay Mishra, question Western audiences for accepting Brook's "universalistic interpretation of the text at face value" and for ignoring the fact that for Indians this epic is mediated through specific cultural practices and forms (Mishra 1991: 201). Thus, Mishra argues that "whilst conceding that

The Mahabharata remains to this day, the very basis of cultural life in India, Peter Brook nevertheless succumbs to the power of the seductive extension of the Sanskrit words *maha* and *bharata* to mean 'The Great History of Mankind'" (Brook 1991: 203). Interestingly the sense of polyphony created by its international, multi-racial cast and its Oriental setting does not entirely conform with the universal, humanistic interpretations advanced in its favor. Yet ultimately, the monumental scope and encyclopedic approach of Brook's production, in contrast to Bharati's focus on one representative moment, weakens the complexities of the text—especially as this version of *The Mahabharata* is underpinned by Brook's unwavering equation between the epic and "truth."

Ultimately Brook's vision of the East in his version of *The Mahabharata*—as well as its reception in the West—remains imbricated in colonial Orientalizing, even while he presents the work in humanistic, ahistorical terms. Like the eighteenth-century British Orientalists, Brook "discovers" a shared history of the East and West in a complex, though idealized epic past, while ignoring the specific relation between *The Mahabharata* and India through history. Thus, unlike Bharati's *Andha Yug*, Brook's visually powerful production does not call its Western audiences to re-consider the relation between India's past and present; the Western *Mahabharata* then, becomes a harmonizing ideal that overlooks the more contingent aspects of history and myth, as well as the more wrenching realities of the post-epic, and postcolonial, "Blind Age." While Brook's aim may have been to bring the ancient epic into an egalitarian modernity, that very gesture recuperates the colonial trope of "discovery" with its attendant teleology of progress. In this contrasting interplay between Brook's and Bharati's "discoveries" of ancient India lies the dynamic of the cultural struggles that continue to shape the postcolonial Indian nation-state. Orientalist revivals of "tradition" appear frequently in postcolonial articulations of Indian nationalism as it mediates between a "real" and imagined India. The trajectory from Coryate's discovery of the fabled India/Indies—following the footsteps of Tamburlaine—to William Jones's Hindu golden age and Nehru's evocations of the ancient Indian *Ram Rajya* is uneven. So is the trajectory from tradition to modernity. The recurring desire for a monolithic definition of India proves elusive, while colonial tropes continue to cast their long shadow on an India in search of its identity.